The Truth About Seventh-day Adventism

Works by Walter R. Martin
in
"THE MODERN CULT LIBRARY" SERIES

Jehovah of the Watchtower
The Christian Science Myth
The Rise of the Cults
The Christian and the Cults
The Maze of Mormonism
The Errors of Romanism

BOOKLET SERIES

Jehovah's Witnesses
Christian Science
Mormonism
Unity
Spiritualism

The Truth About Seventh-day Adventism

WALTER R. MARTIN
Contributing Editor, *Eternity Magazine*

ZONDERVAN PUBLISHING HOUSE
GRAND RAPIDS, MICHIGAN

Library of Congress Catalog Card No. 60–10154

Printed in the United States of America

DEDICATION

To the memory of my father,

JUDGE GEORGE W. MARTIN,

who well taught me that the truth is its own best defense,

this volume is affectionately dedicated.

FOREWORD

As the result of our studies of Seventh-day Adventism, Walter Martin and I reached the conclusion that Seventh-day Adventists are a truly Christian group, rather than an antichristian cult. When we published our conclusion in *Eternity* Magazine (September 1956), we were greeted by a storm of protest from people who had not had our opportunity to consider the evidence.

Let it be understood that we made only one claim; i.e., *that those Seventh-day Adventists who follow the Lord in the same way as their leaders who have interpreted for us the doctrinal position of their church, are to be considered true members of the body of Christ.* We did not, and do not, accept some of their theological positions which we consider to be extravagant, or others which we consider to be non-biblical.

We celebrate the first day of the week, the day of the resurrection of our Lord Jesus Christ, and we keep no sabbath on any day of the week. We believe that every soul has eternal existence and that those who have been redeemed by the Lord Jesus Christ also have eternal life. There is no suspension of consciousness after death, for "to be absent from the body is to be present with the Lord" (II Cor. 5:8). I believe that the ideas of investigative judgment and a secondary sanctuary ministry have no basis in Scripture.

We must realize, however, that many true believers have kept a seventh-day Sabbath and that many true believers have believed in the doctrine of soul sleep. The doctrine of investigative judgment, however, is held by no other group of Christians, and was unknown until the middle of the nineteenth century. It was promulgated at that time, in my opinion, as a means of softening the harsh blow of "The Great Disappointment," which "disappointment" is portrayed so clearly by the noted Adventist historian Dr. LeRoy Froom.

Although my knowledge of Seventh-day Adventism is not confined to the evidence presented in this study, I am indebted to Walter Martin for his thorough and painstaking research. We had the great joy and privilege of twice entertaining several representatives of the General Conference of Seventh-day Adventists for two or three days of prayer and discussion. The Holy Spirit bore witness to our spirits that these men are godly, sincere, Christ-centered, Bible-loving Christians.

Out of these days of meditation, communion and discussion came their own volume, *Seventh-day Adventists Answer Questions on Doctrine,* described by Mr. Martin in his introduction to this book. Mr. Martin is completing the work for the doctorate in philosophy in the field of history of religious movements which had their origin in the United States: Christian Science, Mormonism, Jehovah's Witnesses, Unity and other non-Christian groups. I know of no authority who equals him in this field.

Since leaders of Adventism agree that this book fairly presents their theological position, this work is a milestone in Christian apologetics; for, during this study, brethren talked and prayed together, assessed each other's position and agreed to disagree while still obeying the Lord's command to love one another.

In the present context, I am sure that Adventist leaders will not take it amiss if I express the hope that Mr. Martin's incisive refutation of Adventist doctrinal differences will keep wavering souls from embracing those errors! And they probably hope that their volume will have a corresponding effect!

May the Lord draw all members of His body to each other in mutual respect and love, knowing that each of us is answerable to Him alone.

DONALD GREY BARNHOUSE

PREFACE

While an undergraduate student in New York City in 1949, the writer extensively studied Seventh-day Adventist history and theology, and concluded that "Adventists" were a cult of Christian extraction but with enough heretical error in their doctrine to exclude them from the Body of Christ. In the summer of 1955, however, the writer began a serious research project to discover just what comprises Seventh-day Adventist theology. As he burrowed under the surface of Adventist semantics and teaching, the number of doctrinal "heresies" markedly diminished. He read every major anti-Adventist publication, and was considerably disturbed because quotations from some Adventist books were at variance with statements made by the great majority of Adventist writers. This condition, however, is now being remedied by the Adventist church with a renewed effort toward consistency.

The Truth about Seventh-day Adventism, then, is based upon seven years of intensive reading of primary sources, and of every available anti- and pro-Adventist book and pamphlet. The writer has also had personal interviews with hundreds of Adventist leaders* and laymen, and has enjoyed the full cooperation of the General Conference (the central governing body) of the Seventh-day Adventist Church. The officials graciously gave whatever information was requested, even when findings did *not* favor their cause. The information in this book has also been checked and cross-checked with authoritative Adventist and non-Adventist sources, so that there can be little doubt of its validity. To eliminate misunderstanding of the true position of the Seventh-day Adventist Church with regard to theology, history, and prophetic interpretation, the writer has drawn heavily from recognized Adventist writers and the latest and most authoritative volume on Adventist theology entitled, *Seventh-day Adventists Answer Questions on Doctrine.*[1] This definitive work, which

*Including a mission field survey of some 2 months in Europe and Asia.

[1] Publication of the General Conference of Seventh-day Adventists, Washington, D. C. (1957): 720 pp. It is referred to throughout this book under the abbreviated title, *Questions on Doctrine.*

presents the true position of the Seventh-day Adventist Church, was written to answer questions about their theology and doctrine. Its very title indicates willingness to meet evangelicals halfway, and nowhere is this better illustrated than in the following quotation from the Introduction where, speaking of this writer's questions and their answers, they state:

"The replies were prepared by a group of recognized leaders in close counsel with Bible teachers, editors and administrators. . . . This was *not* to be a new statement of faith, but rather an answer to specific questions concerning our faith. It was natural that these answers would come within the framework of the official statement of Fundamental Beliefs of Seventh-day Adventists which appears in the *Church Manual.* In view of this fact, these answers represent the position of our denomination in the area of church doctrine and prophetic interpretation. . . .

"The writers, counselors and editors who produced the answers to these questions have labored conscientiously to state accurately the beliefs of Seventh-day Adventists. . . . The statement of Fundamental Beliefs as mentioned above is our only official statement. The answers in this volume are an expansion of doctrinal positions contained in that official statement of Fundamental Beliefs. Hence this volume can be viewed as truly representative of the faith and beliefs of the Seventh-day Adventist Church" (*Questions on Doctrine,* pp. 8, 9).

The author has labored conscientiously to present accurately the history and theology of the Seventh-day Adventist denomination. He has based his findings squarely upon what the leaders of Adventism have stated to be the true position of their church today. He has also assumed the basic honesty of the leaders whose Christian cooperation and fellowship he has enjoyed. Since the General Conference issued *Questions on Doctrine,* and it is fully empowered to represent Adventist thought, this volume certainly is *the* primary source upon which to ground an evaluation of Adventist theology.

To better understand the problems connected with our study of Seventh-day Adventism, we must understand the New Testament teaching concerning the Body of Christ, and the divine command of love uttered by Christ. Of all the commandments of the Lord Jesus Christ, none has been more neglected than that which might be called the "lost commandment": "A new commandment I give unto you, That ye love one another; as I have loved you, that ye also love one another" (John 13:34). Many people have the idea that the Ten Commandments are the sum of the moral law of God, but this is not the case. The Lord Jesus Christ uttered approximately 150 commandments which touch every aspect of human life, and either all His commandments have equal claim to our obedience, or the question logically follows, Why obey any of them?

The Lord Jesus Christ made obedience the test of our love for Him when He said, "If ye love me, keep my commandments"; and further, "He that hath my commandments and keepeth them, he it is that loveth me" (John 14:15, 21).

Not only does the New Testament record Christ's great command to love, but it also records the reason why Christians fail to obey. Hebrews 12:14, 15, says: "Follow peace with all men, and holiness, without which no man shall see the Lord. Looking diligently lest any man fail of the grace of God; lest any *root of bitterness* springing up trouble you, and thereby many be defiled." Verse 15 reveals the main cause of friction between Christians; it is a "root of bitterness." What causes this?

First, the verse counsels us to look diligently lest *any one* fail, or literally, *fall back* from the grace of God. To fall back from the grace of God, then, is to make place for "a root of bitterness"—the springing up of spiritual hostility, that is, spiritual maladjustment among members of the Body of Christ. Further, we see in this verse the twofold effect on the Christian: He is "troubled" and "defiled." So when the Christian falls back from the grace of God and allows spiritual hostility to spring up, trouble arises among the brethren and many are spiritually defiled.

Each one of us who knows Christ as Saviour must confess that at times he is guilty of hostility toward other Christians. We have felt distrust and suspicion toward those of "like precious faith," and have exhibited enmity, jealousy and envy, to the disgrace of the Christian Church. And many times our own self-righteous pride, our desire to "be right," regardless of the price others must perhaps pay for our stubbornness, precludes repentance and prevents reconciliation with those who are at odds with us.

Through the years of the controversy between Adventism and

Orthodoxy, such a "root of bitterness" has grown and flourished because the opposing forces have been attacking each other at long range, and only recently have they drawn near enough to learn each other's true character. The only cure for this "root of bitterness," then, is obedience to "the lost commandment."

Jesus did not say that men would know that we are His disciples by the day we keep for worship, by the type of food we eat, by the mode of baptism we practice, or by our views on the eternal security of the believer or the final state of the wicked. The test of fellowship, the proof of the genuineness of our conversion, and the witness to the world that we are His followers is our love for one another.

By no means, however, is love to be made a substitute for "sound doctrine"; rather, they are to complement one another. We fully recognize that "life in Christ" cannot be had without adherence to sound doctrine of the great foundational truths of the Gospel. However, conversely it is more than possible to hold and defend such doctrines without ever having experienced "life in Christ" as evidenced by those whose lack of love for others reveals them to be disobedient or even false Christians in the light of God's Word (I John 4:20).

Christ made love the acid test, so to speak, of one's conversion. In John 14:23 and 24 Jesus said: "If a man love me, he will keep my words: and my Father will love him, and we will come unto him, and make our abode with him. He that loveth me not keepeth not my sayings: and the word which ye hear is not mine, but the Father's which sent me." Here the Lord Jesus Christ plainly taught that if a man did not keep His words, that man did *not* love Him, and those engaged in the Orthodoxy versus Adventism controversy are responsible to heed the words of their one Lord, ". . . the word which ye hear is not mine, but the Father's which sent me."

Thus, love is the proof of conversion, and obedience to the Lord Jesus Christ is the proof of love; for if we love Him we will obey His law of love and love one another, even as He loved us.

John 15:17 should pierce the soul of every believer: "These things I command you, that ye love one another," for our Lord is referring to His earlier words in verse 12: "Love one another, as I have loved you." This is the command of the Son of God to those who name

His Name and profess to trust in His redeeming sacrifice and glorious resurrection. We are to love one another *exactly* as He has loved us.

Both Adventist and non-Adventist need to consider afresh these words of Jesus. In the absence of this love, the "root of bitterness" has grown up and to that extent the Body of Christ is defiled. Filled with Christ's love, we would be as generous as He was in manifesting that love, and we could do no less than love one another as He has loved us.

Still to be healed are many wounds caused by ignorance, prejudice, and an unforgiving spirit, of which both Adventists and non-Adventists are guilty. But the place of healing is the very foundation of Christian faith, the love of God as manifested in the Cross of Calvary. Meeting at the Cross, we shall find it possible to obey His command, "that ye love one another; as I have loved you, that ye also love one another."

In the fifth chapter of Matthew's Gospel, the Lord Jesus gave specific instructions for destroying the "root of bitterness": "If thou bring thy gift to the altar, and there rememberest that thy brother hath ought against thee; leave there thy gift before the altar, and go thy way; first be reconciled to thy brother, and then come and offer thy gift" (verses 23, 24). Reconciliation, therefore, implies forgiveness, mutual love, obedience to the Word of God, and fellowship.

The lost commandment must be restored through repentance and reconciliation: "Be ye kind one to another, tender hearted, forgiving one another, even as God for Christ's sake hath forgiven you" (Eph. 4:32). The Scripture flatly states that if a man claims to love God, but hates his brother, he lies; for as John puts it, "He that loveth not his brother whom he hath seen, how can he love God whom he hath not seen?" (I John 4:20). Reconciliation must be the gateway to solving the Adventist vs. Orthodoxy conflict and it must be genuine; both sides must admit past misdeeds, and truly seek to live and work together in harmony where possible.

To conclude our observations, let us note that the result of love between Christians is true unity. In chapter 3 of Ephesians, Paul states his desire, "That Christ might dwell in your hearts by faith; that ye, being rooted and grounded in love, may be able to comprehend with all saints what is the breadth, and length, and depth, and height; and to know the love of Christ which passeth knowledge, that ye might be filled with all the fulness of God" (verses 17-19). This is the prologue to his great discourse on unity in chapter 4: "I therefore, the prisoner of the Lord, beseech you that ye walk worthy of the vocation wherewith ye are called, with all lowliness and meekness, with longsuffering, forbearing one another in love; endeavoring to keep the unity of the Spirit in the bond of peace. There is one body, and one Spirit, even as ye are called in one hope of your calling; one Lord, one faith, one baptism, one God and Father of all, who is above all, and through all, and in you all."

If Seventh-day Adventists are in basic agreement with their fellow Christians on all the foundational Christian doctrines regarding the salvation of the soul and growth in the Christian life, give evidence of life in Christ and manifest Christian love, then they are *part* of that one body, *indwelt* by that one Spirit, *called* by that one hope, *ruled* by the same Lord, *partakers* of the same faith, *recipients* of the one baptism, and *servants* of the one God and Father of all who confess the Son of God as Lord and Saviour.

Since Scripture commands "that there should be no schism in the body" (I Cor. 12:25), unless we recognize the absolute claim of love upon the Christian life we "become as sounding brass or a tinkling cymbal," even though both Adventists and non-Adventists "speak with the tongues of men and angels."

Let us then remember the mystical Body of Christ to which we belong, and no longer be deluded into believing the devilish lie that one part of the Body is less important to its unity than another.

With these thoughts we commit the following pages to the judgment of the reader confident that "the Truth as it is in Jesus" and the unity of the Church "which is His body" will be served by honest conclusions reached on the basis of verifiable facts and under the guidance of the Holy Spirit of God.

WALTER R. MARTIN

Philadelphia, Pa.
March, 1959

A STATEMENT

For more than a century, Seventh-day Adventists have been proclaiming their beliefs to the world. During the years their motives and teachings have all too often been misunderstood and at times misrepresented. A number of books have been written in criticism of their doctrines, many of which books have been filled with inaccuracies, both historic and doctrinal.

The author of this present volume came directly to Seventh-day Adventists in a sincere desire to study fully at firsthand what they really do believe. This we wholeheartedly welcomed. We appreciate deeply the kindly Christian attitude displayed throughout this book, even in those areas where he is in marked disagreement with us. His presentation of our doctrines and prophetic interpretations as found on pages 47-86 is accurate and comprehensive.

There are places, however, in this book where we believe the author has erroneously criticized some features of our early history and our contemporary theological teachings. His interpretation and criticism of Ellen G. White in quite a few instances are we believe unfounded. We are naturally in disagreement with his critical arguments in certain areas of our theology and it is also incorrect when he says that Adventists equate eternal life with immortality, pages 118-122, 130. We emphatically teach that a true believer in Christ has eternal life abiding in him now, "and this life is in his Son," I John 5:11. We believe that immortality, or that quality of being that makes death impossible, is something bestowed on the believer at the resurrection when our Lord returns.

We trust that in studying the latter chapters of this volume, with which we naturally do not agree, where the author expresses his own beliefs and registers certain definite disagreements with Adventism, the reader will not overlook the fair and accurate statement of Adventist teachings so clearly set forth on pages mentioned above, 47-86.

For one to be completely objective when stating the beliefs of another is perhaps impossible, especially in those areas where there is definite divergence of interpretation. But this author has earned our gratitude and respect by his earnest endeavor to set forth correctly our doctrinal positions and by his attitude of Christian brotherhood.

November 4, 1959

H. W. Lowe, Chairman
Biblical Study and Research Group
General Conference of Seventh-day Adventists
Takoma Park, Washington 12, D. C.

ACKNOWLEDGMENTS

The author wishes to express his profound gratitude to The Rev. George E. Cannon, Professor of New Testament at St. Paul Bible Institute, St. Paul, Minnesota, my research companion and friend. My thanks also go to The Rev. Gilbert Peterson, Mr. Anthony Collarile, Miss Antha E. Card and Mr. Paul A. Hopkins, all of whom contributed greatly to the correction of the manuscript and proofs, and to many many others who have painstakingly provided primary source material without which this volume could never have been effectively written.

My deep appreciation, as always, goes to my wife who encouraged me to publish this work irrespective of the pressures involved and the final outcome.

CONTENTS

Part I

An Introduction to Contemporary Seventh-day Adventism

PART II

An Examination of Seventh-day Adventist Theology

Part III

In Retrospect

The Truth About Seventh-day Adventism

Part I

An Introduction to Contemporary Seventh-day Adventism

CHAPTER ONE

THE HISTORICAL BACKGROUND OF SEVENTH-DAY ADVENTISM

Seventh-day Adventism sprang from the "great second advent awakening" which shook the religious world about the middle of the nineteenth century, when a re-emphasis about the second advent of Jesus Christ was rampant in Britain and on the continent of Europe. Before long, many of the Old World views of prophetic interpretation crossed the Atlantic and penetrated American theological circles.

Based largely upon the apocalyptic books of Daniel and Revelation, the theology of the Advent Movement was discussed in the newspapers as well as in theological journals. New Testament eschatology competed with stock market quotations for front-page space, and the "seventy weeks," "twenty-three hundred days," and "the abomination of desolation" (Dan. 8, 9) were common subjects of conversation.

Following the chronology of Archbishop Ussher, and interpreting the 2300 days of Daniel as 2300 years, many Bible students of various denominations concluded that Christ would come back about the year 1843. Of this studious number was one William Miller, a Baptist minister and resident of Low Hampton, New York. The great second advent movement which swept the United States in the 1840's stemmed largely from the activities of this William Miller, who confidently taught in the year 1818, that in "about" twenty-five years, i.e. 1843, Jesus Christ would come again. As Miller himself put it, "I was thus brought in 1818 at the close of my two-year study of the Scriptures to the solemn conclusion that in about twenty-five years from that time all the affairs of our present state would be wound up."[1]

[1] Francis D. Nichol, *The Midnight Cry* (Washington, D. C.: Review and Herald, 1944), p. 35.

Miller further wrote, "I believe the time can be known by all who desire to understand and to be ready for His coming. And I am fully convinced that some time between March 21, 1843 and March 21, 1844, according to the Jewish mode of computation of time, Christ will come and bring all His saints with Him; and that then He will reward every man as His work shall be."[2] At length his associates set October 22, 1844, as the final date when Jesus Christ would return for His saints, visit judgment upon sin, and establish the Kingdom of God upon earth.

One need only read the words of the Lord Jesus Christ to realize that Miller was teaching in contradiction to the Word of God. Jesus said, "But of that day and hour knoweth no man, no, not the angels of heaven, but my Father only" (Matt. 24:36); "Watch therefore: for ye know not what hour your Lord doth come" (Matt. 24:42); "Therefore be ye also ready; for in such an hour as ye think not the Son of man cometh" (Matt. 24:44). "Watch therefore, for ye know neither the day nor the hour wherein the Son of man cometh" (Matt. 25:13).

The Gospel of Mark also shows that dates cannot be set, for in verse 33 of chapter 13 our Lord stated, "Take ye heed, watch and pray: for ye know not when the time is." And almost His last words to His disciples are a rebuke to those who set dates: "It is not for you to know the times or the seasons, which the Father hath put in his own power" (Acts 1:7). Certainly this should have been deterrent enough for William Miller and his associates, but sad to say it was not.

Compare the two positions, Miller versus the Scriptures: God declared that no man would know the time; Miller stated that he did know the time. God said the times and seasons were within His own Power; the Millerites declared that they had the prophetic key to them. Jesus Christ stated, "No man knows the day or the hour," but the Millerites set the exact day (October 22, 1844). And history bears a bitter record of their terrible disappointment.

Lest anyone reading the various accounts of the rise of Millerism in the United States come to the conclusion that Miller and his followers were "crackpots" or "uneducated tools of Satan," the fol-

2 *Signs of the Times,* Jan. 25, 1843.

lowing facts should be known:[3] The great advent awakening movement which spanned the Atlantic from Europe was bolstered by a tremendous wave of contemporary Biblical scholarship. Although Miller himself lacked academic theological training, actually scores of prophetic scholars in Europe and the United States had espoused Miller's view before he himself announced it. In reality, his was only one more voice proclaiming the 1843/1844 fulfillment of Daniel 8:14, or the 2300 days period allegedly dating from 457 B.C. and ending in 1843-1844.

William Miller was born in Pittsfield, Massachusetts, on February 15, 1782, and while still a young child his family moved to Low Hampton, New York, close to the Vermont State borderline. Miller was raised by a deeply religious mother, but despite her zeal for his conversion Miller himself became a deist. Only after a soul-searching experience which culminated in his conversion did he begin his preparation for the ministry in the Baptist church. A great many books have been written about William Miller and the Millerite movement, but to this writer's knowledge none of them has justly accused Miller of being dishonest or deceptive in his prophetic interpretation of Scripture. Indeed, he enjoyed the reputation, among all who knew him, of being an honest, forthright Christian. One does not have to endorse the errors of Millerism, therefore, to respect the historical figure of William Miller. Regardless of his shortcomings, Miller was a deeply religious Christian who, had he had a more extensive understanding of the Scriptures, most probably would never have embarked upon his disastrous date-setting career.

Clearly it may be seen that although Miller popularized the 1843-1844 concept of Christ coming again, he was by no means alone. If we condemn him, we must also condemn a large number of internationally known scholars who were among the most highly educated men of their day. Yet they too had a blind spot in prophetic interpretation and endorsed this fallacious system of date-setting.

[3] The various charges to the effect that the Millerites were fanatics who waited on rooftops attired in white "ascension robes" anticipating the return of Christ; and further that insanity swept the Millerite ranks in 1843-4 in the wake of the "Great Disappointment" are purely mythological in character and have little basis in verifiable facts. (See F. D. Nichol, *The Midnight Cry*, Review and Herald, Takoma Park, 1944, pp. 321-498, for a documented study of the evidence.)

Regardless of the number of scholars who confirmed his errors, however, the fact remains that Miller and the Millerite movement operated contrary to the express injunctions of Scripture. Both Miller and his followers lived to reap the reward of their foolhardy quest and to suffer crushing humiliation, ridicule and abject despair.

William Miller set the time for the return of the Lord between March 21, 1843 and March 21, 1844 reckoning according to the Jewish calendar.[4] As the first-named date approached, religious frenzy shook the Millerite world—the Lord was coming back!

Zealous and sincere though the followers of Miller were, stark disappointment awaited them as the Jewish year 1843 faded from time and the Lord did not come. When the dream closest to their hearts failed to materialize, they eagerly sought enlightenment from William Miller, who replied with characteristic honesty. Wrote Miller, in the very shadow of spiritual anguish: "Were I to live my life over again, with the same evidence that I then had, to be honest with God and man I should have to do as I have done. Although opposers said it would not come, they produced no weighty arguments. It was evidently guess-work with them; and I then thought, and do now, that their denial was based more on an unwillingness for the Lord to come than on any arguments leading to such conclusion. I confess my error, and acknowledge my disappointment; yet I still believe that the Day of the Lord is near, even at the door; and I exhort you, my brethren, to be watchful and not let that day come upon you unawares."[5]

In the wake of this stunning declaration, the Millerites strove vainly to reconcile their interpretations of the prophetic Scripture with the stark truth that Christ had not returned. With one last gasp, so to speak, Miller reluctantly endorsed "The Seventh-month Movement," or the belief that Christ would come on October 22, 1844, the tenth day of the seventh month according to the Karaite reckoning of the Jewish Sacred Calendar.[6] Once again the Millerites' hopes were lifted, and October 22, 1844 became the watchword for the return of the Lord Jesus Christ. The outcome can best be summed up in the words of Dr. Josiah Litch, a Millerite leader in

[4] *The Midnight Cry*, p. 169.
[5] Sylvester Bliss, *Memoirs of William Miller*, p. 256.
[6] *The Midnight Cry*, p. 243.

Philadelphia, who wrote on October 24: "It is a cloudy and dark day here—the sheep are scattered—the Lord has not come yet."[7]

From Litch's statement, it is easy to piece together the psychological framework of the Millerites in the wake of these two disappointments. They were a shattered and disillusioned people—Christ had not come to cleanse the "sanctuary" (the earth), to usher in judgment, and to bring the world into subjugation to the "everlasting gospel." Instead, the sky was cloudy and dark, and the historical horizons were black with the failure of the Millerite movement. There was, of course, terrible confusion, of which God, Scripture tells us, is not the author (I Cor. 14:33).

The final phase of the movement, then, closed with the "Great Disappointment" of 1844, but as the Millerites disbanded, there emerged other groups, such as the First-day Adventists. However, in our study we are concerned primarily with three segments which later fused to produce the Seventh-day Adventist denomination. William Miller, it should be noted, was *never* a Seventh-day Adventist and stated that he had "no confidence" in the "new theories" which emerged from the shambles of the Millerite movement. Dr. LeRoy Froom, Professor of Prophetic Interpretation at the Seventh-day Adventist Theological Seminary, Takoma Park, Washington, D. C., in the fourth volume of his masterful series *The Prophetic Faith of our Fathers,* pages 828-29,[8] succinctly states exactly what Miller's position was: "Miller was outspokenly opposed to the various new theories that had developed following October 22, 1844, in an endeavor to explain the disappointment. He deplored the call to come out to the churches that had been given, and he never accepted the distinctive positions of the Sabbatarians. The doctrine of the unconscious sleep of the dead and the final destruction of the wicked was not, he maintained, part of the original Millerite position, but was introduced personally by George Storrs and Charles Fitch. He even came to deny the application of the parable in *The Midnight Cry* to the Seventh-month Movement and eventually went so far as to declare unequivocally that the movement was not 'a fulfillment of prophecy in any sense.'"

[7] *The Midnight Cry,* p. 256.

[8] Review and Herald Publishing Association, Takoma Park, Washington, D. C., 1950.

Aside from chronological speculation, therefore, the theology of William Miller differed from Seventh-day Adventist theology in three distinct points: he denied the Seventh-day Sabbath, the doctrine of the sleep of the soul, and the final, utter destruction of the wicked—all doctrines held by the Seventh-day Adventist denomination. And he never embraced the "sanctuary" and "investigative judgment" theories developed by Seventh-day Adventists. For William Miller the era of chronological speculation was over, and he died shortly after the fiasco, a broken and disillusioned man who was, nevertheless, honest and forthright when in error or when repudiating error. I believe he now enjoys the presence of the Lord whose appearing he so anxiously awaited.

In order to understand the background of Seventh-day Adventist history and theology, let us look at the three segments of Millerism which eventually united to form the Seventh-day Adventist denomination. Each of these groups held a distinctive doctrine. The group headed by Hiram Edson in western New York proclaimed the doctrine of the sanctuary "as embracing a special or final ministry of Christ in the Holy of Holies in the *heavenly* sanctuary," thus giving new meaning to the message, "The Hour of God's Judgment has come." The second group, headed by Joseph Bates, whose main following was in Massachusetts and New Hampshire, advocated the observance of the Seventh-day "as involved in the keeping of the commandments of God." The third group, in Maine, emphasized the "spirit of prophecy" or "the testimony of Jesus," which they believed was to be manifest in the "remnant" (Rev. 14:6-12; also Rev. 12:17, 19:10), or "the last segment of God's church of the centuries." Between the years of 1844 and 1847 the thinking of these groups crystallized and was actively declared and promulgated in the writings of their respective leaders, Hiram Edson, O. R. L. Crosier, Joseph Bates, James White and Ellen G. White.

At this point in our historical analysis of Seventh-day Adventism, we believe it will be profitable to briefly review what is discussed in detail later on, "The Great Disappointment of 1844" and its relationship to the Seventh-day Adventist doctrines of the heavenly sanctuary and the investigative judgment. The entire superstructure of the Millerites' prophetic interpretation was based upon their view of the Book of Daniel, chapters eight and nine, with particular emphasis upon Daniel 8:14 and 9:24-27. The Millerites believed that the prophecy of the seventy weeks of Daniel nine must date from the year 457 B.C., which, as recent archeological evidence confirms,[9] was the exact date of the decree of King Artaxerxes to rebuild Jerusalem (Dan. 9:25). Tracing the seventy weeks of Daniel on the theory that, as the Hebrew indicated, it should be rendered "seventy weeks of years" or 490 years, the Millerites arrived at the date A.D. 33; that is, from B.C. 457 to A.D. 33. Since this date reliably refers to Christ's crucifixion, Millerites then linked it to Daniel 8:14, "Unto two thousand and three hundred days; then shall the sanctuary be cleansed" with the seventy weeks of years prophecy, and the 2300 days became 2300 years. Thus if you subtract 490 years (adding of course, A.D. 1 to 33) the figure 1843 is arrived at. Many Biblical scholars have historically shown that in Scripture a day frequently symbolizes a year; further, that the seventy weeks and 2300 days of Daniel could have begun on the same date. And that date, according to the Millerites, was B.C. 457. In *The Prophetic Faith of Our Fathers,* Dr. LeRoy Froom shows that many expositors had embraced the same method of interpretation, which is no argument for accepting it, but a strong argument for the *right* of the Millerites to do so.

As we have seen, when the Millerite calculations failed, all appeared to be lost; but a singular event took place the very next day in a cornfield near Port Gibson, New York, which changed the face of Adventist history and brought about a reinterpretation of the eighth and ninth chapters of the Book of Daniel, an interpretation which is a keystone in the arch of the Seventh-day Adventist view of prophecy.

On October 23, 1844, the morning following the Great Disappointment, Hiram Edson, a devout Adventist and follower of William Miller, was wending his way homeward with his friend, O. R. L. Crosier. In order to avoid the mocking gazes and taunts of their neighbors, they cut across a cornfield.

As they walked through the cornfield in deep silence and meditation, Hiram Edson stopped, became more deeply immersed in meditation, and then with upturned face indicative of a heartfelt prayer

[9] *The Chronology of Ezra 7,* Siegfried H. Horn and Lynn H. Wood, Review and Herald Publishing Association, Takoma Park, Washington, D. C. (1953).

for spiritual light, he suddenly received a great spiritual "revelation." In the words of Dr. Froom, "Suddenly there burst upon his mind the thought that there were two phases to Christ's ministry in the Heaven of Heavens, just as in the earthly sanctuary of old. In his own words, an overwhelming conviction came over him 'that instead of our high priest coming out of the most holy of the heavenly sanctuary to come to this earth on the tenth day of the seventh month at the end of the twenty-three hundred days, He for the first time entered on that day the second apartment of that sanctuary, and that He had a work to perform in the most holy before coming to this earth.' "[10]

In that instant, according to Seventh-day Adventist history, Hiram Edson found the reason why the Millerites had been disappointed the day before. They had expected Christ to come to earth to cleanse the sanctuary, but the sanctuary was not the earth but was located in Heaven! Instead of coming to earth, therefore, Christ had passed from one "apartment" of the sanctuary into the other "apartment" to perform a closing work now known as the "investigative judgment." In the year 1846 this new interpretation of Daniel was convincingly put forth by O. R. L. Crosier,[11] who outlined and defended Hiram Edson's concept in a lengthy article in a special number of *The Day Star,* a Millerite publication in Cincinnati, Ohio. F. D. Nichol in *The Midnight Cry* refers to "a fragment" which Edson wrote about his experience in the cornfield. But as Dr. Froom has pointed out, Edson himself really believed that Christ had passed from the "holy place" to the "most holy" place in the heavenly sanctuary. The Old Testament tabernacle was divided by a veil into two apartments, the holy place, and the most holy place. In the most holy place was the Ark of the Covenant. Into this apartment the high priest went once a year to sprinkle blood upon the mercy seat to make atonement for the sins of the people. In Christian

[10] *The Prophetic Faith of Our Fathers,* Vol. IV, p. 881. An extremely literalistic concept, which is refuted by Hebrews 9:12, 24 and Acts 1, which show that at His ascension Christ entered into the "holy places" not the "second apartment" of the heavenly sanctuary in 1844. Seventh-day Adventists have re-defined their teaching in terms of "phases." See *Questions on Doctrine,* p. 381.

[11] Crosier later rejected this concept though it was endorsed by Ellen G. White and other prominent Adventist leaders. (See D. M. Canright, *Life of Mrs. E. G. White,* p. 107; also, *A Word to the Little Flock* (pamphlet), pp. 11-12.)

theology, this blood symbolized prophetically the death of the Lord Jesus Christ, the Lamb of God, for the sins of all the world.

Transferring this Old Testament ceremonial to the New Testament, and making an extremely literalistic interpretation of the Book of Hebrews, Edson and Crosier formulated the doctrine of "the heavenly sanctuary and investigative judgment." This concept is now understood to mean that in 1844 Christ entered the "second phase" of His ministry in the heavenly sanctuary, and ever since has been reviewing the cases of believers to determine their worthiness for eternal life (a rather literalistic Arminian interpretation). Further, He will come forth from the "second apartment," or finish the "second phase" of His ministry in the sanctuary, to usher in judgment upon the world at His great second advent. This in essence was the interpretation which shaped the later concept of the "heavenly sanctuary" and the "investigative judgment" in Seventh-day Adventist theology. Thus, good Millerite-Adventists were justified in endorsing the work of William Miller. They even maintained that God had allowed Miller to make mistakes for the greater blessing of the "little flock." In her *Early Writings* Ellen G. White made this assertion: "I have seen that the 1843 chart was directed by the hand of the Lord, and that it should not be altered; that the figures were as He wanted them, that His hand was over and hid a mistake in some of the figures so that none could see it until His hand was removed" (p. 74). In this context Mrs. White was distinctly referring to Fitch's prophetic chart utilized by the Millerites, which led them to the year 1843 instead of the date which she considered to be correct—October 22, 1844.

F. D. Nichol in *Ellen G. White and Her Critics* (pp. 332-34), attempts to explain Mrs. White's statement in the light of Acts 24, Mark 16, Exodus 8:15 and Exodus 10. Of course any are at liberty to accept his interpretation of the problem, which I do not. The fact remains, however, that the Millerites erred in their prophetic, chronological interpretation of the Book of Daniel, and only the concept of Hiram Edson in the cornfield and the explanatory writings of O. R. L. Crosier buttressed by the "revelations" of Ellen G. White saved the day.

Although I do not accept Ellen White's explanation, or the interpretations of Edson, Crosier, Froom or Nichol, I would be at a loss to account for the growth and development of Seventh-day Adventism apart from the psychological framework of the "Great Disappointment of 1844." Therefore, I have carefully reviewed the doctrines which evolved from the Edson-Crosier-White pronouncements and set forth the results in Chapter VI. Suffice it to say here that the psychological factor is very important in Seventh-day Adventist history.

The second of the three Millerite-Adventist groups mentioned, is also of great historical import. In Fairhaven, Massachusetts, following the "Great Disappointment of 1844," one Joseph Bates, a retired sea captain, issued a 48-page pamphlet entitled *The Seventh-day Sabbath a Perpetual Sign* (1846). In it he argued for the Sabbath as a divine institution ordained in Eden, prefigured in Creation, and buttressed at Mt. Sinai. Some three years later Bates wrote a second pamphlet entitled, "A Seal of the Living God," based largely upon Revelation 14:9-12. Bates' Sabbatarianism exerted a great influence upon what later became the Seventh-day Adventist denomination.

In Volume IV of *The Prophetic Faith of Our Fathers* (pp. 957-58), Dr. Froom sums it up: "This became henceforth a characteristic and separating feature of Sabbatarian Adventist preaching. Bates here held that the message of Revelation 14 is the foundation of the full Advent message 'Fear God and give glory to Him, for the hour of His judgment is come.' This, he maintained, began to be fulfilled in the preaching of the Millerite movement. And the second angel's message on the fall of Babylon, with its climax in the call 'Come out of her my people' was likewise initially sounded in 1843-1844 . . . They must not stop with the first two messages. There is a third inseparable in the series to be received and obeyed—namely, full obedience to God's holy commandments, including the observance of the Seventh day as a Sabbath. But that obedience is by faith. The Sabbath was next set forth as the 'seal of God' as based on the sealing work of Revelation 7. On January 8, 1849 Bates issued his tract, 'A Seal of the Living God.' From the fact of John's declaration that the number of the sealed was 144,000, Bates drew the conclusion that the 'remnant' who keeps the commandments of God and have the testimony of Jesus Christ would number 144,000.[12]

[12] A position held by Uriah Smith and certain earlier Adventists, long since repudiated by the denominational leadership and majority of members.

So, to the concept of Christ entering the most holy place in the heavenly sanctuary on October 22, 1844 for the final work of judgment and the receiving of His kingdom, was added the Sabbath as involved in the third of this commission series of special 'latter-day' messages. This concept of the 'seal' was likewise built into the message of the Sabbath, as an added prophetic element. And this thought was similarly attested by Ellen White who wrote: 'This seal is the Sabbath,' and described the 'most holy place' in which was the ark (Rev. 11:19), containing the Ten Commandments with a halo of light surrounding the fourth! Thus the Sabbath and the sanctuary became inseparably tied together."

The third group, which fused with the other two to form the Seventh-day Adventist church, emphasized "the spirit of prophecy" (Rev. 19:10). This body of former Millerites accepted the interpretations of one Ellen G. Harmon of Portland, Maine. Ellen Harmon, later Mrs. James White, was recognized by this group as the possessor of the "Spirit of Prophecy," a restoration of the spiritual gift of prophecy (I Cor. 12) or counsel to the Seventh-day Adventist church. Mrs. White had numerous visions which confirmed many Adventist doctrines. We shall discuss her relationship to the Adventist denomination in Chapter Four. When the Edson-Crosier, Bates, and White adherents joined forces, the Seventh-day Adventist denomination was launched.

Although the name "Seventh-day Adventist" denomination was not officially assumed until 1860 at a conference held in Battle Creek, Michigan, nevertheless Seventh-day Adventism had been launched. In 1855, Adventist headquarters were established in Battle Creek and remained there until 1903, when they were transferred to Takoma Park, Washington, D. C.

The three distinctive doctrines of Seventh-day Adventism—the Sabbath, the Sanctuary and the "Spirit of Prophecy"—will be discussed in later chapters. The Adventists had a definite theological platform, which for many years remained almost constant. In recent years, however, there has been a definite movement toward a more explicit declaration of belief in the principles of the Christian faith and the tenets of Christian theology. In short, "clarification" and "redefinition" have characterized recent Seventh-day Adventist theological activities.

Today the Seventh-day Adventist denomination numbers over 1,150,000 adult baptized members, while they have over 1,500,000 Sabbath school members throughout the world. There are some 6,000 ordained ministers and more than 3,200 licensed ministers. The Adventists have 44 publishing houses producing literature in about 220 languages, while they are preaching and teaching in about 800 languages and dialects. They publish 385 periodicals and more than 60 new books yearly, and have enrolled more than 3,000,000 persons in their Bible study courses offered over the radio. Their *Voice of Prophecy* radio program is heard on 860 stations and is reaching people in some 65 languages. *Faith for Today* their official TV program is heard on 153 stations in the U.S. and many stations abroad. The *Signs of the Times* and *These Times* their largest missionary magazines have a combined circulation of 400,000 copies a month.

During 1958 Seventh-day Adventists contributed more than $83,-000,000 for their church work at home and abroad, while the literature sales of the denomination amounted to $22,000,000. They contributed on the average of over $216 per person. In addition the Adventists maintain 220 medical units employing over 420 doctors in 107 sanitariums and hospitals with 114 clinics and dispensaries. They have numerous medical launches in areas like the Amazon, and welfare projects all over the globe.

It is interesting to note by way of contrast that the average per capita contribution for all denominations in the United States is $48.81! Though still a relatively small denomination, the Seventh-day Adventists are said to have actually more missionaries active on foreign fields than any other mission body except Methodists who have a few over 1500; the Adventists in excess of 1400.

To round out the picture where this zealous group of Christians is concerned, it should be remembered that Adventists have a working force of more than 46,000 with a total of 12,500 churches organized into 425 conferences and union conferences. The Adventist school system comprising 5,216 schools and colleges employs more than 12,000 teachers. Approximately 275,000 students are attending their schools.

We cannot hope to cover the entire scope of Seventh-day Adventism's historical development in this chapter but we see that from meager beginnings in the wake of the "Great Disappointment of 1844" and the collapse of the Millerite movement, the Seventh-day Adventist denomination has pressed forward and expanded until today it constitutes an important albeit controversial segment of American Protestantism.

Succeeding chapters will tell more of Seventh-day Adventist history as it is related to their theology. Although this chapter is but a background sketch, the reader can readily see that in Seventh-day Adventism, religious historians have an interesting subject for study, a subject from which many unusual theological speculations have emerged and continue to emerge.

CHAPTER TWO

PSYCHOLOGICAL FACTORS

One of the principal problems in understanding the Seventh-day Adventist movement is to discover the psychological motivation and basis of this thriving denomination of Christian zealots.

I. Early Handicaps

From the beginning, the Adventists were regarded with grave suspicion by the great majority of evangelical Christians, principally because the Seventh-day Adventists were premillennial in their eschatology. That is, they believed that Christ would come before the millennium and so placed themselves squarely in opposition to the predominant post- and a-millennial schools of thought of that era. The "Great Disappointment" of 1844 and the collapse of the Millerite movement, naturally brought premillennialism into disrepute. Certain authors of the time considered premillennarians "peculiar" even to the point of condemning premillennialism outright and dubbed as "Adventists" all who held that view of eschatology. This is especially interesting when we consider that premillennialism is an accepted school of thought in eschatology today and that those who hold postmillennial and amillennial views are considered by the premillenarians to be peculiar.

Thus the Adventists started out with two great psychological handicaps: They had incurred disapproval of the group or the mainstream of Christianity and the Millerites from which they sprang had been publicly humiliated by the failure of their chronological calculations. These two factors and the constant jeering by opposing schools of eschatology united the Seventh-day Adventists in a closely-knit group, habitually on the defensive and suspicious of the motives and intentions of other Christians.

Moreover, the Adventists were drawn together by the "special truths" of the Advent message. They were convinced that they had a proclamation for the world—a great "last-day message." In the next chapter we shall describe how this attitude widened the chasm between Adventists and Christians of other denominations, so it is sufficient here to note that the Adventists considered themselves a special "remnant people" ordained by God to revive certain neglected truths of the Christian message. Filled with burning zeal to fulfill this mission, they laid themselves open to serious misunderstanding by Christians of other denominations who did not agree with them about the proper day of worship, the state of the dead, and investigative judgment.

Engaged in open conflict with Christians of virtually all denominations, the Adventists retreated into an "exclusivistic shell," despising what they termed "certain antinomian tendencies in contemporary Christian theology." They laid strong emphasis upon man's responsibility to the moral law of God, which eventually brought upon them the label, "Galatianists" or "legalists." Now, as we shall see, there can be little doubt that there was and still is legalism in Adventism, as in other Christian communions; but when we consider these early psychological factors, certain of which still obtain today, their reactions are understandable, though hardly defensible.

Of course the aforementioned "neglected" truths made few friends for the Adventists with Christians of other denominations, mainly because these truths were frequently presented in such manner as to arouse opposition instead of inviting investigation. Seventh-day Adventism has woefully demonstrated many times the old but true adage, "Not what we say but how we say it makes or breaks a case."

II. Identity Concealed

In his book, *Answers to Objections,* F. D. Nichol demonstrates how the psychological defense which Adventists erected in their early days has carried over into modern times. Nichol quotes the charge: "When Seventh-day Adventist ministers go into a community to hold a series of lectures they conceal at first their denominational connection. They thus hope to draw into their audience people who would never have come if they knew that Seventh-day Adventists were conducting the meetings. This is a form of deception. There is something the matter with a religious body that is afraid to identify itself as soon as it begins to carry on any activity in a community."

Nichol answers: "Now it is a fact that during most of the history of the Seventh-day Adventist church, the very word Adventist has conveyed to the minds of most people a picture of a deluded band of fanatics sitting on housetops in ascension robes, awaiting the opening of the heavens. This story of ascension robes has become a part of American folklore and has been embalmed in impressive encyclopedias. And the ascension robe story is only part of the fanciful picture that has come to the minds of many when they have heard the word Adventist.

"The ascension robe story is a myth, and ninety-nine percent of related stories are likewise myths—as has now been proved—but that has not prevented people from believing them. The net result has been that many people have seen Seventh-day Adventists only through the distorting mists of slanderous myths. This is nothing new in religious history; witness, for example, the early history of the Quakers and the Baptists.

"It should not be difficult, therefore, for any reasonable person to see why Adventist ministers through the past years have sought first to cause people to see them simply as Christian preachers before announcing their Adventist connection. After all, we seek to be first, and before all else, Christian preachers of righteousness. Then we hope to build on that the timely messages from Bible prophecy that may be described in the words of the Apostle Peter as 'present truth' for these last days of earth's history.

"It has undoubtedly been true in years past that Adventists could not have gotten a crowd out to hear them in certain cities, at least, if they had revealed their identity at the outset. But we think that that proves not the weakness of the Adventist case, but the strength of distorted ideas founded on fanciful myths. The other side of the picture is that many people, after they have attended Adventist meetings for a time, frankly admit that they have changed their ideas about us and are glad that they first came to the meeting not knowing who was conducting them.

"In more recent years our activities have become so much better known that in many places the former distorted picture has been largely corrected. Accordingly, we are increasingly following the plan of announcing at the outset the Adventist sponsorship of the public meetings.[1] That is what we like to do, and what we hope ere long to be able to do everywhere. We are not ashamed of our Adventism, far from it . . . No, we don't want to boast, we simply want to proclaim to the world a message that we earnestly believe should be given at this time. And if, in order to secure an initial hearing, we must at first conceal the name, we do so for a brief period only with a view to a clear-cut announcement of our Adventist connections a little later in the meetings. Then those who have been coming may decline to come further, if they desire. They generally decide to stay!

"Unhappily, as the literature of many objectors to Adventism reveals, it is they who have often been most active in spreading the distorting myths regarding us. And then they are wont to add, as though to prove conclusively their case against us, that we sometimes fail to reveal our Adventist connection at the outset of a series of evangelistic lectures! If they will help us to clear away completely the slanderous myths which folklore has often thrown around the name Adventist, we will be most happy to preface every one of our public meetings with the announcement of its Adventist sponsorship! In the meantime we shall, in such instances and areas as the situation necessitates, follow the precedent set by our Lord's instruction to His disciples as regards the time of disclosing our name" (pp. 421-22).

Thus we see that some Adventist leaders, at least, maintain the premise that everyone's prejudice against them is based on myths and folklore, and on the fact that they deliberately disguise them-

[1] Research has revealed that in some cases this is true. However, it is encouraging to note that the *Voice of Prophecy*, the official Seventh-day Adventist radio program, and *Faith for Today*, as well as *It Is Written*, both Seventh-day Adventist TV programs, have publicly identified themselves to offset the charge of concealment. These are singular instances of keeping faith with their statements that they have nothing to hide as Adventists and wish to deceive no one. The literature program has not kept pace with radio or TV and will undoubtedly take time for full identification. In certain instances disclosure of denominational ties has been withheld by denominations other than Seventh-day Adventists, particularly on the mission field and this chiefly because Adventists as well as some other Christian denominations believe that in certain sections of the world where Protestantism, or even Christianity is looked upon with contempt, that it is in harmony with the Word of God that they do not make too prominent their identification in the beginning. This is done to avoid prejudice and false accusations which might hinder the honest in heart from hearing the Gospel of Jesus.

selves until they can obtain a hearing and demonstrate that they are Christians. These practices have given rise to the charge of proselyting and it is not without foundation. In general, however, Nichol makes some very good points, though inadvertently he reveals only too clearly that he and many Adventists have been reared in this unhealthy climate of distrust, prejudice and suspicion.

Nichol declares, "If they will help us to clear away completely the slanderous myths that folklore has so often thrown around the name Adventist, we will be most happy to preface every one of our public meetings with the announcement of its Adventist sponsorship!"

The only difficulty with Nichol's statement is that the burden of proof lies not upon the other denominations, but upon the Adventists themselves. By openly identifying themselves, they can refute these charges of deception and proselyting.

On page 420, Nichol makes the mistake of using passages in the Gospel of Matthew (8:4; 9:30; 16:20) where Christ enjoined secrecy, to prove that Adventists are only following Him when they conceal their identity, and he unfortunately tries to establish that such a behavior pattern on the part of Adventists is "honorable." Says Nichol, "We have yet to hear any devout Christian expressing misgivings and doubts about the ministry of Christ or declaring that He was ashamed or afraid because He concealed His identity for a time. Evidently, then, this much at least may be established at the outset as being proved by these texts; concealing one's identity is not an insult or proof that one is either ashamed or afraid. There may be honorable and altogether reasonable grounds for such concealment."

Although Nichol's argument appears plausible, the cases are not parallel, for over against the incidents which he cites, the Lord Jesus did many miracles in public and taught openly in the Temple as He Himself declared before Caiaphas (John 18:20). But to compare the motives of Adventists with the motives of the Lord Jesus Christ is just a bit more than this writer is willing to concede.

True, there is much misinformation about Adventist history and theology, but not infrequently it can be traced to unfortunate statements in their own official publications. Although other denominations are likewise guilty, Adventists have largely been outside the main stream of Christian fellowship and so are in an unenviable position. They must go the "second mile" in this respect.

It is evident, then, that because of the opposition and abuse suffered in their early days, and also because of the "special truths" of the Advent message and emphasis upon certain areas of theology, the Adventists have been at a distinct psychological disadvantage and so have tended to band together against other churches. Other denominations, of course, have encouraged this recluse-like behavior by endless repetition of some of the Millerite myths. These factors, therefore, must be soberly evaluated if we are to understand Seventh-day Adventism.

III. Ellen G. White on Interdenominational Fellowship

There is a most interesting sidelight in the psychological study of Seventh-day Adventism which has been overlooked by nearly all students of Seventh-day Adventism and even by the Adventists themselves, who of all people should have heeded it. It is the fact that in her writings Ellen G. White counseled the Adventists to make an effort to establish fellowship and find common ground with ministers and peoples of other denominations. Since Mrs. White is looked upon as a special messenger of God to these people, it is amazing that the average Seventh-day Adventist does not seem to be aware of her counsel in this connection.

As we will see in succeeding chapters, the basic theology of Seventh-day Adventism is essentially orthodox; nevertheless, the Adventists have consistently overemphasized their differences in theology. Indeed, they have tended to magnify these differences, with the result that other Christian denominations regard them with distrust.

No informed student of Adventism can deny that Mrs. White herself, as well as other prominent leaders, in the early days of the movement, encouraged the divisive attitude that Mrs. White, at least, openly deplored during the last three decades of her life. To establish this point beyond doubt, we have carefully catalogued her principal statements on this subject, and present them here so that both Adventists and non-Adventists may have a better criterion by which to evaluate this area of Adventist thought and relationship.

1. "We are to do all we can to remove the prejudice that exists

in the minds of man against our work and against the Bible Sabbath" (*Testimonies to the Church,* Vol. 9, p. 238).

2. "There is to be a time of trouble such as never was since there was a nation. Our work is to study, to weed out of all our discourses everything that savors of retaliation and defiance and making a drive against churches and individuals, because this is not Christ's way and method" (*Testimonies,* Vol. 9, p. 244).

3. "Our ministers and teachers are to present the love of God to a fallen world. With hearts melted in tenderness let the Word of Truth be spoken. Let all who are in error be treated with the gentleness of Christ. If those for whom you labor do not immediately grasp the truth, do not censure, do not criticize or condemn. Remember that you are to represent Christ in His meekness and gentleness and love." "We must expect to meet unbelief and opposition. The truth has always had to contend with these elements. But though you should meet the bitterest opposition, do not denounce your opponents. They may think, as did Paul, that they are doing God service; and to such we must manifest patience, meekness and long-suffering" (*Gospel Workers,* p. 372).

4. "The Lord wants His people to follow other methods than that of condemning wrong, even though the condemnation is just. He wants us to do something more than to hurl at our adversaries charges that only drive them farther from the truth. The work which Christ came to do in our world was not to erect barriers and constantly thrust upon the people the fact that they are wrong . . . The very last work of the controversy may be the enlightenment of those who have not rejected light and evidence but who have been in midnight darkness and have in ignorance worked against the truth. Therefore, treat every man as honest. Speak no word, do no deed that will confirm any in unbelief. If anyone shall seek to draw the workers into debate or controversy on political or other questions, take no heed to either persuasion or challenge" (*Gospel Workers,* pp. 373, 374).

5. "Our brethren should be cautioned to make no moves that will stir up the powers that be so that they will make moves that will limit and cut us off from proclaiming the message in different localities" (*Testimonies to Ministers,* pp. 219, 220).

6. "As workers for Christ we want sanctified tact. Study to be

skillful when there are no rules to meet the case. Win hearts, not repulse them" (*Review and Herald,* December 16, 1884).

7. "Let not those who write for our papers make unkind thrusts and allusions that will certainly do harm, and that will hedge up the way and hinder us from performing the work that we should do in order to reach all classes, the Catholics included. It is our work to speak the truth in love and not to mix in with the truth the unsanctified elements of the natural heart, and speak things that savor of the same spirit possessed by our enemies. All sharp thrusts will come back upon us in double measure when the power is in the hands of those who can exercise it for our injury. Over and over the message has been given to me that we are not to say one word, not to publish one sentence especially by way of personalities unless positively essential in vindicating the truth that will stir up our enemies against us and arouse their passions to a white heat" (*Testimonies,* Vol. 9, p. 241).

8. "The time will come when unguarded expressions of a denunciatory character that have been carelessly spoken or written by our brethren will be used by our enemies to condemn us. These . . . will be charged upon the whole body of Adventists. Our accusers will say that such and such a day one of our responsible men said thus and so against the administration and the laws of this government. Many will be astonished to see how many things have been cherished and remembered that will give point to the arguments of our adversaries. Many will be surprised to hear their own words strained into a meaning that they did not intend them to have. Then let our workers be careful to speak guardedly at all times and under all circumstances. Let all beware lest by reckless expressions they bring on a time of trouble before the great crisis which is to try men's souls" (*Testimonies,* Vol. 6, pp. 394, 395).

9. "It is not our work to attack individuals or institutions . . . We should not be turned aside to lines that will encourage controversy, or arouse antagonism in those not of our faith" (*Ibid.,* p. 394).

10. "Let the ready writers be careful how they use their pens, lest they seem to cast ridicule upon the positions of believers or unbelievers" (*Testimonies to Ministers,* p. 219).

11. "The people must be given the truth, straightforward, positive truth. This truth is to be presented in the Spirit of Christ. We

are to be as sheep in the midst of wolves. . . . The Lord has not given His people the work of making a tirade against those who are transgressing His law. In no case are we to make a raid on the other churches. Let us remember that as a people entrusted with sacred truth we have been neglectful and positively unfaithful" (*Ibid.*, p. 236).

12. "We should not go out of our way to make hard thrusts at the Catholics. Among the Catholics there are many who are most conscientious Christians and who walk in all the light that shines upon them, and God will work in their behalf. . . . Let everyone bear in mind that we are in no case to invite persecution. We are not to use harsh and cutting words. Keep them out of every article written. Drop them out of every address given. . . . Let the Spirit of Christ appear. Let all be guarded in their words lest they place those not of our faith in deadly opposition against us, and give Satan an opportunity to use the unadvised words to hedge up our ways" (*Testimonies,* Vol. 9, pp. 243, 244).

These quotations, from the highest authority outside the Bible where Seventh-day Adventism is concerned, show that Adventists as a denomination have largely ignored what they themselves consider to be the inspired counsel of Mrs. White in this specific area. Although much progress has been made in recent years, some of the earlier attitudes still persist, and until they are corrected in line with Mrs. White's counsel to the Adventist church, they will doubtless present difficulties and obstacles to fellowship between Adventists and Christians of other denominations. So, this writer is quite willing to acknowledge that Adventists have labored under severe psychological handicaps in their founding and development. But Adventists cannot escape the fact that their chief counselor, Ellen G. White, is also chief witness to the fact that they have been guilty of exclusivism. To be consistent in their acceptance of Mrs. White's authority, they must heed her counsel before they can charge the rest of the Christian church with failure to exercise understanding or tolerance, where the propagation of their "special truths" is involved.

CHAPTER THREE

THE HEART OF ADVENTIST THEOLOGY

For many years, Seventh-day Adventists have been handicapped by the lack of a comprehensive volume which adequately defines their doctrinal position. Many excellent publications clearly set forth certain aspects of Adventism, but for doctrinal information one has had to rely upon statements by Ellen G. White, Uriah Smith, J. N. Andrews, F. M. Wilcox, F. D. Nichol, W. H. Branson, Carlyle B. Haynes, L. E. Froom, and others. Except for the brief statement of fundamentals in the Seventh-day Adventist yearbook, the average Adventist has been somewhat handicapped because of conflicting theological opinions within the denomination, and even expressions in the writings of Ellen G. White were sometimes ambiguous. So Seventh-day Adventists have found considerable difficulty in presenting a definite, comprehensive explanation of their faith. In 1957, however, the General Conference of Seventh-day Adventists released the first such authoritative volume, entitled *Questions on Doctrine.*

This book truthfully presents the theology and doctrine which the leaders of Seventh-day Adventism affirm they have always held. Members of other denominations will find it a reliable source to consult when seeking to understand what the Adventists themselves describe as "the position of our denomination in the area of church doctrine and prophetic interpretation."[1]

This present chapter is divided into sixteen sections, each of which contains statements of the recognized Adventist position on a particular aspect of theology, and is thoroughly documented from the primary source material provided in *Questions on Doctrine.* I hope that the reader will weigh carefully the declarations of the Seventh-day Adventist church, for in the study of any religious movement a clear, unbiased picture may be obtained *only* by going to the source of authority, in this case the General Conference of Seventh-day Adven-

[1] Introduction, p. 8.

tists. Thus the Seventh-day Adventists here speak for themselves; let us examine their statements in the light of honest scholarship and Christian ethics. All page numbers refer to *Questions on Doctrine* and a special Author's Note has been added to this chapter to present the facts concerning some of the inaccurate "stock arguments" raised by critics of Seventh-day Adventism relative to their adherence to the foundational doctrines of Christianity.

I. Inspiration and Authority of the Scriptures

I-1. "Seventh-day Adventists believe that all Scripture, both Old and New Testament, from Genesis to Revelation was 'given by inspiration of God' (2 Tim. 3:16), and constitutes the very word of God—the truth that 'liveth and abideth forever' (1 Pet. 1:23). We recognize the Bible as the ultimate and final authority on what is truth" (p. 26).

I-2. "The Holy Scriptures came to us through the ministry of the prophets who spake and wrote 'as they were moved by the Holy Ghost' (2 Pet. 1:21)" (p. 26).

I-3. "We take the Bible in its entirety believing that it not merely *contains* the Word of God but *is* the Word of God" (p. 27).

I-4. "We believe in the authority, veracity, reliability, and truth of the Holy Scriptures. The same union of the divine and the human that is manifested in Christ, exists in the Bible. Its truths, revealed, are 'given by inspiration of God' (2 Tim. 3:16), yet are couched in the words of men" (pp. 27, 28).

I-5. "Seventh-day Adventists hold the Protestant position that the Bible and the Bible only is the sole rule of faith and practice for Christians. We believe that all theological beliefs must be measured by the living Word, judged by its truth, and whatsoever is unable to pass this test, or is found to be out of harmony with its message, is to be rejected" (p. 28).

II. The Godhead

II-1. "The Godhead or Trinity, consists of the Eternal Father, a personal spiritual Being, omnipotent, omnipresent, omniscient, infinite in wisdom and love; the Lord Jesus Christ, the Son of the Eternal Father, through whom all things were created and through whom the salvation of the redeemed hosts will be accomplished; the

Holy Spirit, the third person of the Godhead, the great regenerating power in the work of redemption (Matt. 28:19)" (p. 11).

II - 2. "The Godhead, the Trinity, comprises God the Father, Christ the Son, and the Holy Spirit" (p. 22).

II - 3. "There are three living persons of the heavenly trio; in the name of these three great powers—the Father, the Son, and the Holy Spirit—those who receive Christ by living faith are baptized, and these powers will cooperate with the obedient subjects of heaven in their efforts to live the new life in Christ" (pp. 645-46).

II - 4. "The eternal heavenly dignitaries—God, and Christ, and the Holy Spirit. . . . We are to cooperate with the three highest powers in heaven,—the Father, the Son and the Holy Ghost,—and these powers will work through us, making us workers together with God" (p. 646).

III. The Nature of Christ

III - 1. "Jesus Christ is very God, being of the same nature and essence as the Eternal Father. While retaining His divine nature He took upon Himself the nature of the human family, lived on the earth as a man, exemplified in His life as our example the principles of righteousness, attested His relationship to God by many mighty miracles, died for our sins on the cross, was raised from the dead, and ascended to the Father, where He ever lives to make intercession for us (John 1:1, 14; Heb. 2:9-18; Heb. 8:1, 2; Heb. 4:14-16; Heb. 7:25)" (pp. 11, 12).

III - 2. "Jesus Christ is very God, and He has existed with the Father from all eternity" (p. 22).

III - 3. "Christ, the Word of God, became incarnate through the miraculous conception and the virgin birth; and He lived an absolutely sinless life here on earth" (p. 22).

III - 4. "As to Christ's place in the Godhead, we believe Him to be the second person in the heavenly Trinity—comprised of Father, Son and Holy Spirit. . . . Christ is one with the Eternal Father—one in nature, equal in power and authority, God in the highest sense, eternal and self-existent, with life original, unborrowed, underived. . . . Christ existed from all eternity, distinct from, but united with, the Father, possessing the same glory, and all the divine attributes" (p. 36).

III-5. "Christ was God essentially, and in the highest sense. He was with God from all eternity, 'God over all, blessed forevermore. . . .'" (pp. 642, 647).

III-6. "From all eternity Christ was united with the Father, and when He took upon Himself human nature, He was still one with God" (p. 644).

III-7. "Christ was a real man; He gave proof of His humility in becoming a man. Yet He was God in the flesh" (p. 647).

III-8. "Christ is called the Second Adam. In purity and holiness, connected with God and beloved by God. He began where the first Adam began. Willingly He passed over the ground where Adam fell, and redeemed Adam's failure" (p. 650).

III-9. "In the fullness of time He was to be revealed in human form. He was to take His position at the head of humanity by taking the nature but not the sinfulness of man" (p. 651).

III-10. "When Christ bowed His head and died, He bore the pillars of Satan's kingdom with Him to the earth. He vanquished Satan in the same nature over which in Eden Satan obtained the victory. The enemy was overcome by Christ in His human nature" (p. 651).

III-11. "In taking upon Himself man's nature in its fallen condition, Christ did not in the least participate in its sin. He was subject to the infirmities and weaknesses by which man is encompassed. . . . He was touched with the feeling of our infirmities, and was in all points tempted like as we are. And yet He 'knew no sin.' He was the Lamb 'without blemish and without spot.' . . . We should have no misgivings in regard to the perfect sinlessness of the human nature of Christ" (p. 651).

III-12. "Be careful, exceedingly careful as to how you dwell upon the human nature of Christ. Do not set Him before the people as a man with the propensities of sin. He is the Second Adam. The first Adam was created a pure, sinless being without a taint of sin upon him; he was in the image of God. He could fall, and he did fall through transgressing. Because of sin his posterity was born with inherent propensities of disobedience. But Jesus Christ was the only begotten Son of God. He took upon Himself human nature, and was tempted in all points as human nature is tempted. He could have sinned; He could have fallen; but not for one moment was there in Him an evil propensity" (p. 651).

III - 13. "In treating upon the humanity of Christ, you need to guard strenuously every assertion, lest your words be taken to mean more than they imply, and thus you lose or dim the clear perceptions of His humanity as combined with divinity. His birth was a miracle of God. . . . Never, in any way, leave the slightest impression upon human minds that a taint of, or inclination to, corruption rested upon Christ, or that He in any way yielded to corruption. . . . Let every human being be warned from the ground of making Christ altogether human, such an one as ourselves; for it cannot be" (p. 652).

III - 14. "While He was free from the taint of sin, the refined sensibilities of His holy nature rendered contact with evil unspeakably painful to Him. . . . Christ declared of Himself 'The prince of this world cometh and hath nothing in Me.' . . . On not one occasion was there a response to his [Satan's] manifold temptations" (p. 655).

III - 15. "He was born without a taint of sin, but came into the world in like manner as the human family" (p. 657).

III - 16. "In His human nature He maintained the purity of His divine character. . . . He was unsullied with corruption, a stranger to sin. . . . He was a mighty petitioner, not possessing the passions of our human, fallen natures, but compassed with like infirmities, tempted in all points like as we are" (pp. 658-59).[2]

III - 17. "He was perfect, and undefiled by sin, He was without spot or blemish. . . . Jesus, coming to dwell in humanity, receives no pollution" (p. 660).

IV. The Atonement

IV - 1. "Those who teach that a completed atonement was made on the cross view the term in its popular theological sense, but really what is meant by them is that on Calvary the all-sufficient atoning sacrifice of Christ was offered for our salvation. With this concept all true Christians readily and heartily agree. 'We are sanctified through the offering of the body of Jesus Christ, once for all' (Heb. 10:10). Those who view this aspect of the work of Christ as a completed atonement, apply this term *only* to what Christ accomplished on the cross. They do not include in their definition the

[2] See Author's Note at end of chapter.

application of the benefits of the atonement made on the cross to the individual sinner" (p. 342).

IV-2. "There are those, however, who believe the atonement has a much wider connotation. They fully agree with those who stress a completed atonement on the cross in the sense of an all-sufficient, once-for-all, atoning sacrifice for sin. They believe that nothing less than this took place on the cross of Calvary" (pp. 342-43).

IV-3. "In God's eternal purpose, He who makes the atonement is the Mediator. Everything in the typical service—the sacrifices and the work of the priesthood—pointed forward to Christ Jesus, our Lord. He took our place and died in our stead. In doing this, He became our substitute. In dying on the cross, in yielding his life an atonement for sin, He made adequate compensation for the wrong done; He met in full the penalty of the broken law of God. 'Christ's sacrifice in behalf of man was full and complete. The condition of the atonement had been fulfilled. The work for which He had come to this world had been accomplished.'—Ellen G. White. But the work accomplished on Calvary involves also the application of the atoning sacrifice of Christ to the seeking soul. This is provided for in the priestly ministry of our blessed Lord, our great High Priest in the sanctuary above.

"Not only are His people cleansed from sin by the sacrifice of the Son of God and saved for time and eternity, but the entire universe is to be purified from the very taint of iniquity with the author of sin utterly destroyed. Then will follow a new heaven and a new earth (II Pet. 3:13) which will be the eternal home of the ransomed of all ages, those who have been redeemed by the precious blood of the Lamb" (p. 347).

IV-4. "Some of our earlier Seventh-day Adventist writers, believing that the word 'atonement' had a wider meaning than many of their fellow Christians attached to it, expressed themselves as indicating that the atonement was not made on the cross of Calvary, but was made rather by Christ after He entered upon His priestly ministry in heaven. They believed fully in the efficacy of the sacrifice of Christ for the salvation of men, and they believed most assuredly that this sacrifice was made once for all and forever, but they preferred not to use the word 'atonement' as relating *only* to the sacrificial work of Christ at Calvary. We repeat, they believed as fully as we do that the sacrificial work of our blessed Lord on Golgotha's hill was full and complete, never again to be offered, and that it was done once and for all. Their concept was that the sacrifice of Jesus *provided* the means of the atonement, and that the atonement itself was made only when the priests *ministered* the sacrificial offering on behalf of the sinner. Viewed in this light, it will be seen that the question after all is a matter of a definition of terms. Today, not meeting the same issues that our earlier writers had to meet, we believe that the sacrificial atonement was made on the cross and was *provided* for all men but that in the heavenly priestly ministry of Christ our Lord, this sacrificial atonement is *applied* to the seeking soul.

"Stressing this wider concept, however, in no way detracts from the full efficacy of the death of the Son of God, once for all for the sins of men. It is unfortunate that a lack of a definition of terms so often leads to misunderstanding on the greatest theme of the Christian message" (p. 348).

IV-5. "Seventh-day Adventists do *not* believe that Christ made but partial or incomplete sacrificial atonement on the cross" (p. 349).[3]

IV-6. "Most decidedly the all-sufficient atoning sacrifice of Jesus our Lord was *offered and completed* on the cross of Calvary. This was done for all mankind, for 'he is the propitiation . . . for the sins of the whole world' (I John 2:2). This sacrificial work will actually benefit human hearts *only* as we surrender our lives to God and experience the miracle of the new birth. In this experience Jesus our High Priest, applies to us the benefits of His atoning sacrifice. Our sins are forgiven and we become the children of God by faith in Christ Jesus, and the peace of God dwells in our hearts.

"Hence, the divine plan of redemption involves more than the vicarious atoning death of Christ though this is its very core; also it includes the ministry of our Lord as our heavenly High Priest. Having completed His sacrifice, He rose from the dead 'for our justification' (Rom. 4:25) and then entered into the sanctuary above, there to perform His priestly service for needy men. 'Having obtained eternal redemption for us' (Heb. 9:12) on the cross, He now ministers the benefits of that atonement for those who accept of His mighty

[3] See Appendix A No. 2 for comments on the completed Atonement.

provision of grace. Thus the atoning sacrifice, having been completed on Calvary, must now be applied and appropriated to those who are heirs of salvation. Our Lord's ministry is thus involved in the great work of atonement. So as we think of the mighty sweep of the atonement, in its provisions and its efficacy, it is seen to be vastly more comprehensive than many have thought" (p. 350-51).

IV-7. "The atonement therefore involves not only the transcendent act of the cross, but also the benefits of Christ's sacrifice which are continually being applied to needy man. This will continue until the close of human probation. . . .

"In common with conservative Christians, Adventists teach an atonement that necessitated the incarnation of the eternal Word—the Son of God—in order that He might become the Son of Man; and living His life among men as our kinsman in the flesh, might die in our stead to redeem us. We believe that the atonement provides an all-sufficient, perfect, substitutionary sacrifice for sin, which completely satisfies the justice of God and fulfills every requirement, so that mercy, grace, and forgiveness can freely be extended to the repentant sinner without compromising the holiness of God or jeopardizing the equity of His rule.

"In this way God completely justifies the repentant sinner, however vile, and imputes the perfect righteousness of Christ to cover his unrighteousness; and then imparts, through sanctification, His own righteousness to the sinner, so that he is transformed into the very likeness of Christ. . . .

"Christ, then, is in Himself the sacrificial offering, the ministering priest, and the coming King. That covers past, present, and future" (pp. 352-53).

IV-8. "We feel it to be most important that Christians sense the difference between the atoning act of Christ on the cross as a forever completed sacrifice, and His work in the sanctuary as officiating high priest, ministering the benefits of that sacrifice. What He did on the cross was for all men (I John 2:2). What He does in the sanctuary is for those only who *accept* His great salvation.

"Both aspects are integral and inseparable phases of God's infinite work of redemption. The one provides the sacrificial offering; the other provides the application of the sacrifice to the repentant soul. The one was made by Christ as victim; the other, by Christ as priest.

Both are aspects of God's great redemptive plan for man" (pp. 353-54).

IV-9. "When, therefore, one hears an Adventist say, or reads in Adventist literature—even in the writings of Ellen G. White—that Christ is making atonement[4] now, it should be understood that we mean simply that Christ is now making application of the benefits of the sacrificial atonement He made on the cross; that is He is making it efficacious for us individually, according to our needs and requests. Mrs. White herself, as far back as 1857, clearly explained what she means when she writes of Christ's making atonement for us in His ministry:

" 'The great Sacrifice had been offered and has been accepted, and the Holy Spirit which descended on the day of Pentecost carried the minds of the disciples from the earthly sanctuary to the heavenly, where Jesus entered by His own blood to shed upon His disciples the *benefits* of His atonement' " (pp. 354-55).

IV-10. "*When the Father beheld the sacrifice of His Son,* He bowed before it in recognition of its perfection. 'It is enough,' He said, 'the Atonement is complete' " (p. 663).

IV-11. "Type met antitype in the death of Christ, the Lamb slain for the sins of the world. Our great High Priest has made the only sacrifice that is of any value in our salvation. *When He offered Himself on the cross a perfect atonement was made for the sins of the people.* . . . Our great High Priest completed the sacrificial offering of Himself *when He suffered without the gate. Then a perfect atonement was made for the sins of the people*" (p. 663).

IV-12. "No language could convey the rejoicing of heaven or God's expression of satisfaction and delight in His only begotten Son as He saw the completion of the atonement" (p. 664).

IV-13. "The seal of heaven has been affixed to Christ's atonement. His sacrifice is in every way satisfactory" (p. 664).

IV-14. "Christ could not have done this work had he not been *personally spotless. Only One who was Himself perfection could be at once the sin bearer and the sin pardoner.* He stands before the congregation of His redeemed as their sin-burdened, sin-stained surety, *but it is their sins He is bearing. All through His life* of humilia-

[4] See author's note 2 at end of chapter.

tion and suffering, *from the time that He was born an infant in Bethlehem till He hung on the cross* of Calvary, and cried in a voice that shook the universe 'It is finished,' *the Saviour was pure and spotless. Christ was without sin,* else His life in human flesh and His death on the cross *would have been of no more value in procuring grace for the sinner than the death of any other man*" (pp. 665-66).

IV - 15. "In our behalf He died on the cross of Calvary. He has paid the price. *Justice is satisfied. Those who believe in Christ,* those who realize that they are sinners, and that as sinners they must confess their sins, *will receive pardon full and free. . . . Jesus Christ died upon the cross* of Calvary, bearing in His body the sins of the whole world; and *the gulf between heaven and earth was bridged by that cross. . . . Christ died to make an atoning sacrifice for our sins. At the Father's right hand He is interceding for us as our High Priest. By the sacrifice of His life He purchased redemption for us*" (pp. 669, 681).

V. The Resurrection

V - 1. "Jesus Christ arose literally and bodily from the grave. He ascended literally and bodily into heaven. He now serves as our advocate in priestly ministry and mediation before the Father" (p. 22).

V - 2. "There shall be a resurrection both of the just and the unjust. The resurrection of the just will take place at the second coming of Christ; the resurrection of the unjust will take place a thousand years later, at the close of the millennium (John 5:28, 29; I Thess. 4:13-18; Rev. 20:5-10)" (p. 14).

V - 3. "Seventh-day Adventists believe in the physical, or bodily, resurrection of Jesus Christ from the dead as verily as they believe in His atoning death on Calvary. This is a cardinal doctrine of the Christian faith, for Christianity rests upon the undisputable fact that Christ rose from the dead (I Cor. 15:17)" (p. 66).

V - 4. "The resurrection of Christ is not to be understood merely in the spiritual sense. He actually rose from the dead. He who came from the tomb was the *same* Jesus who lived here in the flesh. He came forth with a glorified body, but it was real — so real that the women who went to the sepulcher, as well as the disciples, saw Him (Matt. 28:17; Mark 16:9, 12, 14). The two disciples on the way to Emmaus talked with Him (Luke 24). He Himself said to the disciples, 'Behold my hands and my feet' (Luke 24:39). He had 'flesh and bones' (verse 39). He ate with them (verse 43).

"Thomas had reason to know it was the same Jesus, for he was invited to 'reach hither thy finger, and behold my hands; and reach hither thy hand, and thrust it into my side' (John 20:27). Yes it was the Saviour Himself. It was not a spirit, not a ghost. It was the real divine Son of God who came forth from the grave" (pp. 66, 67).

V-5. "The resurrection of Jesus our Lord was a vital part of the message of the early church. . . . The resurrection of Jesus Christ is of vital importance in God's great plan of salvation. Even the death of Jesus, sublime as it was, would have been of no avail, were it not for His resurrection from the dead" (p. 67).

V-6. "Seventh-day Adventists hold the Christian doctrine of the future life to be based on the resurrection (I Cor. 15:51-55; I Thess. 4:16). The righteous, made alive through the first resurrection, have no part in the second death, which is for the wicked only. After the second death there is no resurrection, or future life, for the wicked. The second advent resurrection marks the beginning of the immortality of the saints (I Cor. 15:51-57)" (p. 501).

VI. The Second Coming

VI-1. "[Jesus Christ] will return in a premillennial, personal, imminent second advent" (p. 22).

VI-2. "As our denominational name indicates, the second coming of Christ is one of the cardinal doctrines of the Adventist faith. We give it such prominence in our beliefs because it occupies a pivotal place in Holy Scripture, not only in the New Testament, but also in the Old" (p. 449).

VI-3. "Jesus will assuredly come the second time. . . . [His] second advent will be visible, audible, and personal. . . . Seventh-day Adventists believe on the evidence of Scripture that there will be one visible, personal, glorious second coming of Christ" (pp. 451-52, 459).

VI-4. "In summation: Seventh-day Adventists believe that Christ's second advent will be personal, visible, audible, bodily, glorious, and premillenial, and will make the completion of our redemption. And we believe that our Lord's return is imminent, at a time that is near but not disclosed" (p. 463).

VI-5. "There is good reason, we therefore believe, for calling the advent of Jesus the 'blessed hope' (Titus 2:13). In a very real sense it is the supreme hope of the church, for it is at the return of our Lord that the sleeping saints are called forth to immortality.

"Further, those who are translated at the second advent (I Thess. 4:15) will meet those raised from the dead, and together they meet their Lord in the air (verse 17), and so shall they 'ever be with the Lord.' . . . In Revelation 19 Christ is pictured at His second coming as a mighty warrior leading the armies of heaven to battle against the hosts of evil (verses 11-16). This emphasizes the effect of his coming upon the unsaved" (pp. 452, 490).

VII. The Plan of Salvation[5]

VII-1. "The vicarious, atoning death of Jesus Christ, once for all, is all-sufficient for the redemption of a lost race. . . . Man was created sinless, but by his subsequent fall entered a state of alienation and depravity. . . . Salvation through Christ is by grace alone and through faith in His blood. . . . Entrance upon the new life in Christ is by regeneration, or the new birth. . . . Man is justified by Faith . . . sanctified by the indwelling Christ through the Holy Spirit" (pp. 22, 23).

VII-2. "Every person in order to obtain salvation must experience the new birth. . . . This comprises an entire transformation of life and character by the recreative power of God through faith in the Lord Jesus Christ (John 3:16; Matt. 18:3; Acts 2:37-39)" (p. 12).

VII-3. ". . . . The law of ten commandments points out sin, the penalty of which is death. The law cannot save the transgressor from his sin, nor impart power to keep him from sinning. In infinite love and mercy, God provides a way whereby this may be done. He furnishes a substitute, even Christ the Righteous One, to die in man's stead, making 'him to be sin for us, who knew no sin; that we might be made the righteousness of God in Him' (II Cor. 5:21). That one is justified, not by obedience to the law, but by the grace that is in Christ Jesus. By accepting Christ, man is reconciled to God, justified by His blood for the sins of the past, and saved from the power of sin by His indwelling life. Thus the gospel becomes 'the power

[5] **Consult Author's Note at end of Chapter Eight for resumé of law and grace where salvation in Seventh-day Adventism is included.**

of God unto salvation to every one that believeth' (Rom. 1:16). This experience is wrought by the divine agency of the Holy Spirit, who convinces of sin and leads to the Sin Bearer, inducting the believer into the new covenant relationship, where the law of God is written on his heart, and through the enabling power of the indwelling Christ, his life is brought into conformity to the divine precepts. The honor and merit of this wonderful transformation belong wholly to Christ. (I John 2:1, 2; 3:4; Rom. 3:20; 5:8-10; 7:7; Eph. 2:8-10; 3:17; Gal. 2:20; Heb. 8:8-12.)" (p. 13).

VII-4. "The will of God as it relates to moral conduct is comprehended in His law of ten commandments. . . . These are great moral, unchangeable precepts, binding upon all men in every age (Ex. 20:1-17)" (p. 12).

VII-5. "One who truly understands and accepts the teachings of the Seventh-day Adventist Church can assuredly know that he is born again, and that he is fully accepted by the Lord. He has in his soul the assurance of present salvation, and need be in no uncertainty whatsoever. In fact, he may know this so fully that he can truly 'rejoice in the Lord' (Phil. 4:4); and in 'the God of his salvation' (Psalm 24:5)" (p. 105).

VII-6. "The initiative in the plan of salvation is from God, not from man. 'All things,' we read, are 'of [out of] God' (II Cor. 5:18). We know that He 'hath reconciled us' (verse 18); that '*God* was in Christ, reconciling the world unto himself' (verse 19); that it was *not we* who first loved God, but *He* loved us (I John 4:9, 10); that *Christ* is the 'propitiation for our sins' (I John 2:2); and that 'we are reconciled to God by the death of his Son' (Rom. 5:10). All this comes to us 'according to the gift of the grace of God' (Eph. 3:7)" (p. 105-6).

VII-7. "Grace is an attribute of God exercised towards undeserving human beings. We did not seek for it, but it was sent in search of us. God rejoices to bestow His grace upon us, not because we are worthy, but because we are so utterly unworthy. Our only claim to His mercy is our great need" (p. 106).

VII-8. "Christ is the only Saviour of lost mankind. There is, and can be, no other Saviour. . . . Jesus Christ our Lord is the only foundation (I Cor. 3:11). His name is the only name 'whereby we must be saved' (Acts 4:12). . . . 'Christ Jesus came into the world to save sinners' (I Tim. 1:5); He alone 'is able also to save them to the uttermost' (Heb. 7:25). That understanding is basic. Only in and through Christ can we be saved" (pp. 106-7).

VII-9. "Man cannot save himself; in and of himself he is hopelessly lost. . . . Since man is dead in sin, even the initial promptings to a better life must come from God. Christ is the true light who 'lighteth every man that cometh into the world' (John 1:9). This light, in some way known only to Divine Providence, penetrates the darkness of human hearts and kindles the first spark of desire after God. . . . So even the desire to repent comes from above, for Jesus our Saviour *gives* 'repentance' and *grants* 'forgiveness of sins' (Acts 5:31). The complete change thus wrought in the human heart is not by an act of our own wills and certainly not by ethical uplift or social reform endeavor, but wholly by the new birth. . . . In the act of 'regeneration' God *saves us;* it is *He* who sheds on us the Holy Spirit (Titus 3:5, 6)" (pp. 107-8).

VII-10. "Nothing we can ever do will merit the favor of God. Salvation is of grace. It is grace that 'bringeth salvation' (Titus 2:11). It is 'through the grace of the Lord Jesus Christ we shall be saved' (Acts 15:11). We are not saved by 'works' (Romans 4:6; Eph. 2:8; II Tim. 1:9) even though they be *good* works. . . . Neither can we be saved by 'law' (Rom. 8:3), nor by the 'deeds' or the 'works' of the law (Rom. 3:20, Gal. 3:2, 5, 10). The law of God was never designed to save men. It is a looking glass, in which, when we gaze, we see our sinfulness. That is as far as the law of God can go with a sinful man. It can reveal his sin but is powerless to remove it, or to save him from its guilt and penalty and power" (pp. 108-9).

VII-11. "But, thank God, 'what the law could not do, in that it was weak through the flesh' (Rom. 8:3), God did—*in the person of His Son.* In Him a fountain is open 'for sin and for uncleanness' (Zech. 13:1). And into this fount all may plunge and be 'washed' from their sins by Christ's own blood. . . . True it is that by *His* grace, *His* mercy, *His* gift, *His* gospel, and according to *His* purpose, we are saved (Eph. 2:5, 8; Titus 3:5, Eph. 2:8, Rom. 1:16, 8:28)" (p. 109).

VII-12. "Adventists share with hundreds of eminent men of various faiths—Calvin, Wesley, Clark, Barnes, Spurgeon, Moody,

G. Campbell Morgan, Henry Clay Trumbull, Billy Graham—belief in the perpetuity of God's moral law of ten commandments and in its being in force in all dispensations. . . ." (p. 125).

VII-13. "For a true and full understanding of what God means by His moral law, the Christian must turn to Christ. He it is who enables the newborn soul to live the new life. This is really the indwelling of Christ in his heart, and hence the believer, because of his submission to his Lord lives out the principles of God's character in his heart and life" (pp. 122-23).

VII-14. "It is not safe to be occasional Christians. We must be Christ-like in our actions all the time. Then, through grace, we are safe for time and for eternity. . . . Divine grace is needed at the beginning, divine grace at every step of advance, and divine grace alone can complete the work. . . . We may have had a measure of the Spirit of God but by prayer and faith we are continually to seek more of the Spirit" (p. 111).

VII-15. "Doing right, complying with God's commandments, meeting any or all of the conditions we have mentioned, has never saved a soul—nor can it ever preserve a saint. Salvation proceeds wholly from God, and is a gift from God received by faith. Yet having accepted that gift of grace, and with Christ dwelling within his heart, the believer lives a life of victory over sin. By the grace of God he walks in the path of righteousness. While Adventists rejoice that we receive salvation by grace, and grace alone, we also rejoice that by that same grace we obtain present victory over our sins, as well as over our sinful nature. And through that same grace we are enabled to endure unto the end and be presented 'faultless before the presence of his glory with exceeding joy' (Jude 24)" (p. 417).

VIII. The Spiritual Nature of Man

VIII-1. "Some have maintained that man was created mortal, so far as his body was concerned, and that he possessed an immortal entity called either a 'soul' or a 'spirit.' Others have felt equally certain that man was not in any sense created immortal. They have been convinced that man was not in possession of an ethereal soul, or spirit, which survived death as a conscious entity, apart from the body. . . . We as Adventists believe that, in general, the Scriptures teach that the soul of man represents the whole man, and not a particular part independent of the other component parts of man's nature; and further, that the soul cannot exist apart from the body, for man is a unit" (p. 511, 515).

VIII-2. "There is nothing in the word psuchē [soul] itself that even remotely implies a conscious entity that is able to survive the death of the body. And there is nothing in the Bible use of the word indicating that the Bible writers held any such belief" (p. 514).

VIII-3. "There is nothing inherent in the word *pneuma* [spirit] by which it may be taken to mean some supposed conscious entity of man capable of existing apart from the body, nor does the usage of the word *with respect to man* in the New Testament in any way imply such a concept" (p. 517).

VIII-4. "As far as the Bible is concerned, the word 'immortal' is applied only to God: 'Now unto the King eternal, immortal, invisible, the only wise God be honor and glory for ever and ever' (I Tim. 1:17). This is the only occurrence of the word in the Scriptures. Innate immortality is ascribed only to Deity. 'I give thee charge in the sight of God . . . who is the blessed and only potentate, the King of kings, and Lord of lords; who only hath immortality' (I Tim. 6:13, 15, 16)" (p. 517).

VIII-5. "A careful study of all the adjectives used in the Scripture to qualify the word 'spirit' as applied to man indicates that not one even remotely approaches the idea of immortality. This [mortality] is one of the qualities of the human spirit" (p. 518).

VIII-6. "Seventh-day Adventists do not believe that the whole man or any part of him is inherently immortal. We believe that the Bible picture of man is of a creature subject to death and the possibility of eternal life only because Christ has paid the penalty for sin and offers *His life* to the repentant sinner" (pp. 518-19).

VIII-7. "We as Adventists have reached a definite conclusion that man rests in the tomb until the resurrection morning. Then at the first resurrection (Rev. 20:4, 5), the resurrection of the just (Acts 24:15), the righteous come forth immortalized at the call of Christ the Life-giver. And they then enter into life everlasting in their eternal home in the kingdom of glory. Such is our understanding" (p. 520).

VIII-8. "The Scriptures clearly set forth the condition of man in death. . . . The resurrection of the righteous takes place at the time our Saviour returns from heaven to gather His people (Matt. 16:2; Isa. 40:10; II Tim. 4:8; etc.). . . . Another important factor is that, at death, the saints go to the grave. They will live again, but they come to life and live with Jesus after they are raised from the dead. While asleep in the tomb the child of God knows nothing. Time matters not to him. If he should be there a thousand years the time would be to him as but a moment. One who serves God closes his eyes in death and whether the one day or two thousand years elapse the next instant in his consciousness will be when he opens his eyes and beholds his blessed Lord. To him it is death—then sudden glory" (pp. 521-22, 523-24).

IX. Punishment of the Wicked

IX-1. "Everlasting bliss for the righteous and eternal punishment for the ungodly are plainly taught in the Scriptures. That God should reward His people with eternal life and mete out just retribution to the wicked for their evil deeds appears to most men as reasonable and equitable and in harmony with both the love and the justice of God" (p. 533).

IX-2. "The fate of the unrighteous is likewise emphasized in many places in Holy Writ. There will surely be punishment, according to the Word, and there will also be degrees of punishment. And this punishment, moreover, will not be remedial, but punitive and final" (p. 534).

IX-3. "It is commonly believed that at death the righteous go immediately to heaven, and the wicked forthwith to hell, where they are punished. . . . Punishment for sin as such will finally be meted out when the wicked stand before the bar of God and receive the just rewards of their deeds. Neither evil angels nor wicked men are *now* receiving final punishment for their transgressions. Such punishments are still future. . . . Concerning the wicked we read that God reserves 'the unjust unto the day of judgment to be punished' (II Peter 2)" (pp. 534-35).

IX-4. "In the expression 'eternal punishment,' just as in 'eternal redemption' and 'eternal judgment,' the Bible is referring to all eternity—not as of process but as of *result*. It is not an endless process of punishment, but an effectual punishment which will be final and forever" (p. 540).

IX-5. "We reject the doctrine of eternal torment for the following major reasons: 1. Because everlasting life is a gift of God (Rom. 6:23). The wicked do not possess this—they 'shall not see life' (John 3:36); 'no murderer hath eternal life abiding in him' (John 3:15). 2. Because eternal torment would perpetuate and immortalize sin, as suffering, and woe, and contradict, we believe, divine revelation, which envisions the time when these things shall be no more (Rev. 21:4). 3. Because it seems to us to provide a plague spot in the universe of God throughout eternity, and would seem to indicate that it is impossible for God himself ever to abolish it. 4. Because in our thinking, it would detract from the attribute of love as seen in the character of God, and postulates the concept of a wrath which is never appeased. 5. Because the Scriptures teach that the atoning work of Christ is to 'put away sin' (Heb. 9:26)—first from the individual, and ultimately from the universe. The full fruition of Christ's sacrificial, atoning work will be seen not only in a redeemed people but in a restored heaven and earth (Eph. 1:14)" (p. 543).

X. The Sanctuary and the Investigative Judgment[6]

X-1. *"Does your teaching of the sanctuary service mean that the work of Christ on Calvary was not an all-sufficient, complete, once-for-all sacrifice—a sacrifice that obtains for us eternal redemption? Or was something subsequently necessary to make the sacrificial work of Christ effective for the salvation of man?*

"To the first part of the question our answer is an unequivocal No. The death of Christ on Calvary's cross provided the only sacrifice by which man can be saved. . . . This 'one sacrifice' (Heb. 10:12), or 'one offering' (verse 14), of Christ was 'for ever' (verse 12), and wrought 'eternal redemption' (Heb. 9:12) for man. The sacrifice was completely efficacious. It provided a complete atonement for all mankind, and will never be repeated, for it was all-sufficient and covered the needs of every soul" (pp. 356-57).

X-2. *"Relevant to the doctrine of the atonement, do Seventh-day Adventists believe that the sanctuary in heaven is literal, or figurative?*

"Before attempting to answer this question, it seems that there should be some understanding as to the meaning of the words 'literal'

[6] See Chapter Seven for further discussion of these doctrines.

and 'figurative.' If by the word 'literal' it is thought that we conceive of a heavenly sanctuary made of brick and mortar, with all that we associate with such literalness in our everyday life, the answer is, We do not. If, on the other hand, in the use of the word 'figurative' the thought conveyed is that of something unreal, mythical, imaginary, or visionary, the answer would again be, We do not conceive of the sanctuary in this sense.

"We believe the following statements from Holy Writ: 'We have such an high priest, who is set on the right hand of the throne of the Majesty in the heavens; a minister of the *sanctuary* and of the *true tabernacle*, which the Lord pitched, and not man' (Heb. 8:1, 2). We understand from these Scriptures that as the throne of God is real, and Jesus who sits there is real, the sanctuary or tabernacle in heaven would be just as real. As to its form, we know only what is revealed in the Scriptures. We know nothing of what entered into its construction. This does not seem to be revealed, and we just let it rest there, without seeking to probe further into the question" (pp. 365-66).

X-3. "Hence we may regard the earthly tabernacle as but the shadow of the reality; the real sanctuary was in heaven, but it cast its shadow on the earth. The earthly could be seen by men, but not the heavenly. We do, however, in this word 'shadow' catch glimpses of what the heavenly sanctuary is like by looking at its shadow on the earth. It is in this sense that we believe there is a real sanctuary in heaven" (p. 368).

X-4. "The priesthood of Christ is a cardinal doctrine in New Testament teaching. The atoning death of Christ, and His all-sufficient sacrifice for man's redemption is for us, as for all evangelical Christians, the central truth of Christianity. Yet without our Lord's resurrection and ascension, the provisions of His atoning sacrifice would not be available to man (I Cor. 15:17). The victory of our Lord at Calvary was decisive and eternal. Not only did He conquer sin, but He conquered death. And these tremendous truths became the focal point of the apostolic ministry" (p. 369).

X-5. "The expression 'once' or 'once for all,' in connection with the sacrifice of Christ, is deeply significant. . . . 'He died to sin *once for all*' (Rom. 6:10); 'offering of the body of Jesus Christ *once for all*' (Heb. 10:10). He did this not by 'the blood of goats and calves,' but by 'his own blood.' He entered *once for all* into the holy places (or, 'holiest'), 'thus securing an eternal redemption' for us (Heb. 9:12, R.S.V.).

"The Greek word here translated 'holy place' is *hagia,* and is in the plural form. A correct translation would be 'the holies,' or 'holy places,' as in Hebrews 9:24. This entrance, Scripture teaches, occurred at His ascension to glory (Acts 1), having already finished His sacrificial work on the cross. The word translated 'obtained,' in the Greek, is from *heurisko* and is rendered 'found,' 'procured,' 'gained,' or, in R.S.V., 'secured'" (pp. 380-81).

X-6. "Jesus our surety entered the 'holy places,' and appeared in the presence of God for us. But it was not with the *hope* of obtaining something for us at that time or at some future time. No! *He had already obtained it for us on the cross.* And now as our High Priest He ministers the virtues of His atoning sacrifice to us" (p. 381).

X-7. "This priestly ministry of our Lord, we believe, climaxes in a work of judgment. And this takes place just before He returns in glory. While He does not minister in 'places made with hands' (Heb. 9:24), seeing He is sovereign Lord, yet the two types of ministry carried out in the ancient sanctuary—first, that of reconciliation in the holy place, and second, that of judgment in the most holy—illustrate very graphically the two phases of our Lord's ministry as High Priest. And then, that ministry finished, He comes in glory, bringing His rewards with Him" (p. 389).

X-8. "No prophetic period is given in the Bible to reach the second advent, but that the longest one, the 2300 days of Daniel 8:14, terminated in 1844 and brought us to an event called the cleansing of the sanctuary. . . . The true sanctuary of which the tabernacle on earth was a type is the temple of God in heaven, of which Paul speaks in Hebrews eight and onward, and of which the Lord Jesus, as our great high priest, is minister; . . . the priestly work of our Lord is the antitype of the work of the Jewish priests of the former dispensation; . . . this heavenly sanctuary is the one to be cleansed at the end of the 2300 days of Daniel 8:14, its cleansing being, as in the type, a work of judgment, beginning with the entrance of Christ as the high priest upon the judgment phase of His ministry in the heavenly sanctuary, foreshadowed in the earthly service of cleansing the sanctuary on the day of atonement.

This work of judgment in the heavenly sanctuary began in 1844. Its completion will close human probation. . . .

"God, in the time of the judgment and in accordance with His uniform dealing with the human family in warning them of coming events vitally affecting their destiny (Amos 3:6, 7), sends forth a proclamation of the approach of the second advent of Christ; . . . this work is symbolized by the three angels of Revelation 14; and . . . their threefold message brings to view a work of reform to prepare a people to meet Him at His coming" (pp. 14, 15).

X-9. "The time of the cleansing of the sanctuary, synchronizing with the period of the proclamation of the message of Revelation 14, is a time of investigative judgment; first, with reference to the dead, and second, with reference to the living. This investigative judgment determines who of the myriads sleeping in the dust of the earth are worthy of a part in the first resurrection, and who of its living multitudes are worthy of translation (I Peter 4:17, 18; Dan. 7:9, 10; Rev. 14:6, 7; Luke 20:35)" (p. 15).

X-10. "The great judgment scene of heaven will clearly reveal those who have been growing in grace and developing Christ-like characters. Some will have professed to be God's people, but who have disregarded His counsel, will in amazement say to the Lord, 'Have we not prophesied in thy name? and in thy name have cast out devils? and in thy name done many wonderful works?' His reply to such will be brief but emphatic: 'I never knew you. Depart from me, ye that work iniquity' (Matt. 7:22, 23). Since they have proved themselves unworthy of His kingdom, the Lord in His justice can do nothing else but reject them. *They could have done the will of God* but they *chose their own willful way*" (p. 417).

X-11. "In view of the principles here set forth, it seems to us abundantly clear that the acceptance of Christ at conversion does not seal a person's destiny. His life record after conversion is also important. A man may go back on his repentance, or by careless inattention let slip the very life he has espoused. Nor can it be said that a man's record is closed when he comes to the end of his days. He is responsible for his influence during life, and is just as surely responsible for his evil influence after he is dead. To quote the words of the poet, 'The evil that men do lives after them,' leaving a trail of sin to be charged to the account. In order to be just, it would seem that God would need to take all these things to account in the judgment" (p. 420).

X-12. "That there should be a judgment is not strange; the Scriptures reveal it as part of the eternal purpose of God (Acts 17:31), and all His ways are just. Were God alone concerned, there would be no need of an investigation of the life records of men in this judgment, for as our eternal sovereign God, He is omniscient. He knows the end from the beginning. Even before the creation of the world He knew man would sin and that he would need a Saviour. Moreover as Sovereign God, He also knows just who will accept and who will reject his 'great salvation' (Heb. 2:3).

"If God alone were concerned, there would certainly be no need of records. But that the inhabitants of the whole universe, the good and evil angels, and all who have ever lived on this earth might understand His love and His justice, the life history of every individual who has ever lived on the earth has been recorded, and in the judgment these records will be disclosed—for every man will be judged according to what is revealed in 'the books' of record (Dan. 7:10; Rev. 20:12).

"God's love and justice have been challenged by Satan and his hosts. The arch deceiver and enemy of all righteousness has made it appear that God is unjust. Therefore in infinite wisdom God has determined to resolve every doubt forever. He does this by making bare before the entire universe the full story of sin, its inception and its history. It will then be apparent why He as the God of love and of justice must ultimately reject the impenitent, who have allied themselves with the forces of rebellion.

"Just what these books are like, we do not know. That has not been revealed. But the Scriptures make it plain that whatever the nature of these records, they play a vital role in the judgment scene. Moreover, it is only those who have overcome by the blood of the Lamb whose names are retained in the Lamb's book of life" (pp. 420-21).

X-13. "It is our understanding that Christ as High Priest, concludes His intercessory ministry in heaven in a work of judgment. He begins His great work of judgment in the investigative phase. At the conclusion of the investigation the *sentence* of judgment is pronounced. Then as judge Christ descends to *execute* or carry into effect, that sentence. . . . When God's final sentence of judgment is consummated the redeemed will be singing the song of Moses and the Lamb" (p. 422).

X-14. "The blotting of names out of the book of life is, we believe, a work of the investigative judgment. A complete and thorough check of all the candidates for eternal life will need to be completed before Christ comes in the clouds of heaven, for when He appears, the decisions for life and death are already made. The dead in Christ are called to life, and the living followers of Christ are translated (I Thess. 4:15-17)—the entire citizenry of the everlasting kingdom. There's no time subsequent to the second advent for such decisions. . . .

"In Scripture a difference is to be noted between the *forgiveness* of sin and the *blotting out* of sin. The forgiveness of our sins is very real, and is something that can be known and experienced by living faith in our Lord. In the divine act of forgiveness our sins are removed from us, and we are freed, delivered, saved. But the final destruction of sin awaits the day of God's reckoning, when sin will be blotted out forever from the universe of God" (pp. 438-39).

X-15. "When Christ takes a case in the heavenly court, there is not the slightest possibility of His losing, for He knows all the facts, and He is able to supply the remedy. When He confesses before God and the holy angels that the repentant sinner is clothed in the robe of His own spotless character (this is the white robe that will be given him), no one in the universe can deny to that saved man an entrance into the eternal kingdom of righteousness. Then, of course, is the time for his sins to be blotted out forever, for Christ has claimed him for His own. When every case is decided, the decree can issue forth from the throne: 'He that is unjust, let him be unjust still: and he which is filthy, let him be filthy still: and he that is righteous, let him be righteous still: and he that is holy, let him be holy still' (Rev. 22:11)" (p. 442).

X-16. "The following description of the investigative judgment, penned by Ellen G. White, is, we believe, based entirely upon the revealed truths of God's Word as we have set them forth in the preceding pages:

"'As the books of record are opened in the judgment, the lives of all who have believed on Jesus come in review before God. Beginning with those who first lived upon the earth, our Advocate presents the cases of each successive generation, and closes with the living. Every name is mentioned, every case closely investigated. Names are accepted, names rejected. When any have sins remaining upon the books of record, unrepented of and unforgiven, their names will be blotted out of the book of life, and the record of their good deeds will be erased from the books of God's remembrance. . . . All who have truly repented of sin, and by faith claimed the blood of Christ as their atoning sacrifice, have had pardon entered against their names in the books of heaven: as they have become partakers of the righteousness of Christ and their characters are found to be in harmony with the law of God, their sins will be blotted out, and they themselves will be accounted worthy of eternal life'" (p. 443).

X-17. "When the high priest in the typical service had concluded his work in the earthly sanctuary on the Day of the Atonement, he came to the door of the sanctuary. Then the final act with the second goat, Azazel, took place. In like manner, when our Lord completes His ministry in the heavenly sanctuary, He, too, will come forth. When He does this, the day of salvation will have closed forever. Every soul will have thus made his decision for or against the divine Son of God. Then upon Satan, the instigator of sin, is rolled back his responsibility for having initiated and introduced iniquity into the universe. *But he in no sense vicariously atones for the sins of God's people.* All this Christ fully bore, and vicariously atoned for, on Calvary's Cross" (p. 444).

XI. The Scapegoat Teaching

XI-1. "Now comes the climactic act of this great day [of atonement]. After *full and complete atonement has been provided for the people, and they are safe and secure from the wiles of the deceiver,* God gives His people a preview of the way in which He is going to banish iniquity from His great universe. Here, in type, the author of sin is taken and is judged. He who introduced iniquity into the government of God receives his just deserts. The responsibility for conceiving, for introducing, and for inducing men and women to rebellion against God is rolled back upon his head. As the goat is consigned to the wilderness to death, so, near the end of all things, God will consign Satan to the 'bottomless pit' (Rev. 20:1), and later to the lake of fire where he goes down in utter and irrevocable destruction. These we believe are some of the lessons of the great Day of Atonement in the long ago" (pp. 363-64).

XI-2. *"Are not Seventh-day Adventists alone in teaching that the scapegoat or Azazel represents Satan?*

"No, Seventh-day Adventists are not alone in believing that Azazel represents Satan. . . . Many scholars feel that the word 'scapegoat' does not properly convey the thought of the Hebrew text: some even feel it is misleading. The critical scholar, Dr. S. R. Driver comments: 'An evil spirit, supposed to dwell in the wilderness. The word occurs only here in the O.T. . . . However, the marked antithesis between *for Azazel* and *for JHVH* does not leave it open to doubt that the former is conceived as a personal being' (*Book of Leviticus*, p. 81).

"*Samuel M. Zwemer*—'The devil (Sheitan, or Iblis) has a proper name—Azazel. He was expelled from Eden' (*Islam, A Challenge to Faith*, p. 89).

"*J. B. Rotherham*—'And one lot for Azazel' (Lev. xvi:8). 'It seems impossible to dissent from the opinion that "Azazel," instead of being a name for the scapegoat, is the name or title of an evil Being opposed to Yahweh, to whom the live goat on the great Day of Propitiation was sent. . . . It is most important to observe that there is here no sacrifice offered to the evil spirit' (*The Emphasized Bible*).

"*Abingdon Bible Commentary*—'On the goats lots are to be cast, one for *Jehovah*, and the other for Azazel. The translation *dismissal* in the R.V. margin here (cf. removal in ASV margin) is inadmissible, being based on a false etymology. What the word meant is unknown, but it should be retained as the proper name of a wilderness demon.'

"Mention might be made also of William Milligan, James Hastings, . . . James M. Gray, . . . and a host of others who have expressed themselves in the same way. Adventists during the years, have been in full accord with the expressions of such eminent theologians and scholars on this matter" (pp. 391, 393-95).

XI-3. *"What is the actual teaching of Seventh-day Adventists regarding the scapegoat in the sanctuary service? Do you hold that the sins of the righteous are rolled back on Satan, so that in the end he becomes your sin bearer?*

"We take our stand without qualification on the gospel platform that the death of Jesus Christ provides the sole propitiation for our sins (I John 2:2, 4:10); that there is salvation through no other means or medium, and no other name by which we may be saved (Acts 4:12); and that the shed blood of Jesus Christ *alone* brings remission for our sins (Matt. 26:28). That is foundational" (p. 396).

XI-4. "In Leviticus 16, two goats entered into the service of the great Day of Atonement. One, in type, made atonement for sin. The other goat, for Azazel, was not slain, but was kept alive, and hence made no atonement for anyone's sins.

"The first goat represented our Lord Jesus Christ, who, on the cross, made atonement for our sins. The other goat, in *antithesis,* symbolized Satan, who must bear the responsibility not only for his own sins but for his part in all the sins he has caused others, both righteous and wicked, to commit. This live goat, it is to be remembered, was not slain. (Many outstanding authorities support our understanding that the live goat, or Azazel, typified Satan.)

"Two goats were obviously required, and used, on the Day of Atonement, because there is a *twofold responsibility for sin*—first, my responsibility as the *perpetrator,* agent, or medium; and second, Satan's responsibility as the *instigator,* or tempter, in whose heart sin was first conceived.

"Now, concerning my sin, Christ died for *my* sins (Rom. 5:8). . . . He assumed *my* responsibilities, and His blood alone cleanses *me* from all sin. . . . The atonement for *my* sin is made solely by the shed blood of Christ.

"And concerning Satan's sin, and his responsibility as instigator and tempter, no salvation is provided for him. He must be punished for his responsibility. There is no savior, or substitute, to bear his punishment. He must himself 'atone' for his sin in causing men to transgress, in the same way that a master criminal suffers on the gallows or in the electric chair for his responsibility in the crimes that he has caused others to commit. *It is in this sense only that we can understand the words of Leviticus 16:10 concerning the scapegoat, 'To make an atonement with him'" (pp.* 397-98).

XI-5. "Under criminal law, the instigator, or master mind, may be punished more severely than his agents. . . . Satan is the responsible master mind in the great crime of sin, and his responsibility will return upon his own head. *The crushing weight of his responsi-*

bility in the sins of the whole world—of the wicked as well as the righteous—must be rolled back upon him. Simple justice demands that while Christ suffers for my guilt, *Satan must also be punished as the instigator of sin.*

"That is why, on the Day of Atonement, two goats were necessary. One was 'for the Lord, (Lev. 16:7) to provide the atonement through the shedding of his blood, the other was for Azazel' (Lev. 16:8, margin). These two were, in the text, placed *in antithesis.* One typified our Lord and Saviour Jesus Christ, who was slain as our substitute and vicariously bore our sins, with all the guilt and punishment entailed. Thus He made complete atonement for our sins. The other goat, we believe, stood for Satan, who is eventually to have rolled back upon his own head, not only his own sins, but the responsibility for all the sins he has caused others to commit" (pp. 397-99).

XI-6. "The transaction with the live goat (or Azazel) took place *after* the atonement for the sins of the people had been accomplished, and the reconciliation completed; and . . . the live goat was *not slain* and did not provide any propitiation or make any vicarious atonement. And without the shedding of blood there is no remission (Heb. 9:22). None of the blood of the live goat was shed or poured out in propitiation, and none was taken into the sanctuary and sprinkled before the Lord, or placed on the horns of the altar.

"Satan makes no atonement for our sins. But Satan will ultimately have to bear the retributive punishment for his responsibility in the sins of all men, both righteous and wicked. Seventh-day Adventists, therefore, repudiate *in toto* any idea, suggestions, or implication that Satan is in any sense or degree our sin bearer. The thought is abhorrent to us, and appallingly sacrilegious. Such a concept is a dreadful disparagement of the efficacy of Christ and His salvation, and vitiates the whole glorious provision of salvation solely through our Saviour.

"Satan's death a thousand times over could never make him a saviour in any sense whatsoever. He is the archsinner of the universe, the author and instigator of sin. . . . Only Christ, the Creator, the one and only God man would make a substitutionary atonement for men's transgressions. And this Christ did completely, perfectly, and once for all, on Golgotha" (pp. 399-400).

XII. The Sabbath and the Mark of the Beast

XII-1. "We believe that the Sabbath was instituted in Eden before sin entered, that it was honored of God, set apart by divine appointment, and given to mankind as a perpetual memorial of a finished creation. It was based upon the fact that God himself had rested from His work of creation, had blessed His Sabbath, or rest day, and had sanctified it, or set it apart for man (Genesis 2:1-3; Mark 2:2-7)" (p. 149).

XII-2. "So the Sabbath, established in Eden, was kept by patriarch, prophet and people of God throughout the centuries of pagan darkness. When Christ came, at His incarnation, He likewise observed the seventh day as the Sabbath (Mark 6:1, 2; Luke 4:16, 31), and was 'Lord also of the Sabbath' (Mark 2:28)—the Creator who had established the original seventh-day Sabbath of creation week" (p. 151).

XII-3. "The texts in the New Testament specifically mentioning the first day of the week . . . cannot rightly be construed as enjoining the observance of Sunday, or as transferring the Sabbath from the seventh day to the first day" (pp. 151-52).

XII-4. "The revival of seventh-day Sabbath observance was largely brought about in the seventeenth century by the Seventh-day Baptist movement in Britain and on the Continent. Seventh-day Adventism began the promulgation of the Sabbath truth about 1845-46 in America" (p. 153).

XII-5. "We believe that the restoration of the Sabbath is indicated in the Bible prophecy of Revelation 14:9-12. Sincerely believing this, we regard the observance of the Sabbath as a test of our loyalty to Christ as Creator and Redeemer.

"Seventh-day Adventists do not rely upon their Sabbathkeeping as a means of salvation or of winning merit before God. We are saved by grace alone. Hence our Sabbath observance, as also our loyalty to every other command of God, is an expression of our love for our Creator and Redeemer. . . .

"We are saved through the righteousness of Jesus Christ received as a gift of grace, and grace alone. Our Lord's sacrifice on Calvary is mankind's only hope. But having been saved, we rejoice that the righteous requirements of the law are fulfilled in the experience of the Christian 'who walks not after the flesh but after the spirit,' and who by the grace of God lives in harmony with the revealed will of God" (pp. 153, 190).

XII-6. "All Seventh-day Adventists, as creationists, believe in the Genesis record of fiat creation, (Gen. 1:1-2:2), with the seventh day as God's recorded and attested rest day, and the Sabbath given as the perpetual memorial of that creation, blessed and sanctified (or set apart) for man. The Sabbath had its inception *before sin entered the world* (Gen. 2 and 3), and it was given to commemorate a completed creation. If sin had not entered, all would have kept the original Sabbath day" (p. 158).

XII-7. "Our observance of the seventh-day Sabbath is an expression of our belief that Christ created the world. And it is also a sign of our love, loyalty and devotion to Him as our Maker and King. The further fact that the Lord of the Sabbath so loved us that He became man and sacrificed His life to save us from sin's ruin, makes His Sabbath all the more precious and glorious as the Lord's day" (pp. 158-59).

XII-8. "We believe that at His incarnation Jesus Christ came to reveal the perfect character and will and love of God, and to vindicate and fulfill the righteousness of His moral law and government. In this way Christ's perfect obedience and righteousness is first imputed (through justification) and then imparted (through sanctification) to all who accept His atoning death in their stead. Provision was thus made for His perfect Sabbathkeeping to cover all our Sabbathbreaking—as well as the infraction of the nine other precepts of the Ten Commandments" (p. 159).

XII-9. "Sunday observance as a church festival commemorating Christ's resurrection *but as supplementary to, and not in lieu of, the Sabbath,* was introduced at Rome about the middle of the second century. The custom spread gradually from that time onward" (p. 166).

XII-10. "We believe that the seventh day continues as a changeless memorial of God's original creation; and further, that the regenerated believer in Christ who, ceasing from sin, enters into spiritual rest, can keep the Sabbath as a sign of his re-creation. We therefore refuse to recognize, honor and obey what we believe to be the papal substitute of God's unchangeable sabbath" (p. 171).

XII - 11. "We believe, without any reservations, that the Sabbath is the memorial of an immutable historical fact — a finished creation, and that the Creator's rest on the specific seventh day at the close of the creation week. We say it humbly, but we believe that nothing — no person, or group, or power on earth — can change the commemorative, historical fact that God rested on the seventh day of creation week and gave His rest day to mankind as a perpetual memorial-reminder of a finished work — never repealed."

XII - 12. "When Sunday observance shall be enforced by law, and the world shall be enlightened concerning the obligation of the true Sabbath, then whoever shall transgress the command of God, to obey a precept that has no higher authority than that of Rome, will thereby honor popery above God" (p. 178).

XII - 13. "We recognize that the Sabbath was not a test in medieval times. And we do not believe that it was a test in the days of the great sixteenth-century Reformation, or even in Wesley's day. But in these 'last days,' when, we believe, all truth is to be restored before Christ's second coming, and the message with divine import is to come to mankind on the Sabbath of the fourth commandment, there is a moral accountability for obedience on the part of those to whom light and conviction have come. God surely does not hold men accountable for truth that has not yet come to their knowledge and understanding" (p. 178).[7]

XII - 14. "Seventh-day Adventists believe that the prophecies of Daniel 7 and Revelation 13, relating to the beast, refer particularly to the Papacy, and that the activities and further persecuting power will come to sharp focus just before the return of our Lord in glory. It is our understanding that the Sabbath will then become a worldwide test" (p. 181).

XII - 15. "Thus it was that the Adventist heralds of Sabbath reform came to make a further logical application of the mark of the beast — holding it to be, in essence, the attempted change of the Sabbath of the fourth commandment of the Decalogue by the Papacy, its endeavor to impose this change on Christendom, and the acceptance of the papacy's substitute by individuals. We believe that in the end of time, in the light of clear divine prohibitation, all men

[7] **See Author's Note at end of Chapter Six on Sabbathkeeping and salvation.**

will be brought face to face with the decision to accept or reject Sunday observance. . . . That the Roman Catholic Church claims the change as a mark of her authority can be seen from . . . excerpts from her catechisms" (pp. 181-82).

XII-16. *"Do Seventh-day Adventists teach in their authorized literature that those who worship on Sunday and who repudiate in its entirety the Seventh-day Adventist teaching as a consequence have the mark of apostasy, or 'the mark of the beast'? Does not Mrs. White teach that those who now keep Sunday already have the mark of the beast?*

"Our doctrinal positions are based upon the Bible not upon Mrs. White's writings. But since her name has been introduced into the question, an explicit statement from her pen should set the record straight. The following was penned by her in 1899: 'No one has yet received the mark of the beast. Testing time is not yet come. There are true Christians in every church, not excepting the Roman Catholic communion. None are condemned until they have had the light and have seen the obligation of the fourth commandment. But *when the decree shall go forth enforcing the counterfeit sabbath,* and the loud cry of the third angel shall warn men against the worship of the beast and his image, the line will be clearly drawn between the false and the true. *Then those who still continue in transgression will receive the mark of the beast'*" (p. 183).

XII-17. "Christians of past generations observed the Sunday, supposing that in so doing they were keeping the Bible Sabbath; and there are now true Christians in every church, not excepting the Roman Catholic communion, who honestly believe that Sunday is the Sabbath of divine appointment. God accepts their sincerity of purpose and their integrity before Him. . . . As men then reject the institution which God has declared to be the sign of His authority, and honor in its stead that which Rome has chosen as the token of her supremacy, they will thereby accept the sign of allegiance to Rome—'the mark of the beast.' And it is not until the issue is thus plainly set before the people, that they are brought to choose between the commandments of God and the commandment of men, that those who continue in transgression will receive the mark of the beast. . . . Sundaykeeping is not yet the mark of the beast, and will not be until the decree goes forth causing men to worship this idol sabbath. The time will come when this day will be the test, but that time has not come yet" (p. 184).

XII-18. "To your inquiry, then, as to whether Mrs. White maintained that all those who do not see and *observe* the seventh day as the Sabbath *now* have the 'mark of apostasy,' the answer is definitely No" (p. 184).

XII-19. "We hold the firm conviction that millions of devout Christians of all faiths throughout all past centuries, as well as those today who are sincerely trusting in Christ their Savior for salvation and are following Him according to their best light, are unquestionably saved. Thousands of such went to the stake as martyrs for Christ and for their faith. Moreover untold numbers of godly Roman Catholics will surely be included. God reads the heart and deals with the intent and the understanding. . . . Seventh-day Adventists interpret the prophecies relating to the beast, and the reception of his work, as something that will come into sharp focus just before the return of our Lord in glory. *It is our understanding that this issue will then become a worldwide test*" (pp. 184-85).

XIII. The Question of Unclean Foods

XIII-1. "It is true we refrain from eating certain articles, . . . but not because the law of Moses has any binding claims upon us. Far from it. We stand fast in the liberty with which God has set us free" (p. 623).

XIII-2. "It must be remembered that God recognized 'clean' and 'unclean' animals at the time of the Flood long before there was a law of Moses. We reason that if God saw fit at that time to counsel His people against certain articles of diet, these things were not best for human consumption; and since we are physically constituted the same way as are the Jews and all other peoples, we believe that such things are not best for us to use today" (p. 623).

XIII-3. "To us the whole matter of unclean foods is primarily a question of health, for we believe that 'God is as truly the author of physical laws as He is the author of the moral law'" (p. 624).

XIII-4. "Our health teaching is not a matter of religious taboo; in fact it is a much more than careful selection in diet. It is, to us, the following of a well-balanced health program. We feel it to be our

Christian duty to preserve our bodies in the best of health for the service and glory of God. We believe that our bodies are the temples of the Holy Spirit (I Cor. 3:16; II Cor. 6:16), and that whether therefore we eat, or drink, whatsoever we do we should 'do all to the glory of God' (I Cor. 10:31)" (p. 634).

XIV. The "Remnant Church"

XIV-1. *"It is alleged that Seventh-day Adventists teach that they alone constitute the finally completed 'remnant church' mentioned in the Book of Revelation. Is this true, or do Seventh-day Adventists recognize by the 'remnant' those in every denomination who will remain faithful to the Scriptures and the faith once delivered unto the saints? Do Adventists maintain that they alone are the only true witnesses of the living God in our age and that their observance of the seventh-day Sabbath is one of the major marks that identify them as God's remnant church?*

"The answer to this threefold question will depend quite largely on the definition given to the word 'remnant.' If, as is implied in the second part, 'remnant' is taken to mean the church invisible, our answer to the first part is an unqualified No. Seventh-day Adventists have never sought to equate their church with the church invisible—'Those in every denomination who remain faithful to the Scriptures'" (p. 186).

XIV-2. "We believe that the prophecy of Revelation 12:17 points to the experience and work of the Seventh-day Adventist Church, but we do *not* believe that we *alone* constitute the true children of God—that we are the only true Christians—on earth today. We believe that God has a multitude of earnest, faithful, sincere followers *in all Christian communions*, who are, in the words of the question, 'true witnesses of the living God in our age.' Ellen G. White has expressed our view plainly: 'In what religious bodies are the greater part of the followers of Christ to be found? Without doubt, in the various churches professing the Protestant faith'" (p. 187).

XIV-3. "Seventh-day Adventists believe there are special truths for today we have been called of God to give. We definitely feel that we must emphasize certain neglected truths, must restore others that most Protestant bodies no longer stress and must continue the work of the Reformation" (pp. 188, 189).

XIV-4. "Following as we do the principles of this historical school of prophetic interpretation, it is our conviction that the events portrayed in Revelation 14 to 17 are in process of fulfillment, or are about to meet their fulfillment. And to prepare men everywhere for what is coming on the earth, God is sending a special message couched in the terms of the 'everlasting gospel . . . to every nation and kindred and tongue and people' (Rev. 14:6). That message urges men to turn from every false way of life and to worship the true God who created the heavens and the earth. Furthermore, we believe that God has brought the Seventh-day Adventist movement into being to carry His special message to the world at this time" (p. 190).

XIV-5. "Coming to the end of the chapter [Revelation 12] the prophet describes the final struggle, saying 'And the dragon was wroth with the woman [the Christian church] and went to make war with the remnant [the last segment] of her seed, which keep the commandments of God, and have the testimony of Jesus Christ' (verse 17). God will have His loyal and faithful children down to the end of earth's history. In harmony with our understanding of prophecy, we see in verse 17 a graphic description of the *final warfare* between Satan and those 'who keep the commandments of God and have the testimony of Jesus Christ.' Those who will feel the full fury of the dragon's wrath are spoken of as 'the remnant of her seed,' or in Adventist language 'the remnant church'" (p. 191).

XIV-6. "It is in a spirit of deep humility that we apply this Scripture to the Advent Movement and its work, for we recognize the tremendous implications of such an interpretation. While we believe that Revelation 12:17 points to us as a people of prophecy, it is in no spirit of pride that we thus apply the Scripture. To us it is the logical conclusion of our system of prophetic interpretation" (p. 191).

XIV-7. "But the fact that we thus apply this Scripture does not imply in any way that we believe we are the only true Christians in the world, or that we are the only ones who will be saved" (pp. 191, 192).

XIV-8. "Seventh-day Adventists firmly believe that God has a precious remnant, a multitude of earnest, sincere believers, in every church, not excepting the Roman Catholic communion, who are living up to all the light God has given them" (p. 192).

XIV-9. "We believe the majority of God's children are still scattered in this way throughout the world. And of course, the majority of those in Christian churches still conscientiously observe Sunday. We ourselves cannot do so, for we believe that God is calling for a reformation in this matter. But we respect and love those of our fellow Christians who do not interpret God's Word just as we do" (pp. 192, 193).

XIV-10. "In every great crisis God has had loyal, faithful ones whose allegiance to Him has been more precious than life itself. And in this coming hour of test we believe that He will have a loyal 'remnant.' We believe that finally the remnant people will include every true and faithful follower of Christ. We believe God has given us a solemn responsibility to carry His final message of entreaty to the world—'the everlasting gospel' (Rev. 14:6)" (p. 194).

XIV-11. "To sum up the matter: We believe that through all the ages God has had His elect, distinguished by their sincere obedience to Him in terms of all the light revealed to them. These constitute what may be described as the church invisible. We also believe that at various periods of earth's history God has called out a company of people making them uniquely the depositories and exponents of His truth. . . . We believe that in earth's last hour God has a special message for the world, to prepare all who will heed it to withstand the deceptions of the last days and to make ready for the second advent of Christ. We believe that He has raised up a movement—known as the Seventh-day Adventist church—for the express purpose of making it, in a special way, the depository and exponent of this message. While this company of God's children may be described as a church, we believe the term 'movement' more accurately conveys the essential nature and purpose of this distinctive group with its distinctive message.

"We conceive our task to be that of persuading men to make ready for the day of God, by calling on them to accept Heaven's special message and thus to join with us in proclaiming God's great truth for these days. Holding as we do, that God raised up this movement and gave to it its message, we believe that before the final hour of crisis and testing all God's true children — now so widely scattered — will join with us in giving obedience to this message, of which the Seventh-day Sabbath is a basic part.

"Finally, we would say with all the earnestness and directness we can command, that we repudiate any implication that we alone are beloved of God and have a claim upon heaven. We believe that all who serve God in full sincerity in terms of all the revealed will of God they now understand, are presently potential members of that final 'remnant' company as defined in Revelation 12:17. We believe it to be the solemn task and joyous privilege of the Advent movement to make God's last testing truths so clear and so persuasive as to draw all of God's children to that prophetically foretold company making ready for the day of God.

"We fully recognize the heartening fact that the host of the true followers of Christ are scattered all through the various churches of Christendom, including the Roman Catholic communion. These God clearly recognizes as His own. *Such do not form a part of the 'Babylon' portrayed in the Apocalypse*" (*pp. 195-197*).

XV. Past Positions and Conflicting Literature

XV-1. "Seventh-day Adventists believe that the unfolding light of Bible truth is progressive and is to shine 'more and more unto the perfect day' (Prov. 4:18). And we have sought to walk in the advancing light of truth. We have never driven in formal creedal stakes, and said 'This is the truth; thus far, and no farther' . . . . The founding fathers of the Seventh-day Adventist church over a century ago came out of various denominational backgrounds. While all were premillennialists, some were Trinitarian; others were Arian,* the majority were Arminians; a few were Calvinists. Some insisted on immersion; and a few were content with sprinkling. There was diversity on these points. And as with various other religious groups, our early days were characterized by transition and adjustment.

"But with the passage of years earlier diversity of view on certain doctrines gradually gave way to unity of view. Clear and sound positions were then taken by the great majority on such doctrines as the Godhead, the deity and the pre-existence of Christ, and the person-

*Named for Arius of Alexandria, an early church theologian who denied the essential Deity of Jesus Christ.

ality of the Holy Spirit. Clear-cut views were established on righteousness by faith, the true relationship of law and grace, and on the death of Christ as the complete sacrificial atonement for sin. A few however held to some of their former views and at times these ideas got into print. However, for decades now the church has been practically at one on the basic truths of the Christian faith.

"The very fact that our positions were now clarified seemed to us to be sufficient. Our teachings, we felt, were clear. And no particular statement of change from those earlier ideas appeared necessary. Today the primary emphasis of all our leading denominational literature as well as the continuous presentation over radio and television, emphasizes the historic fundamentals of the Christian faith" (pp. 29-31).

XV-2. "All this has made it desirable and necessary for us to declare our position anew upon the great fundamental teachings of the Christian faith, and to deny every statement or implication that Christ, the second person of the Godhead, was not one with the Father from all eternity, and that His death on the cross was not a full and complete sacrificial atonement. Belief of the Seventh-day Adventists on these great truths is clear and emphatic. And *we feel that we should not be identified with or stigmatized for, certain limited and faulty concepts held by some, particularly in our formative years*" (pp. 31, 32).

XV-3. "This statement should therefore nullify the stock 'quotations' that have been circulated against us. We are one with our fellow Christians of denominational groups in the great fundamentals of the faith once delivered unto the saints. Our hope is in a crucified, risen, ministering and soon-returning Savior" (p. 52).

XVI. Foreign Missions Program

XVI-1. "Where different mission groups operate in close proximity, there is always a possibility of the development of a misunderstanding. This is to be deeply regretted, and as Adventists we wish to assure our fellow workers in the gospel of Christ that as far as we are concerned, . . . we will take every precaution to avert such misunderstanding" (p. 627).

XVI-2. "If the matter of proselyting is involved in this question, we would say: According to the Merriam-Webster's New International unabridged dictionary, the verb *proselyte* means 'to convert to some religion, opinion, system or the like; to make a proselyte of; to make proselytes; to convert.' All churches are seeking to make converts. In common with other Christian bodies, we believe that our God-given duty is set forth in the gospel commission, 'Go therefore and make disciples of all nations' (Matt. 28:19, RSV). This we are attempting to do. On the other hand, the Seventh-day Adventists do not believe in obtaining new members by offering financial and other inducements. We condemn such activities wherever they are practiced. The only way men and women can become true members of the body of Christ is through the converting and transforming power of God" (pp. 627-28).

XVI-3. "Our position can best be shown by quoting from the *Working Policy* of the denomination, . . . adopted by the General Conference . . . in 1926 . . . later revised and enlarged. A copy of this is placed in the hands of every missionary sent out to the mission field.

Statement of Relationship to Other Societies

"In the desire to avoid occasion for misunderstanding or friction in the matter of relationship to the work of other [mission] societies the following statement of principles is set forth as a guidance to our workers in mission fields in their contacts with other religious organizations:

"1. We recognize every agency that lifts up Christ before men as a part of the divine plan for the evangelization of the world, and we hold in high esteem the Christian men and women in other communions who are engaging in winning souls to Christ.

"2. Wherever the presentation of the Gospel work brings us into touch with other societies and their work, the spirit of Christian courtesy, frankness and fairness should at all times guide in dealing with mission problems.

"3. We recognize that the essence of true religion is that religion is based on conscience and conviction. It is therefore, to be constantly our purpose that no selfish interest or temporal advantage shall draw any person to our communion, and that no tie shall hold any member save the belief and conviction that in this way he finds true connection with Christ. When change of conviction leads any member of our society to feel no longer in accord with us in faith and practice, we recognize not only his right but his duty to change his religious affiliation to accord with his belief.

"4. Before admitting to church membership anyone who is a member of another church, every care should be exercised to ascertain that the candidate is moved to change his religious affiliation only by force of religious conviction and out of regard to personal relationship to his God; and wherever possible, consultation shall be had with those in charge of the church or mission with which the applicant is connected.

"5. Persons under censure of another mission for clearly established fault in Christian morals or character shall not be considered eligible for membership in our mission until they have given an evidence of repentance and reformation.

"6. An agent [colporteur, teacher, compound helper, etc.] employed or recently employed by another church or mission shall not be employed by our church or mission without preliminary consultation with the church or mission with which the agent is or was formerly connected.

"7. The local mission auditing committees are advised to give consideration, when setting salaries, as to the salaries paid by other missions operating in the same field.

"8. As to the matter of territorial divisions and the restriction of operations to designated areas, our attitude must be shaped by these considerations:

"a. As in generations past, in the providence of God and the historical development of His work for men, denominational bodies and religious movements have arisen to give special emphasis to different phases of gospel truth, so we find in the origin and rise of the Seventh-day Adventist people, the burden laid upon us to emphasize the gospel of Christ's second coming as an event 'even at the door,' calling for the proclamation of the special message of preparation of the way of the Lord as revealed in Holy Scripture.

"b. As this advent proclamation is described in Scripture prophecy, particularly as it is set forth in Revelation 14:6-14, it is commissioned that this special message of the 'everlasting gospel,' which is to precede the coming of the Savior, shall be preached 'to every nation, and kindred, and tongue, and people.' This commission makes it impossible for us to restrict our witness to this phase of the gospel to any limited area, and impels us to call it to the attention of all peoples everywhere" (pp. 625-27).

Author's Note

1. *The Concept of Christ's Sinful Human Nature*

Since almost all critics of Seventh-day Adventism contend that Seventh-day Adventists believe Christ possessed a sinful human nature during the incarnation, a word should be said to clarify this point. These charges are often based on an article in *Signs of the Times,* March 1927, and a statement in *Bible Readings for the Home Circle,* edition of 1944. Regarding the first reference, a critical article states:

"My . . . quotation is from L. A. Wilcox, for many years an editor of *The Signs of the Times,* which according to the latest figures given by the Adventists has been published by them for 82 years. Certainly a statement by an editor of that publication may be considered official. I'm sure that anything that Mr. Wilcox wrote did not just happen to get in. In March 1927 he wrote, 'In His (Christ's) veins was the incubus of a tainted heredity like a caged lion ever seeking to break forth and destroy. Temptation attacked Him where by heredity He was weakest, attacked Him in unexpected times and ways. In spite of bad blood and an inherited meanness, He conquered.'

"And again in the December 1928 issue of *Signs of the Times* this editor Mr. Wilcox stated: 'Jesus took humanity with all its liabilities, with all its dreadful risks of yielding to temptation.'"[8]

First, L. A. Wilcox was never on the editorial staff of *Signs of the Times*. Moreover, Mr. L. A. Wilcox, who wrote the article, in a letter dated April 26, 1957 states:

"The writer of the *Signs* article was a very young man in 1927 and not by any means always felicitous in his phraseology. I know, for I was the writer. The first sentence quoted is crude and shocking and theologically inaccurate, and I was properly spanked for it by Adventist officials, which proves that this article cannot be truly represented as 'official' or 'authoritative.'

"It is no more than fair to point out that no man has taught more

[8] ***The King's Business*, April, 1957.**

earnestly or fervently than I, as an Adventist minister, the deity of the Lord Jesus Christ, the sinlessness of Christ, salvation by grace, righteousness by faith, the finished work of Calvary, a Christ-centered religion, than I—with the 'Amen' of Seventh-day Adventist leadership."

Virtually every critic of Seventh-day Adventism, including the authors quoted above, also uses a statement quoted from *Bible Readings for the Home Circle* (1944 edition, p. 174)—even though in 1945 the statement was expunged by Adventists because it was not in line with official Adventist theology.

A further quotation often seized upon is taken from the book, *Desire of the Ages,* by Ellen G. White. On page 117 she says, "Our Savior took humanity, with all its liabilities. He took the nature of man, with the possibility of yielding to temptation." Mrs. White also speaks of "fallen nature." Understandably, not having read all she has written on the subject, these critics conclude that she means that Christ possessed a sinful, carnal, or degenerate human nature. However, Mrs. White's writings clearly indicate that when she speaks of the fallen nature of Christ, she means the physical properties of the race, which degenerated since the time of Adam who was created perfect without the ravages of sin upon either his physical or spiritual being. Adam did not age before the fall, but Christ was born into the world a true man and with the curse of sin operative upon the physical properties of the human race. For thirty-three years He endured the aging process. He could not have reached the age of thirty-three without organic changes taking place in His body, and were He not subject to the physical decline of the race, he would not have been a true man, "made under the law" (Gal. 4:4). Mrs. White's position has been held by many eminent scholars who have never been accused of being either heretics or non-Christians. Why, then, should she and the Adventists be condemned for holding this view? For centuries Christians have argued about the human nature of Christ. Some have believed that He could have sinned, but did not. Others, including this writer, that He could not have sinned. However, it is a theological issue not likely to be resolved by trite phrases and dogmatic pronouncements.

We have already quoted at length from current official Seventh-day Adventist sources which deny the sinful-nature theory with which critics have relentlessly charged them. Would it not be fairer to consider their publication, *Questions on Doctrine,* released in 1957 and endorsed by the denominational leadership of the Seventh-day Adventist Church, than to cite statements from much older publications that have since been outdated or revised in these respects?

2. *The Incomplete Atonement Concept*

It is also often charged that inherent in SDA theology is the unbiblical teaching that "the atonement was not finished on the cross of Calvary." Certain Seventh-day Adventist sources are cited to bolster these charges. For instance, Uriah Smith, a prominent Adventist of the past, stated in his book *Looking Unto Jesus,* "Christ did not make the atonement when He shed His blood upon the cross." Other earlier writers such as J. H. Waggoner have expressed the same thought. He said, "There is a clear distinction between the death of Christ and the atonement" (f.n. *The Atonement in the Light of Nature and Revelation,* p. 181). Even some later writers like C. H. Watson* have been influenced by these early exponents of Adventism.

However, a little investigation of these writings would show that Smith and Waggoner wrote eighty years ago. As demonstrated elsewhere in this book this concept has been repudiated by the SDA denomination. The current position of the Seventh-day Adventist denomination—not the opinions of a few scattered writers over a hundred-year period — should be considered in judging this charge of "incomplete atonement."

Current Adventist writings teach that the atonement was completed on the cross; and no less an Adventist than Ellen G. White, writing in the *Review and Herald,* September 21, 1901, stated: "Christ planted the cross between Heaven and earth and when the Father beheld the sacrifice of His Son, He bowed before it in recognition of His perfection. 'It is enough,' He said, 'The atonement is completed.'" In the same periodical, under the date of August 16, 1899, Mrs. White stated, "No language could convey the rejoicing of heaven or God's expression of satisfaction and delight in His only begotten Son that He saw the completion of the atonement."

There are, of course, still extant in certain Adventist publications

* See *The Atoning Work of Christ.*

not yet revised, unfortunate statements like those of Smith and Watson, but the Adventists are aware of this and are taking steps to harmonize all such writings with the true position of the denomination. Many more quotations could be cited, but critics usually overlook the greater number of statements relative to the completeness of the atonement which are readily available in past and present Seventh-day Adventist literature.

Nothing could be clearer than the Adventist declaration that *"when one hears an Adventist say or reads in Adventist literature in the writings of Ellen G. White that Christ is making atonement now; it should be understood that we mean simply that Christ is now making application of the benefits of the sacrificial atonement He made on the cross; that is He is making it efficacious for us individually according to our needs and request."* Mrs. White herself, as far back as 1857, clearly explained what she means when she writes of Christ making atonement for us in His ministry: " 'the great sacrifice had been offered and has been accepted and the Holy Spirit which ascended on the Day of Pentecost carried the minds of the disciples from the earthly sanctuary to the Heavenly, where Jesus entered by His own blood to shed upon His disciples the benefits of His atonement.' "[9]

[9] *Questions on Doctrine,* pp. 354-355.

CHAPTER FOUR

ELLEN G. WHITE AND THE SPIRIT OF PROPHECY

In most religious movements, one extraordinary and gifted personality dominates the scene, and so it was with Seventh-day Adventism. This dominant personality was, and is today, through her writings, Ellen G. White. She was one of the most fascinating and controversial personages ever to appear upon the horizon of religious history. Her memory and work have been praised by Adventists and damned by many of their enemies since the early years of the movement. Born Ellen Gould Harmon at Gorham, Maine in 1827, and reared a devout Methodist in the city of Portland, Mrs. White was early recognized as an unusual person, for she bore witness to certain "revelations" which she believed she had received from Heaven.

When Ellen was thirteen, the Harmon family came under the influence of the Millerite movement. William Miller delivered a series of addresses in the Casco Street Christian Church in Portland in 1841 and 1842. At the age of seventeen, Ellen embraced the Adventist faith of the Millerites.[1] Although deeply stirred by Miller's sincerity and his chronological calculations, the Harmon family remained in fellowship with the Chestnut Street Methodist Church of Portland, which in 1843 disfellowshiped them because they believed in the premillennial second advent of Jesus Christ.

Despite her youth, Ellen Harmon passed through trying times, emotionally, physically and spiritually, between 1837 and 1843. In the words of Dr. Froom, "She rebelled against the dismal prospects resulting from an early accident, and its attendant invalidism."[2] In 1840, at a Methodist camp meeting at Buxton, Maine, Ellen Harmon found wonderful deliverance and "her burden rolled from her shoulders," for she experienced great joy in learning that she was truly a child of God, which she publicly confessed afterward by request-

[1] Ellen G. White, *Life Sketches*, pp. 64-68.
[2] *The Prophetic Faith of Our Fathers*, Vol. IV, p. 978.

ing baptism by immersion. Many points still perplexed her, among them the doctrine of the eternal punishment of the wicked, which in subsequent years she surrendered to as well as the concept of conditional immortality and the sleep of the soul while awaiting the resurrection. In December 1844, after "The Great Disappointment," while visiting a friend in Portland, Ellen Harmon experienced what she termed her first vision which portrayed the "vindication" of the Advent faith. In that vision she claimed to see the Adventists triumphant over their critics — pressing upward to Heaven in the face of insuperable obstacles.

For many years controversy has raged about Mrs. White and her "revelations," and there are conflicting opinions within and without Adventism regarding her "revelations" and "inspiration," their extent and nature. The position of Ellen White in Adventist teaching, then, is most significant and must be understood if we are to get a proper picture of this people. The writings and counsels of Ellen Harmon (later Ellen G. White by her marriage to James White, a prominent Adventist leader), are termed the "Spirit of prophecy," an expression taken from Revelation 19:10. Adventists believe that in the last days special counsels from God are to be revealed, which neither add to nor contradict Scripture, and that these counsels are primarily for the Seventh-day Adventist denomination. And while following these counsels, they claim they always test them by the Word of God. Finally, they believe that the visions of Mrs. White, and her counsels to their denomination are the "spirit of prophecy" for their church.

Through the years, some overzealous Adventist writers have given the impression that everything Mrs. White said, or wrote even in private letters was inspired and infallible. This is decidedly *not* the official position. The Adventist denomination readily admits that not everything Mrs. White said or wrote was either inspired or infallible, although some individual Adventists still cling to that idea. In this connection we present statements from the new definitive volume on Seventh-day Adventist theology, *Questions on Doctrine,* in the hope of clearing the way for proper understanding of the life and ministry of Ellen G. White, as viewed by the Seventh-day Adventist church.

I. Seventh-day Adventist Statements — Life and Ministry of Ellen G. White

(Page numbers are in *Questions on Doctrine,* unless otherwise indicated.)

1. "We do not regard the writings of Ellen G. White as an addition to the sacred canon of Scripture. We do not think of them as of universal application as is the Bible, but particularly for the Seventh-day Adventist Church. We do not regard them in the same sense as the Holy Scriptures, which stand alone and unique as the standard by which all other writings must be judged" (p. 89).

2. "Seventh-day Adventists uniformly believe that the canon of Scripture closed with the Book of Revelation. We hold that all other writings and teachings, from whatever source, are to be judged by, and are subject to, the Bible, which is the spring and norm of the Christian faith" (pp. 89-90).

3. "I recommend to you, dear reader, the Word of God as the rule of your faith and practice. By that Word we are to be judged" (Ellen G. White, *Early Writings,* p. 78; *Questions on Doctrine,* p. 90).

4. "The Spirit was not given — nor can it ever be bestowed — to supersede the Bible; for the Scriptures explicitly state that the Word of God is the standard by which all teaching and experience must be tested" (*The Great Controversy*, Introduction, p. vii; *Questions on Doctrine,* p. 90).

5. "We have never considered Ellen G. White to be in the same category as the writers of the canon of Scripture" (p. 90).

6. "It is in . . . the category of messengers [other than the Biblical writers] that we consider Ellen G. White to be. Among Seventh-day Adventists she was recognized as one who possessed the gift of the spirit of prophecy, though she herself never assumed the title of prophetess" (p. 91).

7. "I know that many have called me a prophet, but I have made no claim to this title. . . . Why have I not claimed to be a prophet? — Because in these last days many who boldly claim that they are prophets are a reproach to the cause of Christ; and because my work includes much more than the word 'prophet' signifies. To claim to be a prophetess is something that I have never done. If others call

me by that name I have no controversy with them. But my work has covered so many lines that I cannot call myself other than a messenger" (*Review and Herald,* July 26, 1906, p. 8; *Questions on Doctrine,* p. 92).

8. "Seventh-day Adventists regard her writings as containing inspired counsel concerning personal religion and the conduct of our denominational work. . . . That portion of her writings, however, that might be classified as predictions, actually forms but a small segment. And even when she deals with what is coming on the earth, her statements are only amplifications of clear Bible prophecy" (p. 92).

9. "It is significant that in her counsels, or 'testimonies,' the attention of the reader is constantly directed to the authority of the Word of God, as the sole foundation of faith and doctrine" (p. 92).

10. "In His Word God has committed to men the knowledge necessary for salvation. The Holy Scriptures are to be accepted as an authoritative, infallible revelation of His will. They are the standard of character, the revealer of doctrines, and the test of experience" (pp. 92, 93, quoting E. G. W.).

11. "While Adventists hold the writings of Ellen G. White in highest esteem, yet these are not the source of our expositions. We base our teachings on the Scriptures, the only foundation of all true Christian doctrine. However, it is our belief that the Holy Spirit opened to her mind the important events and called her to give certain instructions for these last days. And inasmuch as these instructions, in our understanding, are in harmony with the Word of God, which Word alone is able to make us wise unto salvation, we as a denomination accept them as inspired counsels from the Lord. But we have never equated them with Scripture as some falsely charge. Mrs. White herself stated explicitly the relation of her writings to the Bible: 'Little heed is given to the Bible, and the Lord has given a lesser light to lead men and women to the greater light'" (*Review and Herald,* Jan. 20, 1903; *Questions on Doctrine,* p. 93).

12. "While Seventh-day Adventists recognize that Scripture canon closed nearly two thousand years ago and that there have been no additions to this compilation of sacred books, yet we believe that the spirit of God, who inspired the Divine Word known to us as the Bible, has pledged to reveal Himself to the Church and through the different gifts of the Spirit. . . . It is not our understanding that

these gifts of the Spirit take the place of the Word of God, nor does their acceptance make unnecessary the Scripture of truth. On the contrary, the acceptance of God's Word will lead God's people to a recognition and a manifestation of the Spirit. Such manifestations will, of course, be in harmony with the Word of God. We know that some earnest Christians have the impression that these gifts ceased with the apostolic church. But Adventists believe that the closing of the Scripture canon did not terminate Heaven's communication with men through the gifts of the Spirit, but rather that Christ by the ministry of His Spirit guides His people, edifying and strengthening them, and especially so in these last challenging days of human history" (pp. 93-95).

13. "The Spirit of prophecy is intimately related to the gift of prophecy, the one being the Spirit which indited the prophecy, the other the evidence of the gift bestowed. They go together, each inseparably connected with the other. The gift is the manifestation of that which the Spirit of God bestows upon him whom, according to His own good purpose and plan, He selects as the one through whom such spiritual guidance is to come. Briefly then, this is the Adventist understanding of Ellen G. White's writings. They have been for a hundred years, to use her own expression, 'a lesser light' leading sincere men and women to 'the greater light'" (p. 96).

14. "Concerning the matter of church fellowship, we would say that while we revere the writings of Ellen G. White, . . . we do not make acceptance of her writings a matter for church discipline. She herself was explicit on this point. Speaking of those who did not fully understand the gift, she said: 'Such should not be deprived of the benefits and privileges of the church, if their Christian course is otherwise correct, and they have formed a good Christian character'" (*Testimonies*, Vol. I, p. 328; *Questions on Doctrine*, pp. 96, 97).

15. "We therefore do not test the world in any manner by these gifts. Nor do we in our intercourse with other religious bodies who are striving to walk in the fear of God, in any way make these a test of Christian character" (J. N. Andrews in *Review and Herald*, Feb. 15, 1870; *Questions on Doctrine*, p. 97).

16. "James White, thrice General Conference president, speaking of the work of Ellen G. White, expressly declares that Adventists be-

lieve that God called her 'to do a special work at this time, among this people! They do not, however, make a belief in this work a test of Christian fellowship'" (*Review and Herald*, June 13, 1871).

"This has been our consistent attitude throughout our history. However, if one who holds membership in our church loses confidence in these counsels and later stirs up enmity among the believers, we reserve the right to disfellowship such from the body. But such action will not be taken because of one's lack of confidence in these writings, but rather because the one disaffected is stirring up strife among the believers" (p. 97).

17. "After men and women have had evidence that the work is of God, and then join hands with those who fight against it, our people claim the right to separate from such" (*Review and Herald*, June 13, 1871; *Questions on Doctrine*, p. 97).

18. "In the practice of the church it has not been customary to disfellowship one because he did not recognize the doctrine of spiritual gifts. . . . A member of the church should not be excluded from membership because of his inability to recognize clearly the doctrine of spiritual gifts and its application to the second advent movement" (F. M. Wilcox, *The Testimony of Jesus*, pp. 141-43; *Questions on Doctrine*, p. 98).

It may be seen from these quotations that Seventh-day Adventists hold to the restoration of the "gift of prophecy" in the last days of the Christian Church, and that they believe this restoration occurred in the life and ministry of Ellen G. White. The Adventists differ from other churches, then, in that while they hold the Bible to be the unique, complete, infallible, inerrant Word of God, they maintain that in specific contexts Ellen White's writings are to be accepted by Adventists as "testimonies" from the Spirit of God to guide their denominational activities.

Dr. Wilbur M. Smith, the esteemed Professor of English Bible at Fuller Theological Seminary, Pasadena, has summed up the objections of most evangelicals where Seventh-day Adventism emphasis upon Mrs. White and "the Spirit of prophecy is involved when he recently observed Mrs. White's place in the new Seventh-day Adventism Bible Commentary."

"I do not know any other denomination in all of Christendom

today that has given such recognition, so slavishly and exclusively, to its founder or principal theologian as has this commentary to the writings of Ellen White. At the conclusion of every chapter in this work is a section headed, 'Ellen G. White Comments.' For example, on Genesis 28, the blessing conferred upon Jacob, there are less than three pages of comment, but at the end, forty references to the various works of Ellen White. In addition, at the end of the first volume of this commentary is a section again headed 'Ellen G. White Comments,' containing eighty columns of material quoted from her writings. There is no section devoted to anyone else, Calvin, Luther, Wesley, or anyone else."

"The Preface to this commentary contains the statement: 'At the close of each chapter is a cross reference or index to those passages in Ellen G. White's writings that comment on the various texts in that chapter.' And the second sentence following reads: 'The Advent movement has grown strong through the study of the Bible; and it can be said with equal truth that the movement has been safely guided in that study by the light shining from the Spirit of prophecy.' I would say that the writers of this commentary believe that 'the Spirit of prophecy' has rested *exclusively* upon Ellen G. White, for no one else is so classified in this work."*

Dr. Smith is correct in his evaluation of the place of Ellen G. White's writings in the denomination. Seventh-day Adventists are of necessity committed to her visions and counsel because they believe that the Spirit of prophecy rested upon her and upon no other person of their group.

This writer rejects this concept of inspiration but one should carefully note that, for Adventists, "inspiration" in connection with Mrs. White's writings has a rather different meaning from the inspiration of the Bible. Adventists freely admit that the Bible is *objectively* the Word of God, the final authority in all matters of faith and morals. But the writings of Mrs. White cannot be so regarded, and they are the first to say so. Apparently, they have adopted a qualified view of inspiration as related to her writings—"a lesser light to lead men and women to the greater light"—which emphasizes subjective interpretation as the criterion for determining specifically

*** In a recent letter to the author.**

where in Mrs. White's writings the "spirit of prophecy" has decisively spoken. There is no doubt in my mind that the Adventists are defending a situation which is at best paradoxical and at times contradictory. But this position, as a matter of religious liberty, they are *entitled* to hold so long as they do not make faith in Mrs. White's writings a test of fellowship between themselves and other denominations, and do not attempt to compel other Christians to accept the "testimonies" of Mrs. White as indispensable to a deeper, richer experience of Christian consecration and living.

If Seventh-day Adventists did indeed claim for Mrs. White inspiration in *every* area of her writings, then we might well be cautious about having fellowship with them. However, this they do not do, as I have amply demonstrated from official denominational sources. Since they do not consider Mrs. White's teachings the source of their expositions of faith, the claim that one has only to refute Ellen G. White and her writings, in order to refute Seventh-day Adventism, falls by its own weight.

II. Mrs. White and Her Critics

Through the years a great deal of literature has appeared, criticizing the life and works of Ellen G. White. These criticisms have ranged from the mild judgment that Mrs. White was a sincere but emotionally disturbed mystic, to the charge that she was a "false prophetess" who sought material gain and deliberately plagiarized much of her writing. In the interest of honest investigation and truth, and since it is impossible in a book of this size to analyze all the conflicting data, we shall present some highlights of the controversy, and let the reader determine the validity of these charges.

The inspiration for 90 per cent of the *destructive* personal criticisms leveled against Mrs. White is found in the writings of Dudley M. Canright, an ex-Adventist leader of great ability, and a one time personal friend of Ellen G. White, her husband James, and a great number of prominent Adventist leaders. Canright, one of the most able of the Seventh-day Adventist writers and debaters of his day, left the movement because he lost faith in the inspiration of Mrs. White, and in many doctrines then held by the Adventist Church. While it is true that Canright thrice ceased to preach, his credentials as a minister were never revoked. He finally resigned from the

Seventh-day Adventist ministry in 1887 to become a Baptist minister. By Canright's own admission, his personality conflicts with Ellen G. White and her advisers were largely responsible for his turning away from the active ministry at the times mentioned. He, however, apparently maintained close personal relations with James White, Mrs. White's husband, and other prominent Seventh-day Adventist leaders as evident from the correspondence quoted below. Canright rebelled violently against Arianism (the denial of the deity of Christ) and extreme legalism, which existed among some of the early Seventh-day Adventists; and his convictions led him later to write two volumes (*Seventh-day Adventism Renounced*, and *Life of Mrs. E. G. White*), which systematically and scathingly denounced Seventh-day Adventism theologically and impugned the personal motives and integrity of Mrs. White.

In these two volumes, D. M. Canright laid the foundation for all future destructive criticism of Seventh-day Adventism, and careful research has confirmed the impression that nearly all subsequent similar publications are little more than repetitions of the destructive areas of Canright's writings, buttressed by standard theological arguments. This is especially true of the writings of a former Seventh-day Adventist missionary printer, E. B. Jones, now editor of a small news sheet, *Guardians of the Faith,* who has issued a number of vitriolic pamphlets against Seventh-day Adventism, all of which are drawn almost exclusively from Canright and other critics, and are for the most part outdated and in some cases both scholastically and ethically unreliable.* It can be seen, therefore, that what D. M. Canright has written about Ellen G. White is of prime importance as first-hand evidence, and no Seventh-day Adventist apologist, regardless of the scope of his knowledge of Adventism or the breadth of his scholastic learning, can gainsay all that Canright has written.[3]

In the March 22, 1887 issue of the *Review and Herald,* his former brethren wrote of Elder Canright, "We have felt exceedingly sad to part in our religious connection with one whom we have long esteemed as a dear brother. . . . In leaving us he has taken a much

* They contain, however, just enough factual criticism of Adventist teaching to give them an air of respectability, making them doubly deceptive.

[3] Recognizing that some of Canright's criticisms are well taken, I, too, have drawn upon them as *prima facie* sources where thoroughly documented.

more manly and commendable course than most of those who have withdrawn from us, coming voluntarily to our leading brethren and frankly stating the condition of mind he was in. He did this before his own church in our presence and so far as we know has taken no unfair underhanded means to injure us in any way. He goes from our midst with no immoral stain upon his character. He chooses associations more pleasant to himself. This is every man's personal privilege if he chooses to take it."

Writing to Canright on May 22, 1881, from Battle Creek, Michigan, James White, Ellen's husband, stated, "It is time there was a change in the offices of the General Conference. I trust that if we are true and faithful, the Lord will be pleased that we should constitute two of that Board." In another letter to Canright, dated July 13, 1881, James White said, "Brother Canright, I feel more interest in you than in any other man because I know your worth when the Lord is with you as a laborer." It is apparent, therefore, that Canright was in good standing with the Adventists, despite his later renunciation of Mrs. White's testimonies and the "special truths" of the Adventist message.

In 1951 a carefully documented volume of almost 700 pages was issued by the Review and Herald Publishing Association of Washington, D. C. The author was Francis D. Nichol, leading apologist of the Seventh-day Adventist denomination. This volume, entitled, *Ellen G. White and Her Critics,* attempts a point-for-point refutation of many of the charges made by D. M. Canright in his *Life of Mrs. E. G. White.* Nichol has dug deep into early Adventist history —even beyond Canright's day, but after reading both Nichol and Canright, the writer concludes that there is much to be said on both sides. But Canright, we believe, has the edge because he can say, "I was there," or "Mrs. White said . . ." and contradictory contemporary statements are not to be found where many of Canright's charges are concerned.

My own conclusion is that in some areas (particularly theology) Canright's statements are irrefutable, especially with regard to his personal relationships with Mrs. White and the leading members of the Adventist denomination. It is also significant to note that many charges which are based on personal experiences and have been well documented have never been refuted.

By this I do not mean that all of Canright's writing is to be trusted, for many of his criticisms of Mrs. White's activities have been neatly undercut by contemporary evidence unearthed by F. D. Nichol and others. Where Nichol is concerned, "methinks he doth protest too much," and he often goes to extremes to defend Mrs. White. This in my judgment has hurt his case and has proved nothing except that he is a devoted disciple of Mrs. White and therefore strongly biased. Nichol is none the less the most able Adventist apologist.

We now turn to two charges which require investigation, if we are to understand Seventh-day Adventism and Mrs. White's part in the movement.

III. Was Mrs. White a Plagiarist?

According to the dictionary, plagiarism is the appropriation of the ideas, writings or inventions of other persons without rendering proper acknowledgment. To put it bluntly, plagiarism is literary theft. Thanks to stringent copyright laws and alert eyes of competent editors, plagiarism is less common today. But in the nineteenth century, plagiarism was not so clearly defined, although it was not an uncommon practice. However, court action was brought against persons who committed literary larceny. Careful reading of the life and the works of Ellen G. White convinces me that she did not intend to plagiarize for profit. Nevertheless, it is evident that she was not guiltless. This conclusion is only in keeping with the facts and reflects no rancor toward Mrs. White or the claims of Seventh-day Adventists on her behalf.

In the year 1907 Dr. Charles E. Stewart, formerly of the Battle Creek Sanitarium (a Seventh-day Adventist institution), a physician of acknowledged talent and an acquaintance of Mrs. White, published an 89-page pamphlet in which he accused Mrs. White of certain plagiarisms, notably in a book she wrote in 1883 entitled, *Sketches from the Life of Paul,* as well as in her *magnum opus, The Great Controversy*. We quote from that pamphlet, as Dr. Stewart says, "in order to make clear what I mean with reference to the similarity in the two books."

Sketches from the Life of Paul
Ellen G. White, 1883

1. "The judges sat in the open air, upon seats hewn out in the rock, on a platform which was ascended by a flight of stone steps from the valley below" (p. 93).

2. "Had his oration been a direct attack upon their gods, and the great men of the city who were before him, he would have been in danger of meeting the fate of Socrates" (p. 97).

3. "An extensive and profitable business had grown up at Ephesus from the manufacture and sale of these shrines and images" (p. 142).

4. "Only their reverence for the temple saved the apostle from being torn in pieces on the spot; with violent blows and shouts of vindictive triumph, they dragged him from the sacred enclosure" (p. 216).

5. "In their excitement they flung off their garments as they had done years before at the martyrdom of Stephen, and threw dust into the air with frantic violence. This fresh outbreak threw the Roman captain into great perplexity. He had not understood Paul's Hebrew address and concluded from the general excitement that his prisoner must be guilty of some great crime. The loud demands of the people that Paul be delivered into their hands made the commander tremble. He ordered him to be immediately taken into the barracks and examined by scourging, that he might be forced to confess his guilt" (p. 220).

6. "Among the disciples who ministered to Paul at Rome was one Onesimus, a fugitive from a city of Colosse. He belonged to a Christian named Philemon, a member of the Colossian church. But he had robbed his master and fled to Rome" (p. 284).

The Life and Epistles of the Apostle Paul
Conybeare and Howson — 3rd Edition
1855

1. "The judges sat in the open air, upon seats hewn out in the rock, on a platform which was ascended by a flight of stone steps immediately from the Agora" (p. 308).

2. "Had he begun by attacking the national gods in the midst of their sanctuaries, and with the areopagites on the seats near him, he would have been in almost as much danger as Socrates before him" (p. 310).

3. "From the expressions used by Luke, it is evident that an extensive and lucrative trade grew up at Ephesus for the manufacture and sale of these shrines" (p. 432).

4. "It was only their reverence for the holy place which preserved him from being torn to pieces on the spot. They hurried him out of the sacred enclosure and assailed him with violent blows" (p. 547).

5. "In their rage and impatience they tossed off their outer garments (as on that other occasion when the garments were laid at the feet of Saul himself) and threw dust into the air with frantic violence. This commotion threw Lysias into new perplexity. He had not been able to understand the apostle's Hebrew speech, and when he saw its results he concluded that his prisoner must be guilty of some enormous crime. He ordered him therefore to be taken immediately from the stairs into the barracks and to be examined by a torturer in order to elicit a confession of his guilt" (p. 557).

6. "But of all the disciples now ministering to Paul at Rome, none has for us a greater interest than the fugitive Asiatic slave, Onesimus. He belonged to a Christian named Philemon, a member of the Colossian church, but he had robbed his master and at last found his way to Rome" (p. 640).

Mrs. White gave no credit to Conybeare and Howson's *Life and Epistles of St. Paul.* She did not set off the passages with quotation marks; neither did she indicate that she had borrowed other sections cited by Dr. Stewart. Adventists maintain that there is a fine line between kinds of plagiarism, but Mrs. White should have been more careful, and her proofreaders should have been more alert. For the fact remains that this is unmistakable plagiarism.

We refer once more to Dr. Stewart's booklet where, in *parallel columns*, he reveals plagiarisms in Mrs. White's 700-page book, *The Great Controversy*.[4]

The Great Controversy
Mrs. E. G. White, Edition 1844

1. "The bull invited all Catholics to take up the cross against heretics. In order to stimulate them in this cruel work, it absolved them from ecclesiastical pains and penalty; it released all who joined the crusade from any oaths they might have taken; it legalized their title to any property which they might have illegally acquired and promised remission of all their sins to such as should kill any heretic. It annulled all contracts made in favor of the Vaudois, ordered their domestics to abandon them, forbade all persons to give them any aid whatever and empowered all persons to take possession of their property" (p. 83).

2. "In the gloom of his dungeon, John Huss had forseen the triumph of true faith. Returning in his dreams to the humble parish where he had preached the gospel he saw the pope and his bishops effacing the pictures of Christ which he had painted on the walls of his chapel. The sight caused him great distress; but the next day he was filled with joy as he beheld many artists busily engaged in replacing the figures in greater numbers and brighter colors. When their work was completed the painters exclaimed to the immense crowd surrounding them, 'Now let the popes and bishops come!' Said the reformer as he related his dream, 'I am certain that the image of Christ will never be effaced. They have wished to destroy it, but it shall be painted in all hearts by much better preachers than myself'" (pp. 91, 92).

History of the Waldenses
Rev. J. A. Wylie

1. "The bull invited all Catholics to take up the cross against the heretics, and to stimulate them in this pious work, it absolved from all ecclesiastical pains and penalties, general and particular; it released all who joined the crusade from any oaths they might have taken; it legitimatized their title to any property they might have illegally acquired and promised remission of all their sins to such as should kill any heretic. It annulled all contracts made in favor of Vaudois, ordered their domestics to abandon them, forbade all persons to give them any aid whatever, and empowered all persons to take possession of their property" (p. 28).

D'Aubigne's "History of the Reformation"

2. "One night the holy martyr saw in his imagination from the depths of his dungeon, the pictures of Christ that he had painted on the walls of his oratory effaced by the pope and his bishops. The vision distressed him but on the next day he saw many painters occupied in restoring these figures in greater numbers and brighter colors. As soon as their task was ended, the painters who were surrounded by an immense crowd exclaimed, 'Now let the popes and bishops come! They shall never efface them any more!' . . . 'I am no dreamer,' replied Huss, 'but I maintain this for certain: that the image of Christ will never be effaced. They have wished to destroy it, but it shall be painted afresh in all hearts by much better preachers than myself'" (p. 3).

[4] Adventists point to Mrs. White's introduction to *The Great Controversy* which gives credit to other authors, but in the first edition of the book this credit was not given. In fact it was not until the plagiarism was discovered that sources other than the *Spirit of Prophecy* were acknowledged.

These quotations from Dr. Stewart's pamphlet are not intended to vilify the character of Mrs. White, but are merely adduced to show that she was altogether human and prone to make mistakes, and that she did make some indefensible mistakes. It is too bad that plagiarism, even though limited, was one of these mistakes.

Dudley M. Canright, in his *Life of Mrs. E. G. White,* repeats Dr. Stewart's charge of plagiarism: "The rights of authorship are recognized and protected by copyright laws the world over. Any infringement of these rights even where credit is given is punishable by severe penalties and frequently by confiscation of the works involved. Plagiarism or literary piracy is the worst form of this offense. It is the appropriating of the writings of another as one's own without quotes or credit. It is indulged in by uneducated, pedantic, and unscrupulous persons who desire to appear what they are not, or to make money from the product of other minds. . . . One of the damaging facts against the claim of divine revelation in the writings of Mrs. White is that she copied extensively from other authors without giving credit" (pp. 192-93).

Now to be perfectly fair, especially since Canright has popularized this charge, let us look at the other side of the coin! In a book published in 1878 entitled, *The Bible From Heaven* (written while he was still a Seventh-day Adventist minister and high official), Canright himself plagiarized not only some of the content but even the title of a book written in 1863 by Moses Hull,[5] also an Adventist and a predecessor of Canright in the ministry.

Recalling the scathing denunciation by Canright of Mrs. White's plagiarism, it can be seen that Canright's displeasure with Mrs. White and Adventism led him to condemn a practice of which he himself was guilty. Let not those who revere the memory of D. M. Canright dismiss such a charge as baseless or an Adventist trick to smear him. I have reproduced below some of Canright's own plagiarisms and I have maintained that, as in the case of Mrs. White's plagiarism, they do not dangerously affect her over-all work as a writer, or her testimony as a Christian, so I maintain that Canright's

[5] He later renounced Christianity and became a Spiritist and a leading figure in that non-Christian cult.

plagiarisms do not markedly lessen his position. Careful students should weigh thoroughly the writings of both Mrs. White and Canright in order to appreciate their respective worth as leaders and contributors to the saga of Advent history in the United States.

The Bible From Heaven
by D. M. Canright, 1878

1. We now come directly to the question. Are the sciences really against the Bible? We answer, no. It is true that the Bible does not abound with lectures upon physiology, anatomy, hygiene, materia medica, chemistry, astronomy, or geology. It is not given to teach these subjects. God has given us the stars to teach astronomy, the earth to teach us geology, and the Bible to teach us religion. Yet we are not willing to admit that anything in the Bible contradicts any of the sciences. As each new science has been discovered it has been supposed by infidels that in it they would find a new ally, but alas for infidelity. The older sciences have all proved to be of heavenly birth, and have given their testimony in behalf of God and the Bible; so will the new ones when more perfectly understood. Of all the sciences, geology, if it may be termed a science, has proved itself the most fallible, and yet its professors are the most noisy in their boasts of what they intend to do (p. 288).

The Bible From Heaven
by Moses Hull, 1863

1. We now come directly to the question. Are the sciences really against the Bible? We answer, No. It is true that the Bible does not abound with lectures upon physiology, anatomy, hygiene, materia medica, chemistry, astronomy, or geology. It is not given to teach these subjects. God has given us the stars to teach astronomy, the earth to teach us geology, and the Bible to teach us religion. Yet we are not willing to admit that anything in the Bible contradicts any of the sciences. As each new science has been discovered it has been supposed by infidels that in it they would find a new ally, but alas for infidelity. The older sciences have all proved to be of heavenly birth, and have given their testimony in behalf of God and the Bible; so will the new ones when more perfectly understood. Of all the sciences, geology—if it may be termed a science—has proved itself the most fallible, and yet its professors are the most noisy in their boasts of what they intend to do (pp. 168, 169).

D. M. Canright's plagiarism does not, of course, excuse Mrs. White's. Far from it! But it is an interesting parallel, especially since Canright is the wellspring of the charge of plagiarism which is still raised against Mrs. White.

There are other instances of plagiarism in the writings of Mrs. White, but this writer has examined enough evidence to recognize that, far from being on the pedestal where she has been placed by some Adventist writers, Ellen G. White was a very human personage. She would doubtless be the first to reject some of the appraisals of her life and ministry by certain of her overzealous supporters! This, of course, is true of practically every other leading religious personality, but in the case of Mrs. White and Seventh-day Adventism, a comparatively young movement, abundant evidence is available to offset many of the exalted concepts of her, promulgated by sincere but uninformed zealots.[6]

IV. Outside Influences and the Spirit of Prophecy

The second and extremely serious charge against Mrs. White which must be noted relates to her inspiration. The claim is that at times she was under influences other than the Spirit of God, which influences strongly affected some of her "Testimonies." By this I do not mean that Mrs. White was influenced by demonic or devilish powers, but rather that the influences of certain older persons surrounding her must be taken into consideration if one is to be true to history and fact.

To illustrate, let us review some instances where influence exerted upon Mrs. White caused her to write *Testimonies* alleged to have their authority in the pronouncements of God.

A. *The Health Reform Institute*

On December 25, 1865 in Rochester, New York, Mrs. White affirmed that she received a vision from the Lord stressing "health reform" and a divine directive to the Adventist people to create facilities for Adventists and others who were ill. This "revelation" was written and delivered in 1867 as Testimony Number Eleven (Volume I) and was the principal instrument in accumulating gifts for expansion of the Health Reform Institute in Battle Creek, Michigan. Throughout Testimony Number Eleven, Mrs. White constantly affirmed, "I was shown," which to any informed Adventist indicates that the "Spirit of prophecy" operated through her. For example, on page 489 of Volume I she states, "I was shown that we should provide a home for the afflicted and those who wish to learn how to take care of their bodies that they may prevent sickness."

On page 492, Mrs. White wrote, "I was shown that there is no lack of means among Sabbath-keeping Adventists. At present their greatest danger is in their accumulations of property. Some are continually increasing their cares and labors; they are over-charged. The result is, God and the wants of His cause are nearly forgotten by

[6] For a discussion of the plagiarism charge and a defense of Mrs. White's activities, see F. D. Nichol, *Ellen G. White and Her Critics,* pp. 403-68, to which this writer takes strong exception.

them; they are spiritually dead. They are required to make a sacrifice to God, an offering. A sacrifice does not increase but decreases and consumes. Here I was shown, was a worthy enterprise for God's people to engage in, one in which they can invest means to His glory in the advancement of His cause. Much of the means among our people is only proving an injury to those who are holding onto it. Our people should have an institution of their own under their own control for the benefit of the diseased and suffering among us who wish to have health and strength that they may glorify God in their bodies and spirits which are His. Such institution rightly conducted would be the means of bringing our views before many whom it would be impossible for us to reach by the common course of advocating the truth."

It may be seen from the foregoing quotations, then, that Mrs. White in 1867 used the 1865 vision to promote the raising of funds for the *expansion* of the Health Institute in Battle Creek, which in itself would not be objectionable from an Adventist standpoint were not other difficult problems involved.

The first of these difficult problems is the fact that in Volume I of *Testimonies,* pages 563 and 564, Mrs. White directly contradicted Testimony Number Eleven concerning the Health Institute, the beginnings of which had been torn down at a cost in excess of $10,000. This evidence would indicate that James White had influenced his wife to issue another Testimony contradicting the first one in regard to the application of the 1865 vision to the Health Institute *expansion* in Battle Creek (1867). Wrote Mrs. White in her retraction:

"What appeared in Testimony Number Eleven concerning the Health Institute should not have been given until I was able to write out all I had seen in regard to it. . . . The brethren at Battle Creek who were especially interested in the Institute knew I had seen that our people should contribute of their means to establish such an institution. They therefore wrote to me that the influence of my Testimony in regard to the Institute was needed immediately to move the brethren on the subject, and that the publication of Number Eleven would be delayed 'till I could write. This was a great trial to me as I knew I could not write out all I had seen, for I was then speaking to the people six or eight times a week, visiting from house to house and writing hundreds of pages of personal testimonies in private letters. This amount of labor with unnecessary burdens and trials thrown upon me unfitted me for labor of any kind. My health was poor, and my mental sufferings were beyond description. Under these circumstances *I yielded my judgment to that of others* and wrote what appeared in Number Eleven in regard to the Health Institute, being unable to give all I had seen. *In this I did wrong.*"[7]

F. D. Nichol in *Ellen G. White and Her Critics,* pages 495-503, puts forth the thesis that Mrs. White's contradiction can be explained on the basis of her statement, "What appeared in Testimony Number Eleven concerning the Health Institute should not have been given until I was able to write out *all* I had seen in regard to it."

Nichol, however, makes two errors in judgment, as can be seen by a careful analysis of his statement. He says, "But nothing in the Bible supports the idea that prophets are infallible when they are exercising their private judgment" (p. 502).

This, however, in no way explains Mrs. White's statement "In this I did wrong" and her contradiction in the two previously-cited quotations. The point that Nichol makes is invalid, because, while we agree that prophets are not infallible when they exercise their own private judgment, according to the language of Testimony Number Eleven, Mrs. White was not exercising her own private judgment for she clearly states, "I was shown." And as the statements cited indicate, she firmly believed God had shown her that the 1867 Testimony, which was based upon the 1865 vision, was decidedly applicable to the Health Institute being constructed in Battle Creek. It could hardly be cited as a matter of private judgment! So it involves then a matter of Mrs. White's inspiration, since by her direct application of the 1865 "vision" to the project, she indicated that the Lord ordained additional construction for the Health Institute.

Second, Nichol states, "We hold that the credentials of the prophet are to be judged only by what he claims to know by revelation from God" (p. 502).

Now if this be true in Mrs. White's case, the Adventists have encountered more than they bargained for in their defense of her claim

[7] *Testimonies,* Vol. I, p. 563; italics mine.

to inspiration, because in Testimony Number Eleven she asserted that she knew by revelation from God that the Health Institute expansion in 1867 was instituted by divine revelation. The argument that the vision of 1865 applied only to some future erection and not specifically to the Institute expansion begun in 1867 is fallacious, because Mrs. White deliberately applied the 1865 vision to the 1867 Health Institute construction program. Then, influenced by her husband, she countermanded her previous Testimony and the work which she said God ordained, was torn down.

Nichol contends that this was done to prevent overexpansion and indebtedness and while this may be true, it does not explain how Mrs. White could have been inspired to endorse the project in the first place, if expansion and debt were against the better interest of the denomination peculiarly guided by the "Spirit of prophecy."

Remember that Mrs. White stated, "Under these circumstances I yielded my judgment to that of others, and wrote what appeared in Number Eleven in regard to the Health Institute, being unable then to give all I had seen. In this I did wrong." Clearly then, Mrs. White wrote, allegedly under divine inspiration, something which she was forced to retract under human influence, while at the same time ascribing her retraction to divine inspiration! Her statement, "In this I did wrong," indicates her fallibility and the futility of Adventists' attempting to defend everything she wrote as divinely inspired, as some have been prone to do. Personally speaking, I believe this incident weakens, if not destroys, the entire basis of the Spirit of Prophecy doctrine and that Adventists would be wise to admit her error in this instance.

On page 503 of *Ellen G. White and Her Critics,* Nichol attempts to vindicate the Whites: "All work was stopped. But not because James White wanted it another way, but because he and others with him believed that it should not be built at all. It was the overextended financial situation of the Health Institute and the inexperience of the management that led to the stopping of the construction, and not James White's overextended sense of pride and importance."

The only difficulty with Nichol's defense is that it is not in keeping with all the facts. Regardless of what James White's motives were, the fact remains that Mrs. White, allegedly under the guidance of the "spirit of prophecy," *endorsed* the expansion of the Health Institute in 1867, and if her counsel was valued at all the work never should have been stopped; but it was! And this particular point even Nichol has not attempted to explain or refute!

Dr. J. H. Kellogg, who headed the famous Battle Creek Sanitarium, an Adventist institution at that time, said, "It was an infamous doing, a crime, tearing that thing down for no reason than because James White was not consulted."[8] Furthermore, Dr. Kellogg's statement was not challenged by contemporary Adventists who were familiar with the facts and we are therefore justified in accepting it as an eyewitness account.

B. *Mrs. White on Tithing*

In *Review and Herald* for November 10, 1896, Mrs. White discussed the subject of tithing: "Let none feel at liberty to retain their tithe to use according to their own judgment. They are not . . . to apply it as they see fit, even in what they may regard as the Lord's work. . . . A minister should not feel that . . . he can retain and apply it according to his own judgment, because he is a minister. It is not his. . . . Let him not give his influence to any plans for the diverting from a legitimate use the tithes and offerings dedicated to God. Let them be placed in His treasury."

Ten years later, on January 22, 1906, in a testimony directed to Elder George F. Watson, Mrs. White wrote: "It has been presented to me for years that my tithe is to be appropriated by myself. . . . I have myself appropriated my tithe to the needy cases brought to my notice. . . . It is a matter that should not be commented upon; for it will necessitate my making known these matters, which I do not desire to do. . . . And if any person should say to me, 'Sister White, will you appropriate my tithe where you know it is most needed?' I shall say, 'Yes,' and I will and have done so. I commend those sisters who have placed their tithe where it is most needed. . . . For years there have been now and then persons who have lost confidence in appropriation of the tithe but have placed their tithe in my hands. . . . I have taken the money, given a receipt for it, and told them where it was to be appropriated. I write this to you

[8] **D. M. Canright, *Life of Mrs. E. G. White*, pp. 78, 79.**

so that you shall keep cool and not become stirred up and give publicity to this matter, lest more shall follow their example."[9]

A careful comparison of these two statements from the pen of Mrs. White reveals contradiction. The question is, what made Mrs. White change her mind during that ten-year period? And for this we must further consult the record.

In a letter postmarked Battle Creek, Michigan, May 24, 1881, Elder James White addressed D. M. Canright as follows: "Brother Canright, the *Review* will tell of our plan. We shall depend on you to help us. . . . We hope you can join us in our labors. There will be efforts made to get you to Wisconsin, to have you go here and there. . . . I hope we shall see our way out and be able to labor in union. . . . Elders *Butler* and *Haskell* have had an influence over *her* that I hope to see broken. It has nearly ruined *her*. These men must not be supported by our people to do as they have done. . . . It is time there was a change in the officers of the General Conference. I trust that if we are true and faithful, the Lord will be pleased that we shall constitute two of that board" (Signed, James White).

It is obvious that the "her" was James White's wife, Ellen, and that these two leading Adventists were exerting a strong "influence" over her mind. As early as 1881, then, people were influencing Mrs. White and her writings. Consider James White's own influence over Ellen regarding the Health Institute, and the pressure exerted by the Battle Creek clique, to make Mrs. White contradict herself in successive Testimonies.

Returning to the conflicting testimonies on tithing, there is evidence that Mrs. White was influenced in this matter by her son, J. E. White. The authority for this is her other son, Elder W. C. White. At a session of the General Conference, speaking of her letter of January 22, 1906, he said, "The letter was written by my mother, and was duplicated, and a copy was sent Brother Watson, and another copy, very unwisely I believe, and I am sorry to say, to my brother. What called it out was a letter from my brother to my mother. I am very sorry that the letter was written."

There has been no evidence to contradict W. C. White's asser-

[9] That Mrs. White paid a tithe none can fairly doubt (See Series A, No. 1, pp. 26-28). But she also appropriated her tithe when she thought it advisable, thus contradicting her own counsel: "Let none feel at liberty to retain their tithe to use according to their own judgment" (*Review and Herald*, Nov. 10, 1896).

tion that his mother issued the contradictory testimony because of a letter received from her other son. W. C. White's statement, "I am very sorry that the letter was written," certainly indicates conflict behind the scenes and is further proof that not all Mrs. White wrote and spoke was divinely inspired.[10]

V. The Verdict of the Evidence

After considering all the evidence obtainable, of which the foregoing is only a part, this writer is convinced that Ellen G. White was a highly impressionable woman, strongly influenced by her associates. That she sincerely believed the Lord spoke to her, none can fairly question, but the evidence set forth in this chapter gives good reason, we believe, to doubt the inspiration of her counsels, whether Seventh-day Adventists will concede this or not.

The writer's personal evaluation of the visions of Ellen G. White is best summed up in the following statement from a friendly critic. In 1847, at the outset of her work, one of Mrs. White's cousins stated: "I cannot endorse Sister Ellen's visions as of Divine inspiration, as you and she think them to be; yet I do not suspect the least shade of dishonesty in either of you in this matter. I may, perhaps, express to you my belief in the latter without harm—it will, doubtless, result either in your good or mine. At the same time I admit the possibility of my being mistaken. I think that what she and you regard as visions from the Lord are only religious reveries in which her imagination runs without control upon themes in which she is most deeply interested. While so absorbed in these reveries she is lost to everything around her. Reveries are of two kinds: Sinful and religious. In either case, the sentiments in the main are obtained from previous teaching, or study. I do not by any means think that her visions are from the Devil."[11] If Seventh-day Adventists are to defend their claim for Mrs. White's inspiration, they must explain a number of contradictions in her writings. They would do better to admit, we believe, that she was very human, capable of errors in judgment, subject to lapses of memory, and possessed of the universal human predisposition toward personal sin (Romans 3:23).

[10] D. M. Canright, *Life of Mrs. E. G. White*, pp. 256-58.
[11] Reproduced in *A Word to the Little Flock*, p. 29 (1847) by Elder James White.

We have seen that Mrs. White was definitely influenced in some of her writings by time and circumstances, and also by the powerful personalities who surrounded her.[12] Some Adventists maintain that this would in no way prevent her conveying messages from the Lord. However, as I see it, anyone who attempts to prove her divinely inspired or infallible (no informed Adventist holds the latter) must first dispose of the evidence here presented, as well as other evidence which space does not admit.[13] F. D. Nichol in *Ellen G. White and Her Critics,* makes a masterful attempt to answer some of these problems, but not all of them can be answered with a good conscience or an airtight defense of Mrs. White and her actions. It does not detract from her stature as a sincere Christian or from the quality of her contribution to insist upon an honest and systematic evaluation of her statements by thinking Adventists, to ascertain just how far Adventists may rightfully maintain that the Lord has "spoken" through Mrs. White. Non-adventists, of course, reject the claims made for Mrs. White and her writings and hope that Adventists will some day amend their questionable view of "Ellen G. White and the Spirit of Prophecy."

After reading the publications of the Seventh-day Adventist denomination and almost all the writings of Ellen G. White, including her *Testimonies,* the writer believes that Mrs. White was truly a regenerate Christian woman who loved the Lord Jesus Christ and dedicated herself unstintingly to the task of bearing witness for Him as she felt led. It should be clearly understood that some tenets of

[12] At various times by Bates, Butler, Haskell, the "Battle Creek Clique," and of course her husband James White, a much older man, of whom Canright states, "He exercised great influence over her."

[13] We refer to such things as Mrs. White's censure of SDA for purchasing life insurance (*Testimonies,* Vol. I, p. 549), a practice most Adventists participate in today; and her counsel regarding eating of meat, although she herself ate meat for almost sixty years (*Ministry of Healing,* pp. 312-17). The problem of life insurance is a very clear instance — at least where this writer is concerned — of the attitude of the SDA Church toward some of Mrs. White's writings, for she definitely stated, "I was shown that Sabbath-keeping Adventists should not engage in life insurance. This is a commerce with the world which God does not approve." No Adventist can deny from the very language used ("I was shown") that this is allegedly a divine dictate, yet SDA's openly engage in the purchase of life insurance, "which God does not approve!" Seventh-day Adventists explain this by declaring that life insurance today is vastly different than when Mrs. White wrote her counsel, but the fact is that up to the time of her death in 1915 she never reversed it and her other counsels stand on the same basis — why not this one?

Christian theology as historically understood and the interpretations of Mrs. White do not agree; indeed, they are at loggerheads. Nevertheless, Ellen G. White was true to the cardinal doctrines of the Christian faith regarding the salvation of the soul and the believer's life in Christ. We must disagree with Mrs. White's interpretation of the sanctuary, the investigative judgment, and the scapegoat; we challenge her stress upon the Sabbath, health reform, the unconscious state of the dead, and the final destruction of the wicked, etc. But no one can dispute the fact that her writings conform to the basic principles of the historic Gospel, for they most certainly do. However, we must not assume as many Adventists do that Mrs. White's writings are free from theological and exegetical errors *for they are not.* Although this writer believes that the influence of Mrs. White's counsels on the Advent denomination parallels the influence of J. N. Darby of the Plymouth Brethren and A. B. Simpson of the Christian and Missionary Alliance, the claim that she possessed a "gift of prophecy" akin to that described in I Corinthians 14 as believed by the Seventh-day Adventist church, we cannot accept.

Many critics of Seventh-day Adventism have assumed, mostly from the writings of professional detractors, that Mrs. White was a fearsome ogre who devoured all who opposed her, and they have never ceased making the false claim that Seventh-day Adventists believe that Mrs. White is infallible, despite the often published authoritative statement to the contrary. Although Seventh-day Adventists do hold Mrs. White and her writings in great esteem, they maintain that the Bible is their only "rule of faith and practice." Christians of all denominations may heatedly disagree with the Seventh-day Adventist attitude toward Mrs. White, but all that she wrote on such subjects as salvation or Christian living characterizes her as a Christian in every sense of the term.

Farther on in this book, we shall discuss Mrs. White's relations with the Adventist denomination, particularly in the field of theology. Enough has been presented here, however, to show that she was a most interesting personality, far different from the "Sister White" idealized beyond reality in certain Seventh-day Adventist publications.

Dudley M. Canright, the chief critic of Seventh-day Adventism, has, we feel, rendered good service in this respect. He has presented the human side of Mrs. White, from the standpoint of a first-hand friendship which lasted through the formative years of the Seventh-day Adventist denomination. Despite his criticisms of Seventh-day Adventism and Mrs. White, Canright himself never ceased to believe that, despite what he believed to be her errors in theology and her mistaken concept of visions, she was a regenerate Christian. With his brother, Canright attended the funeral of Mrs. White in 1915. His brother describes the occasion thus: "We joined the passing throng, and again stood by the bier. My brother rested his hand upon the side of the casket, and with tears rolling down his cheeks, he said brokenly, 'There is a noble Christian woman gone!' "[14]

The controversy between Seventh-day Adventist historians and personal recollections of D. M. Canright[15] will probably never be settled this side of Heaven, but beyond question, Canright has left an indelible mark upon the history of both the denomination and Ellen G. White, a woman of great moral fortitude and indomitable conviction. Her influence will doubtless affect the religious world through the Seventh-day Adventist denomination for many years to come.

In order that the reader may make his own estimate of the merits of the two best books ever written on this subject, we have set forth in Appendix A a sample of the main charges made by D. M. Canright and the answer-references given by F. D. Nichol. If the reader wishes more information he can consult these books.

[14] W. A. Spicer, *Spirit of Prophecy and the Advent Movement,* p. 127.

[15] It has been stated by misinformed Seventh-day Adventists at one time or another that Canright recanted and accepted Seventh-day Adventism shortly before his death. I have examined this story carefully and found it false. Canright did leave the ranks of Adventism at least twice, but returned and preached for them again. In 1887 he left and never returned. He died a Baptist minister, still denouncing the theological deviations of Seventh-day Adventism. As his daughter put it, "Father was more firm in his conviction of the error of their teaching the longer he lived, in spite of Adventist claims that he repudiated his writings against them. I tell you this in anticipation of your having such falsehoods to meet" (*The Christian Standard,* Oct. 16, 1902).

Part II
An Examination of Seventh-day Adventist Theology

CHAPTER FIVE

THE SLEEP OF THE SOUL AND THE DESTRUCTION OF THE WICKED

The doctrine of conditional immortality, commonly called "soul sleep" outside Adventist circles, and its necessary corollary, annihilation,[1] have been cardinal teachings from the beginning of the Seventh-day Adventist Church. They must be dealt with from an exegetical standpoint if the theology underlying the basic premise is to be understood. These positions, incidentally, are held today by the Advent Christian Church, an affiliate of the National Association of Evangelicals, and by outstanding Bible scholars in not a few denominations.

The purpose here is essentially to review the historic position of the Christian church from the days of the apostles to the present, and to examine the teaching of the Scriptures on these subjects. Many noted Christians of the past believed in conditional immortality, among them Martin Luther, William Tyndale, and John Wycliffe, all of whom were competent Greek scholars. Luther even stated that he could not support the doctrine of the immortality of the soul, which he called one of the "endless monstrosities in the Roman dunghill of decretals."[2] Tyndale declared that "in putting them [the souls of the departed dead] in Heaven, hell and purgatory you destroy the arguments wherewith Christ and Paul doth prove the resurrection . . . and again, if the souls be in Heaven, tell me why they be not in as good case as the angels be? And then what cause is there for their resurrection?"[3]

However, in his *Commentary on Genesis*, Luther later categorically stated, "In the interim [between death and resurrection], the soul does *not* sleep but is awake and enjoys the vision of angels and of God, and has converse with them."[4]

1 Adventists do not use this term; they prefer "final destruction."
2 Weimar edition of Luther's *Works*, Vol. VII, pp. 131-32.
3 *An Answer to Sir Thomas More's Dialogue*, Parker's 1850 reprint, Book 4, chapter iv, pp. 180-81.
4 *Works*, XXV, 321.

However, neither preponderance of one opinion, nor the opinions of a few great thinkers can validate theological speculation or interpretation. The Christian Church does not base its belief in the conscious bliss of departed saints on the opinions of individuals, no matter how prominent or learned, *but upon the historic, Biblical foundation of the Christian faith.*

I. Textual Analysis

The Seventh-day Adventist doctrine of the sleep of the soul is best expressed in their own words: "We as Adventists believe that, in general, the Scriptures teach that the soul of man represents the whole man, and not a particular part independent of the other component parts of man's nature; and further, that the soul cannot exist apart from the body, for man is a unit. . . . We, as Adventists, have reached the definite conclusion that man rests in the tomb until the resurrection morning. Then, at the first resurrection (Rev. 20:4, 5), the resurrection of the just (Acts 24:15), the righteous come forth immortalized at the call of Christ, the Lifegiver, and *they then enter into life everlasting,** in their eternal home in the kingdom of glory. Such is our understanding."[5]

The key to the preceding statements, of course, is the last phrase of the second paragraph, "They *then* enter into life everlasting, in their eternal home in the kingdom of glory." Now, the majority of Christians through the centuries have held that this proposition contradicts the teaching of the Word of God contained in the following passages:

1. *I John 5:11-13:* "And this is the record, that God hath given to us eternal life, and this life is in his Son. He that hath the Son hath life; and he that hath not the Son of God hath not life. These things have I written unto you that believe on the name of the Son of God; that ye may know that ye have eternal life, and that ye may believe on the name of the Son of God." In the grammar and context of this passage eternal life (*eionion zoes*) is the present pos-

*See also these standard Adventist publications where this erroneous equation is set forth. 1) *In Defence of the Faith,* W. H. Branson, p. 239 2) *Desires of Ages,* E. G. White, p. 786, paragraph 3 3) *God Speaks to Modern Man,* Arthur Lickey, p. 503 4) *Answers to Objections,* F. D. Nichol, p. 323, paragraph 325. Thus Adventists speak of having eternal life "now," but they do not emphasize that it is suspended at death hence *not* eternal.

[5] *Questions on Doctrine,* pp. 515, 520.

session of every believer in the Lord Jesus Christ, and if the term *eternal life* does not include *conscious fellowship* then the whole New Testament meaning is destroyed. The Holy Spirit used the present indicative active of the verb *echo,* expressing present, continuous action. Thus we see that the believer, having been regenerated by the Holy Spirit, *already* possesses never-ending life as a continuing *quality* of conscious existence.

Through the use of this same Greek tense and verb form, the New Testament many times declares that everlasting life is the *present* possession of the believer. "He that heareth my word, and believeth on him that sent me, *hath* (*echei*) everlasting life, and shall not come into condemnation; but *is* passed from death unto life" (John 5:24). An extremely interesting sidelight in I John 5:11-12 is the contrast between individuals who have spiritual life and those who do not. Thus we see that the unsaved man is *physically* alive but *spiritually* dead: "He that hath not the Son of God *hath not life.*" But the saved man is physically *and* spiritually alive: "He that hath the Son hath life." A parallel case obtains in the context of John 5:24, where the Holy Spirit informs us that a spiritually dead man, passes by faith into spiritual or eternal life, but with no change in his physical nature, thus indicating the dualism of body and soul. This completely refutes the general Adventist contention that everlasting life or immortality is bestowed upon the believer only *at* the resurrection of his body. To make this point even more telling, the Lord Jesus Christ stated in John 6:47, "He that believeth on me (*or,* the one believing on me) *hath* everlasting life." This emphasizes the present continuous operation of eternal life in the soul of the one who is redeemed by Christ. And that redemption guarantees that the immaterial nature of man, created in the image of God, now possesses eternal or never-ending life (conscious fellowship) as the free gift of God (Romans 6:23).*

2. *John 11:25, 26:* "Jesus said unto her, I am the resurrection and the life: he that believeth in me, though he were dead, yet shall he live: and whosoever liveth and believeth in me shall never die. Believest thou this?"

The context here indicates that the Lord Jesus Christ was con-

*Conversely "eternal death" (never-ending death) in Scripture is conscious separation from God, *not* unconsciousness or annihilation (Matt. 25:41, 46).

soling Martha upon the death of her brother Lazarus. Therefore, the words "life" and "dead" must refer to that particular occasion. To attempt to wrest the meanings of these terms from their expressed context, and to teach that the end of the age is primarily in view or somehow close, is a violation of the grammar and context.

All thorough students of the Word of God, including the Adventists, recognize that in any study of the doctrines of eternal life and immortality, it is vitally essential to apply the hermeneutic principle (comparing all texts on a given subject) of interpretation, and the application of this principle, we believe, leads to the following facts. The root meanings for the words "death" and "life" in the New Testament usage ("death" *thanatos,* in its verb form *apothnesko,* and "life" *zoe* or its verb form *zac*) are respectively "separation or to separate," from communion or fellowship. The Scriptures describe two types of death, physical and spiritual, the former being the separation of the body from the soul, and the latter being the separation of the soul from God as the result of sin. Also, two kinds of life are spoken of in the New Testament: physical life (*bios*), which is the union or communion of body and soul; and spiritual life (*zoe*), which is the communion or fellowship of the soul with God. These terms we equate with the Greek of the New Testament, and they are essential to an understanding of Christ's words to Martha.

He was assuring her that, despite the physical evidence of death, Jesus, the eternal Word of God, made flesh was Himself the source of life. And, *as such,* He was able to give life, even though death had actually occurred. Let us therefore take His words literally.

Christ's primary purpose was to comfort Martha. And what better comfort could He give than the knowledge that her family's limited concept of life as dependent upon the resurrection was depriving her of the joyous knowledge that the Prince of Life gives to the believer eternal life, unaffected by physical death.

Now let us look carefully at this context with no violation to hermeneutics or grammar, and this great truth becomes clear. John 11:20 tells us that as soon as Martha heard that Jesus was coming to Bethany, she went out to meet him. In verse 21 she greets Him thus: "Lord, if thou hadst been here, my brother had not died." In answer to her obvious affliction and grief Jesus, with divine compassion, stated, "Thy brother shall rise again." Verse 24 indicates, however, that Martha thought He was referring to the resurrection of the dead which will take place at "the last day."

To dispel her confused and grief-instilling concept of life (spiritual life), Jesus gives comfort beyond measure: "I am the resurrection and the life," He declares; "he that believes in me, even though he were dead, yet shall he live, and the one living and believing in me shall never die."

Now it is apparent from the context of verse 25 that Jesus was referring to Martha's brother Lazarus, one who believed in Him and had physically died. Christ's promise is, "yet shall *he* live." But going beyond this, Jesus lifts the veil and reveals that, in the realm of the physically alive, whoever believes in Him shall never experience the greatest of all terrors, spiritual death.[6]

The Greek is extremely powerful in verse 26 for our Lord deliberately used the double negative, a construction which intensifies with great emphasis that to which it is applied. Jesus *could not* grammatically have been more emphatic in stating that the believer, who is alive both physically and spiritually, can never experience loss of communion of fellowship as a spiritual entity, though his body may "become" dead.

We see, further, that Seventh-day Adventists have no warrant for the idea that death is a state of unconsciousness. The New Testament frequently indicates that the unregenerate man is already "dead," but not even the Adventists would say that he was extinct or unconscious! Some instances of this are: Matthew 8:22, "Let the dead bury their dead"; John 5:25, "The hour is coming and now is, when the dead shall hear the voice of the Son of God, and they that hear shall live"; and Ephesians 2:1, "You hath he quickened, who were dead in trespasses and sins."

Admittedly in the New Testament, death is compared with sleep, but this is recognized by Bible scholars generally as a grammatical metaphor. One does not develop a doctrine from a figure of speech, as conditional immortalitists apparently have done, but upon the sound principles of Biblical hermeneutics, contextual analysis, and linguistic exegesis. The application of these principles leads to the one conclusion which the Scripture unreservedly teaches, that *eternal*

[6] Matthew 25:41 – separation from God's fellowship.

life is vastly different from "immortality"; although immortality *will* be bestowed upon the believer at the resurrection, *in this life* he already possesses "eternal life," a spiritual quality of existence which will at length be united with the physical quality of incorruptibility which the Bible speaks of as immortality, and "we shall be like him, for we shall see him as he is" (I Cor. 12; I John 3:2). A study of these words in any Greek lexicon, and of their use in the New Testament, will show that immortality and eternal life are neither identical nor synonymous. For certain Adventist writers therefore to treat these terms as interchangeable is clearly a linguistic impossibility.

3. *II Timothy 1:10:* The Apostle Paul writes that God's eternal purpose "is now made manifest by the appearing of our Saviour Jesus Christ, who hath abolished death, and hath brought *life* and *immortality* to light through the gospel." In this verse "life" (*zoen*) and "immortality" (*aphtharsian*) are clearly distinguished. Life has been bestowed upon the believer at the moment of regeneration by faith in Jesus Christ (I John 5:11, 12); immortality is a future gift, to be bestowed upon the believer's body at the second advent of our Lord, or as Paul expressed it, "This corruptible must put on incorruption (*aphtharsian*), and this mortal must put on immortality" (*athanasian*).

Again in Romans 2:7, the Apostle clearly distinguishes between "eternal life" as a conscious quality of spiritual existence bestowed upon the believer as a gift; and "immortality," which, in this connection in the New Testament refers to the resurrection bodies of the saints or to the nature of God Himself. Thus, God's Word clearly indicates the difference between "life" as spiritual existence, and "immortality," incorruptibility in a body like that of our risen Lord.

4. *Philippians 1:21-23:* "For to me to live is Christ, and to die is gain. But if I live in the flesh, this is the fruit of my labor: yet what I shall choose I wot not. For I am in a strait betwixt two, having a desire to depart and to be with Christ; which is far better: nevertheless to abide in the flesh is more needful for you."

Seventh-day Adventists say here, "Of course it will be better to be with Christ, but why, it must be asked, should we conclude that the apostle expects immediately upon death to go at once into the presence of Christ? *The Bible does not say so.* It merely states his desire to depart and be with Christ. One might reason that the *implication* is to the effect that being with Christ would be immediately on his departure. But it must be admitted that such is not a necessary implication, and it certainly is not a definite statement of the text. In this particular passage Paul does not tell us *when* he will be with his Lord. In other places he uses an expression similar to one in this passage. For instance, he says 'The Time of my departure is at hand' (II Tim. 4:6). The Greek word used in these two texts, *analuō,* is not used very often in the Greek New Testament, but the word has the meaning 'to be loosened like an anchor.' It is a metaphor drawn from the loosened moorings preparatory to setting sail."[7]

Now, of all the texts in the New Testament on the state of the believer after the death of his body, this one alone[8] gives us Paul's mind on the subject, so we need to pay strict attention to what he says. In the main, Seventh-day Adventists support their arguments with Old Testament passages, most of which, I maintain, are taken out of context, while ignoring metaphorical usages, implications or deductions. To treat literally such words as "sleep," "death" and "destroy," is we feel, unwarranted. However, in the New Testament, when faced with a positive statement like this one by the Apostle Paul, it seems that they refuse to be literal and insist upon metaphors, deductions and implications. They seem unwilling to accept the Apostle's statement at face value. The noted Adventist author F. D. Nichol, in his book *Answers to Objections,* states that if Philippians 1:21-23 were the only passage about the condition of man in death, he would be forced to acknowledge the accepted Orthodox position. Nichol then attempts to strengthen his argument by taking texts out of context to "prove" that Paul does not *mean* what he most decidedly *says.* With this thought in mind, let us examine the context and grammar of the Apostle's statement for it answers the Seventh-day Adventist contention.

In verse 21 Paul states that to continue to live *is* Christ, and to die

[7] *Questions on Doctrine,* pp. 527-28.

[8] II Cor. 5:8 is also a strong passage, but has possible application to the resurrection body and cannot, therefore, be dogmatically adduced to support the historic position — though from a hermeneutic standpoint it does. The sentence "to be absent from the body and to be at home with the Lord" does however, strongly suggest the intermediate state.

"is gain." Since Paul was ordained to preach the Word of God to the Gentiles while enjoying fellowship with the living Christ, what would he gain by death or unconsciousness? According to the Adventist idea, fellowship with Christ would end, and Paul would merely go to sleep until the resurrection. In the very context, this argument violates both context and grammar.

Verse 23 is grammatically uncomplicated. It is a series of coordinate statements tied together by the conjunctions *kai* and *de*. The phrase "to depart and be with Christ, which is far better" (*eis To analusai Kai sun Christo einai*) is grammatically devastating to the Seventh-day Adventist position. The preposition *eis To* plus the infinitive shows "true purpose or end in view"—the strong desire which causes Paul's dilemma. Both infinitives (*analusai and einai*) have one construction, so are *one* thought, *one* grammatical expression; literally, "my desire is unto the, *to depart,* and unto the, *to be with* Christ." In simple English, Paul's one desire has a twofold object: departure and being *with* Christ! If departure did not mean his immediately being with Christ, another construction would have been employed. It therefore seems impossible that soul sleep was in the mind of the Apostle, since he desired to depart *from* his body and to spiritually enjoy the presence of his Lord. The Second Advent could not have been in view in this passage, for the context indicates that Paul expected death—and instantaneous reunion with Christ—*then, not* at the resurrection. There would have been no need of his staying to instruct the Philippians (vs. 24) if he were speaking of the Second Advent, for they would all be glorified together and in need no longer of His presence to strengthen them. Most translators and recognized Greek authorities contend that Philippians 1:21-23 teaches the historic position of the Christian Church, i.e., the conscious presence of the believer with Christ at the death of the body.

As quoted above, the Adventists, in common with all conditionalists, say, but "Why . . . should we conclude from this remark that the Apostle expects, immediately upon death, to go at once into the presence of Christ? The Bible does not say so. It merely states his desire to depart and to be with Christ." We answer that the context of the chapter, the grammatical construction of the verse, and every grammar book on New Testament Greek usage teaches that from the construction utilized the Apostle expected to go *at once* into the presence of His Lord. Nevertheless the Adventists insist, "The Bible does not say so. It merely states his desire to depart and to be with Christ." This statement is not accurate, it is not exegetically sound, and it will not stand the test of contextual criticism. It is only an attempt I believe to justify a doctrine that is *not* supported by the Word of God.

In reply to the Adventist statement, "In this particular passage Paul does not tell us *when* he will be with his Lord," we point out that the Apostle categorically states that his desire *is* "to depart." If this departure did not mean immediate presence with Christ, he would have used a different grammatical construction as previously noted; but as it stands, it can have *no other meaning.* In the face of these facts, Seventh-day Adventists disregard the preponderance of historical scholarship in favor of the doctrine of "soul sleep."

5. *I Thessalonians 4:13-18:* "I would not have you to be ignorant, brethren, concerning them which are asleep, that ye sorrow not, even as others which have no hope. For if we believe that Jesus died and rose again, even so them also which sleep in Jesus will God bring with him. For this we say unto you by the word of the Lord, that we which are alive and remain unto the coming of the Lord shall not prevent them which are asleep. For the Lord himself shall descend from heaven with a shout, with the voice of the archangel, and with the trump of God: and the dead in Christ shall rise first: then we which are alive and remain shall be caught up together with them in the clouds, to meet the Lord in the air: and so shall we ever be with the Lord. Wherefore comfort one another with these words."

This final passage, we believe, refutes the SDA teaching on the intermediate state of the dead, and is marked by explicit emphasis of construction in the Greek and cannot be ignored by any serious student of the language.

The key is the preposition *sun* which carries the primary meaning of "together with." In verse 14, the Holy Spirit tells us that God intends to bring with Him (*sun auto*), that is, with Jesus at His second advent, believing Christians who have experienced physical death. The physical state of their bodies is described as "sleep," a common metaphor in the New Testament. In every instance where the word "sleep" is used to describe death, it always refers to the *body* and cannot be applied to the soul, especially since "sleep" is never used with reference to the soul. This fact Seventh-day Adventists seem to overlook.

The second use of *sun* is in verse 17, which tells us that believers who survive to the coming of the Lord will be caught up together with them (*sun autois*), that is, with the dead in Christ (*oi nekroi en Christe*) to meet the Lord in the air. Here again, *sun* has no meaning other than "together with"; a fact most difficult for Seventh-day Adventists to explain.

The last use of the preposition *sun* is also in verse 17, "and so shall we ever be with the Lord" (*sun kurio*). It is quite obvious, therefore, that at the Second Advent of Christ those who at death departed to be spiritually with the Lord (Phil. 1:21-23) *return* with Him or "together with" Him to claim their resurrected, immortal bodies. Simultaneously, their corrupting bodies in the graves, spoken of as "asleep," are instantly metamorphosed or changed and reunited with the returning personalities. This fact is consistently emphasized by continual use of the preposition *sun*, "together with." Since the preposition *sun* means "together with" both times in verse 17, grammatically it cannot mean something altogether different in the same context and parallel usage of verse 14. Therefore, if at Christ's advent our bodies are to go with Him physically (verse 16) it is obvious that the saints who preceded us in death have been with Him from the moment of death, since they accompany Him in His return (verse 14).

A final grammatical point is the Holy Spirit's use of *nekroi* which throughout the New Testament refers primarily to the physical body of man, and only metaphorically to the soul. We see, then, that the corpses (*nekroi*) of the physically dead saints are to be raised and united with their returning souls (verse 14). Not once does the context or grammar indicate that the souls of departed believers are "asleep." Instead, it categorically states that they are "with Jesus" or returning "together with" Jesus.

The great hope of the believer, then, is the joy of personal union with the Lord, and this union, the Apostle Paul tells us, takes place at the death of the body. That this has been the position of the large majority of the Christian church since the times of the apostles, the Adventists have never denied. In I Thessalonians 4, the Apostle Paul was giving comfort to people who were mourning for departed loved ones; and his words carry the undeniable conclusion that they are not "dead" in the usual pagan sense. Although physically dead, they are spiritually alive and with Christ, and are awaiting the day when they will return "together with him," (verse 14) to claim their inheritance of completion, physical immortality or incorruptibility.

II. "Soul" and "Spirit"

For a fuller treatment of Adventist teaching on soul sleep, we must discuss briefly the Bible use of "soul" and "spirit." In the Old Testament, the words "soul" and "spirit" are the Hebrew *nephesh* and *ruach*. In the New Testament they are the Greek *psuche* and *pneuma*. Although in the Old Testament *nephesh* and *ruach* frequently refer only to the *principle* of life in both men and animals, in many other places they mean the intellectual and spiritual nature of man. Such verses as Isaiah 57:16, Zechariah 12:1, Isaiah 55:3 and Genesis 35:18,[9] belie the Adventists' criterion for determining the spiritual nature of man. On page 522 of *Questions on Doctrine*, the Adventists list eight Scripture passages about death, to show that at the death of the body, the intellect, will, and spirit of man (*nephesh* and *ruach*) lapse into unconsciousness pending the resurrection. However, seven of these are from the Old Testament, and every one of them refers to the *body*. Adventists lean strongly on the Book of Ecclesiastes, especially 9:5-6[10] to substantiate their doctrine. But Ecclesiastes 12:7 tells us that, upon the death of the body, "the spirit [*ruach*] shall return unto God." Unlike the mere principle of life in the animals, man possesses a cognizant, immaterial nature created in God's image.[11]

[9] "For I will not contend for ever, neither will I be always wroth: for the spirit should fail before me, and the souls which I have made" (Isa. 57:16); "The burden of the word of the Lord for Israel, saith the Lord, which stretcheth forth the heavens, and layeth the foundation of the earth, and formeth the spirit of man within him" (Zech. 12:1); "Incline your ear, and come unto me: hear, and your soul shall live; and I will make an everlasting covenant with you, even the sure mercies of David" (Isa. 55:3); "And it came to pass, as her soul was in departing, (for she died) that she called his name Ben-omi: but his father called him Benjamin" (Gen. 35:18).

[10] "For the living know that they shall die: but the dead know not any thing, neither have they any more a reward: for the memory of them is forgotten. Also their love, and their hatred, and their envy, is now perished; neither have they any more a portion for ever in any thing that is done under the sun" (Eccl. 9:5, 6).

[11] It is almost universally agreed among Biblical scholars that Ecclesiastes portrays Solomon's apostasy and is therefore virtually worthless for determining doctrine. It sketches man's life "under the sun" and reveals the hopelessness of the soul apart from God. The conclusion of the Book alone mirrors the true revelation of God (chap. 12).

It is a basic Christian principle, which Adventists share, that the Old Testament must be interpreted by the New Testament, and not the reverse. However, where conditional immortality is involved Adventists do not follow this principle. The New Testament teaches that the immaterial nature of man (soul and spirit) is separate from the body (Matthew 10:28, Luke 8:55, I Thessalonians 5:23, Hebrews 4:12, Revelation 16:3);[12] that it is independent of man's material form, and departs from that form at death, to go either into the presence of the Lord (Phil. 1:23) or into a place of punishment (Luke 16). In Acts 7:59, Stephen committed his spirit (*pneuma*) into the hands of the Lord Jesus Christ. This establishes the fact that the immaterial nature of man is independent of his body; at the same time, the Scripture tells us, "He [Stephen] fell asleep" in death; that is, his physical body took on the appearance of "sleep." But he as a unit did not die; he merely experienced separation of the soul from the body and he went to be with the Lord, into whose hands he had committed his spiritual nature.

In Luke 23:46 the Lord Jesus Christ said, "Father, into thy hands I commend my spirit." This verse would be meaningless if it applied only to the "Breath of Jesus." The classic example of the penitent thief, who in his last moments believed on the Lord Jesus Christ, is proof that eternal life is a *quality including conscious existence*. It does not terminate with the death of the physical but continues in never-ending personal fellowship with our Lord. "Today shalt thou be with me in paradise," is the guarantee of the Son of God that those who trust Him will never be separated from His presence and fellowship. Seventh-day Adventists, in company with other Conditionalists, attempt to explain this by reading the text, "Verily, verily, I say unto thee today, thou shalt be with me in paradise." The reason is that Christ's statement calls in serious question their doctrine of soul

[12] "And fear not them which kill the body, but are not able to kill the soul: but rather fear him which is able to destroy both soul and body in hell" (Matt. 10:28); "And her spirit came again, and she rose straightway: and he commanded to give her meat" (Luke 8:55); "and the very God of peace sanctify you wholly; and I pray God your whole spirit and soul and body be preserved blameless unto the coming of our Lord Jesus Christ" (I Thess. 5:23); "For the word of God is quick, and powerful and sharper than any twoedged sword, piercing even to the dividing asunder of soul and spirit, and of the joints and marrow, and is a discerner of the thoughts and intents of the heart" (Heb. 4:12); "And the second angel poured out his vial upon the sea; and it became as the blood of a dead man: and every living soul died in the sea" (Rev. 16:3).

sleep. Moreover, Adventists seem to overlook the important fact that wherever Jesus used the words, "verily, verily, I say unto you," He never qualified them because qualification was unnecessary. It would have been redundant for Jesus to say, "Verily, verily, I say unto you, that is, *today* I am saying unto you. . . ." By this type of interpretation, the Adventists violate the plain sense of one of Christ's favorite expressions of emphasis.

In Matthew 17:3, we see Moses and Elijah with Christ on the Mount of Transfiguration. We know that Moses died (Deuteronomy 34:5), and Elijah was translated (II Kings 2:11). However, it *was* Moses who was communing with our Lord. Since the Scripture nowhere states that Moses had been raised from the dead for this occasion (Adventists attempt to teach this from the Book of Jude, where such an assertion is *not* made), it is evident that the soul of Moses appeared to our Lord. Thus conscious existence is a necessary predicate of the intermediate state.

It is the strong conviction of the author, based upon Scripture, that the doctrine of soul sleep cannot stand in the light of God's revelation. Perhaps the reader will think that there has been too much space given to the meanings of words and the grammar of the Greek New Testament, but this is most essential because the crux of Adventist argument, it seems to this writer, is a denial of the meaning of terms in their context. For example, they say, "There is nothing in the word *psuche* [soul] itself that even remotely implies a conscious entity that is able to survive the death of the body. And there is nothing in the Bible use of the word indicating that the Bible writers held any such belief. . . . There is nothing inherent in the word *pneuma* [spirit] by which it may be taken to mean some supposed conscious entity of man capable of existing apart from the body, nor does the usage of the word *with respect to man* in the New Testament in any way imply such a concept. . . . A careful study of all the adjectives used in Scripture to qualify the word 'spirit' as applied to man, indicates that *not one* even remotely approaches the idea of immortality as one of the qualities of the human 'spirit.'"[13] In Matthew 10:28 Jesus Christ apparently believed and taught that the soul was more than "body and breath" as Seventh-day Adventism

[13] *Questions on Doctrine*, pp. 514, 517-18.

teaches, for He said, "Fear not them which kill the body, but are not able to kill the soul!"

Seventh-day Adventist writers charge that orthodox theologians have been overly dogmatic about the nature of man while Adventists have maintained a guarded reserve. But Adventists have been equally dogmatic in denouncing the orthodox position. To be dogmatic one should have a sound, scholarly basis for his dogmatism, and such a basis exegetically speaking is conspicuously absent from the historic position of conditional immortalitists. As mentioned above, Adventists generally confuse "immortality" with "eternal life." We quite agree that "a careful study of all the adjectives used in Scripture to qualify the word 'spirit' as applied to man indicates that not one even remotely approaches the idea of immortality," as our Adventist brethren have stated.[14] But as we have shown, "immortality" refers *only* to the resurrection body of the saints and to the nature of God Himself. Therefore, since the saints are to be clothed with their resurrection bodies at the Second Advent, they do not *now* possess "immortality." For Adventists to confuse "immortality" with "eternal life" and then to argue that "immortality" *means* "eternal life" and is never applied to the spirit, is logical and theological error.

The question of soul sleep, however, should cause no serious division between Christians since it does not affect the foundational doctrines of the Christian faith, or the salvation of the soul. It is merely an area of theological debate, and has no direct bearing upon any of the great doctrines of the Bible. The ground of fellowship is not the condition of man in death but faith in the Lord Jesus Christ, and the love He commanded us to have one for another (John 13:34, 35). Seventh-day Adventists are welcome to hold this doctrine, but when one is faced with such concrete Old Testament instances as Samuel's appearance to Saul (I Sam. 28:18, 19) and such New Testament accounts as those given by the Apostle Paul (II Cor. 5:8), "To be absent from the body is to be at home with the Lord," or (Phil. 1:23) ". . . to depart and be with Christ, which is far better," it is difficult to see how our Adventist brethren can long substantiate their claim for the "sleep of the soul." Every instance in the account of I Samuel, for example, indicates that Samuel in his spiritual nature

[14] *Questions on Doctrine,* p. 518.

addressed Saul. Nowhere is it even intimated that it was not Samuel, and any attempt to establish what the Hebrew text simply does not allow is evidence of failure to recognize the hermeneutic principle of interpretation governing the processes of sound exegesis.

III. Hell and Eternal Punishment

The doctrines of Hell and Eternal Punishment are unpleasant topics for any Christian whose heart is filled with the love of Christ and the sanctifying influences of the Holy Spirit, especially when one realizes the horror into which the souls of unregenerate men are plunged at death. The Bible does not tell us the nature of Hell and the lake of fire so vividly recorded in the Book of Revelation, and it is folly to try to discover what God has not seen fit to reveal. But one fact is clear: it required the death of the sinless Son of God to save sinful man from everlasting punishment. Consequently, whatever Hell and the lake of fire are, they must be avoided at all cost. Men must ceaselessly be warned that only by the matchless grace of Christ do they find deliverance from the wrath to come.

There are many references to Hell and eternal punishment in the New Testament,[15] and the Bible speaks plainly about the state of the unsaved. The issue here is, whether the Bible *means* what it plainly *says* about "punishment," "destruction," "torment," and "fire," all these terms accompanied by the great adjective of emphasis, "everlasting" (*aionion*). Scores of Greek scholars, grammar textbooks and commentaries affirm that when Scripture speaks of "everlasting punishment," it means punishment without cessation, i.e., the continuing wrath of God upon those who refuse to believe and be saved.

One of the best statements on the subject was made by the late *Dr. Charles Hodge* in his *Systematic Theology*. Dr. Hodge was especially interested in refuting the contention of conditional immortalitists that the word "everlasting" does not always mean unending, but that it sometimes describes limited periods or ages. To this contention Dr. Hodge replied: "It may be remarked (1) That the Hebrew and Greek words rendered in our version 'eternal' or 'everlasting,' mean duration whose termination is unknown. When used

[15] *See* Matthew 5:22, 29, 30; 7:13; 10:28; 11:21-24; 13:42, 50; 18:7-9; 22:12, 13; 23:33; 25:41, 46; 3:29; 9:43-48; Luke 12:2-5; 16:19-31; John 3:16, 36; 5:24; Acts 17:31; Revelation 20:11.

in reference to perishable things, as when the Bible speaks of 'the everlasting hills,' they simply indicate indefinite existence to which there is no known or assignable limit. But when used in reference to that which is either in its own nature imperishable, or of that of which the unending existence is revealed, as the human soul, or in reference to that for which we have no authority from other sources to assign a limit to, as the future blessedness of the saints, then the words are to be taken in their literal sense. If, because we sometimes say we give a man a thing *forever* without intending that he is to possess it to all eternity, it were argued the word 'forever' expresses limited duration, everyone would see that the inference was unfounded. If the Bible says that the sufferings of the lost are to be everlasting, they are to endure forever unless it can be shown either that the soul is not immortal[16] or that Scriptures elsewhere teach that those sufferings will come to an end. No one argues that the blessedness of the righteous will cease after a term of years because the word 'everlasting' is sometimes used of things which do not continue forever. Our Lord teaches that the punishment of the wicked is everlasting in the same sense that the blessedness of the saints is everlasting.

"(2) It is to be remembered that, admitting the word everlasting to be ever so ambiguous, the Bible says that the worm never dies, that the fire is never quenched. We have therefore the direct assertion of the Word of God that the sufferings of the lost are unending. All the modes of expression used to set forth the perpetuity of salvation of believers and the everlasting duration of the Kingdom of Christ are employed to teach the perpetuity of the future punishment of the wicked. If that doctrine, therefore, be not taught in the Scriptures it is difficult to see how it could be taught in human language."[17]

Conditional Immortalitists try to answer Dr. Hodge's argument by declaring that the soul is not eternal by creation; but the Bible emphatically teaches that it is, since we have seen that the word "death" does not imply unconsciousness as Adventists declare. The soul is

[16] For Hodge, "immortality" of the soul is equal to eternal, conscious existence. His usage is not based on the contextual usages of the terms *aphthartos* and *athanasia*.

[17] Charles Hodge, *Systematic Theology*, p. 876.

exempt from unconsciousness, or death as the Adventists construe the term. An excellent example of how the New Testament destroys the doctrine of the annihilation of the wicked is found in Matthew 25:41, 46.

Verse 41 says, "Then shall he say also unto them on the left hand, Depart from me, ye cursed, into everlasting fire prepared for the devil and his angels." Verse 46 says, "These shall go away into everlasting punishment, but the righteous into life eternal."

Now it is admitted by almost all scholars that hermeneutics and grammar largely determine the meaning of terms. In the 25th chapter of Matthew's Gospel, the Lord Jesus Christ contextually and grammatically establishes the fact that the unrighteous depart from the presence of God into never-ending punishment, and the righteous enjoy never-ending life. Now, since the Adventists maintain that "everlasting" (*aionion*) in the first part of verse 46 refers to punishment of limited duration, or cessation, they would be forced by the laws of grammar to translate the second clause of verse 46 to make the existence of the saints of a limited duration. Thus not only do the unrighteous escape eternal punishment, but the righteous forfeit eternal life. The only escape from this dilemma is to admit that the Greek adjective *aionion* (everlasting) here refers to an eternal state, and establishes the fact that Satan, his angels, and unregenerate men must suffer never-ending punishment, while the redeemed of the Lord enjoy never-ending bliss in His presence. The key problem is the context; and in this the Lord of Life unmistakably describes the destiny of the unregenerate as "everlasting fire" (verse 41); a fire which is to punish everlastingly (verse 46).* Thus if eternal punishment is not a grammatical reality, eternal life becomes at best a limited state of existence. This latter idea the Adventists themselves vehemently deny. How can they affirm the eternal life of the righteous, and vigorously reject the teaching about the state of the unrighteous in the same verse? Both contextually and grammatically, "everlasting" *means* "everlasting"; i.e., never-ending life for the saints and never-ending punishment for the wicked. As Dr. R. A. Torrey put it, "I would like very much to believe that there is no Hell and

***See all major exegetical commentaries on the eternal duration of the flame and the punishment (consciously) of unregenerate souls, etc.**

no eternal punishment, were it not for the fact that the Bible simply does not teach it."

Doubtless one of the chief reasons why many people reject the Biblical doctrine of eternal punishment is because they have acquired a distorted, un-Biblical concept of the doctrine. For instance, Luke 12: 47, 48 teaches that while eternal punishment is forever, not all are punished with identical severity. The Scripture states that some will be beaten with many stripes and some with few, which dissipates the idea that God hurls the souls of rebellious men and angels into one cauldron of fire where all are equally tormented forever. The Word of God teaches that the Judge of all the earth will "do right" (Gen. 18:25), and we can rest secure in the fact that God conducts His punishments in accordance with perfect love and absolute justice.

Frequently, the Lord Jesus Christ Himself warned of the dangers of Hell when He said, "Ye generation of vipers, how can ye escape the damnation of hell?" (Matt. 23:33). And again, "It is better for you to enter the kingdom of God with one eye than with two eyes to be thrown into hell, where their worm does not die and the fire is not quenched" (Mark 9:47, 48).[18] If Christ was not speaking about punishment for the unregenerate soul after death, why did He three times use the Hebraic metaphor "where their worm does not die" which, in our language, means "where their suffering does not cease"?**

Our Adventist brethren sometimes state that they believe in "everlasting punishment" but not in "everlasting *punishing*." This in my opinion is a linguistic evasion, since the words used to describe Hell and everlasting punishment are too clear in the Greek to be used in such a manner. The church of Jesus Christ has always believed that death itself is not "the judgment" but, as the Word of God says, "It is appointed unto men once to die, but after this the judgment" (Heb. 9:27).

Let us now consider an interesting statement made by the Apostle Peter: "The Lord knows how to keep the unrighteous under punishment until the day of judgment" (II Pet. 2:9, literal Greek). This

[18] See also Mark 9:43 and Matt. 13:42, 50.

**See Lange, Jamieson, Fausset and Brown, Clarke, Alexander, on Isa. 66:24 and Lenski plus the aforementioned on Mark 9:44, 46, 48.

statement points out that God is able righteously to punish the unregenerate right up *to* the time of their final judgment (Rev. 20:13-15), and establishes the fact that the unregenerate do not "rest in the tomb until the resurrection" as Adventists hold,[19] but immediately upon death enter a state of alienation and conscious suffering, because of their unbelief.

As stated in our review of Matthew 25:41, 46, it is unnecessary to discuss the meaning of "everlasting" where suffering is concerned. But it should be noted that the Greek word *kolasin*[20] in the Matthew passages is consistently defined as "punishment" and in over one hundred Greek writings of the first century the word carries that the Apostle Peter meant precisely what they said—punishment, not "sleep," is the destiny of the *unregenerate* soul at death.

IV. Hell and Punishment in New Testament Greek

The grammar of the Greek New Testament teaches unquestionably the doctrine of Hell and eternal punishment. Nowhere is this more pointedly brought out than in the following passages:

1. *Matthew 5:22 and 10:28*: "Whosoever shall say, Thou fool, shall be in danger of hell fire." "Fear him which is able to destroy both soul and body in hell."

In both passages the Greek word *gehenna* portrays a place of punishment for the unsaved. *Gehenna* originally meant the Valley of Hinnom, a garbage dump which smoldered perpetually outside Jerusalem. The rabbis believed that punishment after death could be likened to Gehenna, and often threatened their people with punishment after death. The Lord Jesus Christ, however, pointed out to the unbelieving Jews that those who rejected Him could look forward to everlasting Gehenna. In Matthew 10:28 He coupled *gehenna* with *apolesai*, which Thayer's Greek lexicon defines as "to be delivered up to eternal misery." *Gehenna,* then, symbolizes eternal separation and conscious punishment for the spiritual nature of the unregenerate man. This eternity of punishment is also taught in the Old Testament; e.g., "Their worm shall not die, neither shall their fire be quenched" (Isa. 66:24).

[19] *Questions on Doctrine,* p. 520.

[20] Robert C. Trench, *Synonyms of the New Testament* (1950): "The *kolasis aionios* (eternal punishment) of Matt. 25:46, as it is plain, is not merely corrective and therefore temporary discipline."

2. *II Thessalonians 1:8-9:* "In flaming fire taking vengeance on them that know not God, and that obey not the gospel of our Lord Jesus Christ; who shall be punished with everlasting destruction from the presence of the Lord and from the glory of his power."

From the context, especially verse 8, "everlasting destruction" is to be that of "flaming fire," visited upon those who "obey not the gospel of our Lord Jesus Christ." The heart of the problem here is the meaning of the word "destruction," which the Adventists claim is reduction to a state of non-existence (*Questions on Doctrine*, p. 14). As a matter of fact, the Greek word *olethros* used here has the clear meaning of "ruining."[21] We see then, that everlasting destruction or "ruination" is the lot of those who know not God. Many people who are not well versed in Greek try to make "destruction" synonymous with "annihilation"; this does violence to New Testament Greek, which supports no such concept. A common illustration will show the fallacy of this idea.

In the course of her work a housewife changes light bulbs and sometimes one drops to the floor and breaks. Of course the bulb has been "destroyed," but no one would say that it had been annihilated, for there is a difference between the *function* of an object and its *nature*. The function of the bulb is to give forth light. When broken, its function is destroyed, but the glass remains, although in fragments, and so does the metal base. Although the bulb has been "ruined" or "destroyed," it certainly has not been "reduced to nothing."

The Bible teaches that unregenerate men will suffer the eternal wrath of God, and must undergo destruction and ruin of their original function which was "to glorify God and to enjoy Him forever." But the human spirit, created in the image of God (Gen. 1:26, 27) remains intact, a spiritual entity of eternal existence, capable of enduring eternally the righteous judgment of a righteous and just Judge.

3. *Revelation 20:10:* "The devil who deceived them was cast into the lake of fire and brimstone where the beast and the false prophet are, and they will be tormented day and night into the everlasting of the everlasting" (literal translation).

The root meaning of the Greek word *basanizo* is "to torment, to

[21] Thayer, p. 443, on *olethros;* see on *vulnus,* to wound.

be harassed, to torture or to vex with grievous pain,"[22] and is used throughout the New Testament to denote great conscious pain and misery, never annihilation or cessation of consciousness. The reader who wishes to pursue this point may look up the following verses where this word is used: Matthew 8:6, 29; Mark 5:7; Luke 8:28; Revelation 14:10, 11. In each place, *basanizo* means conscious "torment." In Revelation 14:10-11, speaking of the followers of the Beast, unmistakably it means torment or punishment, everlasting or never-ceasing.[23]

In Revelation 20:10, Satan, the beast and the false prophet are described as tormented (*basanis thesontai*) "day and night[24] into the everlasting of the everlasting"; so if language means anything at all, in these contexts alone the theory of the annihilation or, as the Adventists say, the final destruction, of the wicked is itself annihilated.

4. *John 3:36:* "He that believeth on the Son hath everlasting life, and he that believeth not the Son shall not see life, but the wrath of God abideth on him."

Our fourth and final grammatical point relative to the doctrine of annihilation is made by coupling Romans 2:8-9 and Revelation 14:10 with John 3:36. John tells us that the one who believes in the Lord Jesus Christ already *has* everlasting life (present tense); and then, of one who "believes not the Son," he states that he "shall not *see* life, but the wrath of God abides on him." The Greek word *menei*, here translated *abide*, appears several times in the New Testament. It carries the idea of continuous action (see John 1:33, 2:12, 8:31, 15:9). Thus, in John 3:36 the Holy Spirit says that the wrath of God continually abides on the one who "believeth not the Son." Comparing this with Romans 2:8, 9, we see that those who do not obey the truth but do evil are the objects of God's wrath, which Revelation 14:10-11 describes as eternal. "The same shall drink of the wine of the wrath of God . . . and the smoke of their torment ascendeth up for ever and ever: and they have no rest day nor night."

Orges, translated "wrath," appears in each of the verses cited, so

[22] *Ibid.*, p. 96*b*.
[23] *Ibid.*, p. 40, No. 2; also Liddell and Scott on *anapausis*.
[24] Metaphorical usage clearly indicated in the context — i.e., eternal duration.

there can be no doubt that the same subject is being discussed. It is apparent then that, far from the comparatively blissful prospect of total annihilation, those who "have not the Son of God have not life,"[25] and "the wrath of God continues upon them."* God's wrath even now hangs like the sword of Damocles over the heads of those who deny Jesus Christ. It will strike when the rebellious soul goes into eternity and appears before the bar of God's eternal justice.

Seventh-day Adventists should not be ostracized because they cling to this doctrine, since they believe that an undetermined period of punishment will elapse before the actual ultimate destruction of the wicked with Satan and his hosts.

Dr. Francis Pieper, the great Lutheran scholar and author of the monumental *Christian Dogmatics,* states the views of this author in essence when he says: "Holy Scripture teaches the truth of an eternal damnation so clearly and emphatically that one cannot deny it without, at the same time, rejecting the authority of Scripture. Scripture parallels the eternal salvation of the believers and the eternal damnation of the unbelievers. Whoever therefore denies the one must, to be consistent, deny the other (Matt. 25:46). We find the same juxtaposition and antithesis in other passages of Scripture. This parallelism proves that the term *eternity* in the sense of limited duration as sometimes used in Holy Writ, is inapplicable here. We must take the predicate eternal in its proper or strict sense, a sense of *sine fine* in all Scripture texts which use it to describe the duration and the penalties of the wicked in yonder life (see II Thess. 1:9, Matt. 18:8, Mark 3:29). . . . The Objections raised in all ages to the endlessness of the infernal punishment are understandable; for the thought of a never-ending agony of rational beings fully realizing their distressing plight is so appalling that it exceeds comprehension. But all objections are based on the false principle that it is proper and reasonable to make our human sentiments and judgments the measure of God's essence and activity.

"This is the case in particular with those who contend that an everlasting punishment of a part of mankind does not agree with

[25] I.e., personal communion or fellowship with Christ. Spiritual death is the opposite of eternal life in that the soul is deprived of such communion or fellowship and is conscious of it.

*Death (spiritual) far from being unconsciousness is eternal *conscious* endurance of God's just wrath.

the unity of God's world plan, or that it is compatible neither with divine love nor with divine justice, who accordingly substitute for eternal damnation eventual salvation by gradual improvement in the next life, or an immediate or later annihilation of the wicked. Against such views we must maintain the general principle that God's essence, attributes and actions exceed our comprehension, that we can therefore not know *a priori* but only from God's revelation in His Word what agrees or conflicts with God's essence and attributes. The nature of eternal damnation consists in eternal banishment from the sight of God or, in other words, in being forever excluded from communion with God. . . . To illustrate the terrible agony setting in with this banishment from the sight of God, the dogmatician points to the agony of the fish removed from its element. But there is this difference; the fish which is removed from its element soon dies, whereas the man who is banished from communion with God must by God's judgment live on, 'is guilty of eternal judgment,' Mark 3:29."[26]

Seventh-day Adventists would do well to heed Dr. Pieper's observation; they would do well to heed the testimony of the Christian church generally for almost two thousand years; but most important, they should heed the teaching of the Word of God that the soul of man, whether regenerate or unregenerate, exists after the death of the body. The justice of God makes everlasting punishment for the unregenerate and everlasting life for the saved to be two sides of one coin — God's justice and God's love. The Bible then we believe clearly teaches that there is neither authority nor warrant for the doctrines of conditional immortality and annihilation. God grant in the fulness of His wisdom that none of His children will persist in setting up their standards as the criterion to determine His perfect righteousness. It is this writer's opinion that Seventh-day Adventists have done just this; first by predicating that a God of love *would not* eternally punish a conscious being, and second by attempting to force the Scriptures into their frame of thought while seeming to ignore context, hermeneutics and exegesis. Their fellow Christians can only pray that they may soon be led to embrace the historic position of the church, which is the antithesis of the sleep of the soul and the annihilation of the wicked.

[26] Pieper, Francis, *Christian Dogmatics*, pp. 544-545, Vol. III.

CHAPTER SIX

THE SABBATH, THE LORD'S DAY, AND THE MARK OF THE BEAST

I. The Sabbath

Certainly the most distinctive doctrine promulgated by the Seventh-day Adventist denomination, and one of the two from which they derive their name, is the Seventh-day Sabbath. How Adventists came to hold the Sabbath as the true day of worship, and why they continue to champion it and jealously urge it upon all who worship on Sunday, provides the key to understanding their psychological and theological motivations.

A. *Influence of Joseph Bates*

As we have seen, after the "Great Disappointment of 1844," the Millerites divided into various groups, three of which later united to form the Seventh-day Adventist denomination. One group was led by Captain Joseph Bates of Fairhaven, Massachusetts. From his study of the Bible, (influenced by Thomas M. Preble[1]), Captain Bates became convinced that the Seventh-day Sabbath of the fourth commandment was binding upon Christians. To this view he succeeded in "converting" Ellen G. White, her husband James, and other leading Adventists. In 1846 Bates published "The Seventh-day Sabbath, a Perpetual Sign." This tract, which became very popular with the earlier Adventists, contains the core of modern Seventh-day Adventist reasoning about the Sabbath.

Dr. LeRoy Froom best sums up Bates' position which is that of the Denomination today and was endorsed by Ellen G. White (i.e., the Spirit of Prophecy), thereby making it a tenet of Adventist belief. Writes Dr. Froom: "Bates presented his case for the Sabbath almost exclusively on the premise that the Sabbath was instituted at creation and re-enforced at Sinai. He maintained that the Ten Com-

[1] A Freewill Baptist minister of East Weare, N. H., who became a devout Millerite.

mandments are the moral guide and rule for all mankind, including Christians—the historic Protestant position—with the Seventh Day enjoined as the Sabbath. He touched briefly on the prophesied change of the Sabbath, as the papal little horn of Daniel seven, who thinks 'to change times and laws of God, particularly the law of the Sabbath.' It was the typical Seventh-day Baptist presentation. Then, as a prophetic expositor, he asked pointedly: 'Now the Second Advent believers have professed all confidence in his [Daniel's] visions; why, then, doubt this?'

"However, in the second edition of the tract issued in 1847 Bates adds a fuller prophetic argument based primarily on Revelation 14:9-12 in conjunction with the aforementioned argument of Daniel seven. On the basis of the long accepted Protestant identification of the beast with the papacy, he contrasts God's appointed Sabbath with its change as the badge of papal power—therefore finally as the 'mark of the [papal] beast.' This became henceforth a characteristic and separating feature of Sabbatarian Adventist preaching. Bates here held that the message of Revelation 14 is the foundation of the full Advent message—'Fear God and give glory to Him for the hour of his judgment is come.' This, he maintains, began to be fulfilled in the preaching of the Millerite movement. The second angel's message on the fall of Babylon, with its climax in the call, 'Come out of her, my people, was likewise initially sounded in 1843-44.

"Then, Bates continues with logical progression, according to Bible prophecy a third message is to follow those two which will warn against following and worshiping the papal beast and ultimately receiving his 'mark.' And he notes that those who refuse the mark are immediately described thus: 'Here is the patience of the saints: here are they that keep the commandments of God, and the faith of Jesus' (Rev. 14:12). They must not stop at the first two messages. There is the third inseparable in the series to be received and obeyed—namely, full obedience to God's holy commandments including the observance of the Seventh Day as the Sabbath. But that obedience is by faith.

"The Sabbath was next set forth as 'the seal of God,' as based on the sealing work of Revelation seven. In January 1849, Bates issued his tract, 'The Seal of the Living God.' . . . This concept of the seal was likewise built into the message of the Sabbath as an added prophetic element. This thought was similarly attested by Ellen White who wrote, 'This seal is the Sabbath,' [Ellen G. White in broadside, 'To Those Who Are Receiving The Seal Of The Living God,' January 31, 1849] and describes the most holy place in which was the ark (Rev. 11:19) containing the Ten Commandments with a halo of light surrounding the fourth (*A Sketch of the Christian Views and Experiences of Ellen G. White,* p. 16).

"Thus the Sabbath, first received under the claims of the law of God, was now urged by various prophetic passages, particularly Revelation 14:9-12, which gave the Sabbath the significance of a testing, sealing message for the last days."[2]

B. *Apocalyptic Illusions*

Here in the proverbial nutshell we have the heart of Seventh-day Adventist teaching on the Sabbath. We may learn from this account that: (1) They believe the fourth commandment of the Decalogue commending Sabbath observance is binding upon all Christians. (2) Daniel 7:25 refers to the papacy which "changed" said observance to Sunday-keeping. (3) Because they "keep the commandments of God and the faith of Jesus" (Rev. 14:12), they give the impression that they are the only *fully* obedient Christians in these last days. (4) Sabbath observance is the seal of the living God; Sunday observance will *ultimately* become the mark of the papal beast.[3] Responsible Adventists have generally made it clear, however, as has Ellen G. White, that no one who keeps Sunday in good conscience has as yet received the mark of the beast. That comes at a future day, Adventists declare.

A great deal has been written to refute the Adventists' fourth claim listed above (see Bibliography), so it is unnecessary to go into detail here except to point out that the Adventists base their interpretations largely upon purely apocalyptic and prophetic passages in the Books of Daniel and Revelation. Regardless of how many scholars they cite to back up their historicist interpretation[4] of these

[2] *The Prophetic Faith of Our Fathers,* Vol. IV, pp. 957-59.
[3] See Chapter III, section XII, The Sabbath and the Mark of the Beast.
[4] That school of prophetic interpretation which teaches that prophecy is to be understood in the light of continuous historical development.

pages, neither they nor the scholars have done more than speculate. There is no grammatical or contextual foundation in the Word of God for teaching that (a) the Papacy is the power spoken of in Daniel 7:25; (b) the seal of the living God of Revelation seven is the Sabbath observance as opposed to Sunday-keeping; (c) Sunday-keeping in the face of knowledge that the Sabbath is the true day of worship is exaltation of papal edict over divine command (hence ultimately the mark of the beast); or (d) those who "keep the commandments of God and the faith of Jesus" (Rev. 14:12) are Sabbatarian Adventists. It is a totally arbitrary application of apocalyptic symbols whose meaning the Holy Spirit has not been pleased to reveal. We reject the claim that because Ellen White endorsed these theological speculations that that assures their validity. Further, the SDA rely solely upon conjecture, arbitrary application of symbols, and the year-day system of chronological computation.[5] These have all been confirmed by "the spirit of prophecy" allegedly manifested in the writings of Ellen G. White. In my opinion, it cannot be denied that the chief source of these apocalyptic speculations is a failure to consider the fact that God has deliberately hidden some things from human understanding.

The Adventists and certain other Christians claim that the Sabbath is anchored in the Decalogue, that the Decalogue is in effect today as before Calvary, and therefore Christians are obligated to observe the seventh day. We have sought to refute this (Chapter VII) where we point out from Scripture that there are not two laws (moral and ceremonial), but *one* law with several aspects or divisions, all fulfilled at Calvary and superseded by the higher law of love. Dr. Girdlestone has succinctly stated it: "The word *nomos* is very frequently used of the law of Moses which is regarded both in the Old and New Testament as *one,* though containing many *entolai* or specified commandments (see Matt. 22:36). This law is also called, the Law of the Lord, because, though it was given by Moses (John 1:17) and by the disposition of angels (Acts 7:53), it really represented the will of the Lord God (Luke 2:23). In the Four Gospels

[5] An *interpretation* shared by many reformers and scholars. Interpretation, however, is not exegesis, the latter being the most valid approach, resting as it does upon grammatical and contextual foundations.

and Acts the law is referred to fifty times and generally in the sense now mentioned; in some passages, however, it specially designates the books of Moses, according to the ordinary Jewish mode of dividing the Old Testament."[6]

The Seventh-day Adventist argument that if Christians "keep" the other nine commandments they are bound to keep the fourth, is refuted by the Apostle Paul in his epistle to the Galatians as Dr. Girdlestone's expert observation based on the New Testament usage of "Law" has pointed out.

Seventh-day Adventists maintain that they can "prove" from the Bible that they are the "remnant people," that the papacy is the "power" of Daniel seven, and so on; but their "proving" I find to be only arbitrary interpretations of symbols and dates. These are pyramided in a series of deduced propositions, all baseless we believe, when tested by the principles of exegesis and systematic theology. Like everyone else, Adventists are free to interpret the Scriptures as they please; but does this give them the right to discriminate against other Christians who do not subscribe to their exclusiveness and their conviction that they are the "depository" of "special truths" for this age? We not only reject this view (and those enumerated above) but also their teaching on the millennium,* a theory held by many others, including John Wesley, a fact which proves nothing except that Wesley too made errors.

The real issue is not so much a matter of prophetic interpretation as it is a proper understanding of New Testament teaching about the Sabbath and the Lord's Day. In this connection, the Adventists' position is unsound even though they marshal not a few theological "authorities" to give credence to their position. To most exegetical theologians, such appeals to "authority" are largely worthless, for issues are not decided according to how many are *for* or *against* a proposition, but by proper exegesis of Scripture. Here, where the Sabbath is concerned, Seventh-day Adventists are fighting, we believe, for a lost cause. Upon this, the Christian church at large is agreed.

C. *Ellen G. White on the Fourth Commandment*

What was Ellen G. White's role in establishing "Sabbath truth"? Although Mrs. White did not originate any major doctrines of Ad-

[6] R. B. Girdlestone, *Synonyms of the Old Testament*, p. 210.
*I.e., that it would be heavenly.

ventist theology, she placed her seal of approval upon them by exercising the alleged gift of the "spirit of prophecy." She insisted that the Sabbath was the seal of God's creative power which identified Him as Creator and only Law Giver. To emphasize this, she tells of how in "vision," she saw the fourth commandment of the Decalogue encircled by a halo of light. In her writings she stated:

"The seal of God's law is found in the fourth commandment. This *only* of all the ten brings to view both the *name* and the *title* of the law giver. It declares Him to be the *creator* of the heavens and the earth and thus shows His claim to reverence and worship above all others. Aside from this precept there is *nothing* in the Decalogue to show by whose authority the law is given. When the Sabbath was changed by the papal power the seal was taken from the law. The disciples of Jesus are called upon to restore it by exalting the Sabbath of the fourth commandment to its position as the Creator's memorial and the sign of His authority. . . . Hallowed by the Creator's rest and blessing, the Sabbath was kept by Adam in his innocence in holy Eden; by Adam fallen, yet repentant when he was driven from his happy estate. It was kept by all the patriarchs from Abel to righteous Noah, to Abraham to Jacob."[7]

This statement is unique among the writings of Mrs. White, and the reasons for its uniqueness become apparent as one analyzes it.

When she affirms that the fourth commandment "only of all the ten [Commandments] brings to view both the *name* and the *title* of the law giver," she reveals her unfamiliarity with the Hebrew and this is the root of her error. The Hebrew plural noun *Elohim* appears in Genesis 1:1 and designates God as Creator. In Exodus 20:1, which is the preface to the Decalogue, the *same* name and its accompanying *title* appears. In verse 2, the first precept of the Decalogue, and in verses 5 and 7, compounded with *Jehovah* for added emphasis, Elohim, or God (who must be Creator [cf. Gen. 1:1]), is revealed again. These passages also dispose of Mrs. White's claim that "aside from this precept [the fourth commandment] there is nothing in the Decalogue to show by whose authority the law is given." Exodus 20:10, which contains the fourth commandment, has the same compound name, *Jehovah-Elohim,* as Exodus 20:5, 7. Thus the Creator, *Elohim,* and lawgiver, *Jehovah,* is mentioned

[7] *The Great Controversy,* pp. 452-53.

earlier than Mrs. White states He is—an unanswerable linguistic argument. In addition to this, Mrs. White's assertion that the seal of God was removed by the papacy by the "changing" of the fourth commandment is refuted by the appearance of the name Elohim, designated *Creator* in Gen. 1:1, because even if the fourth commandment were "removed," the "seal," as she puts it, would remain in the third and fifth commandments.

It is true that God hallowed the seventh day, but many scholars from the church fathers down have debated the meaning of the word "hallowed" and some have questioned whether a literal 24-hour day was meant at all. Many scholars agree that there is no direct or verifiable Biblical evidence that Adam, Abel, Noah, Abraham, or Jacob kept the Sabbath day as a memorial to God's creative power as Mrs. White's statement declares. We know, of course, that Abraham kept God's laws and commandments as did the other patriarchs, but there is no proof that these laws and commandments included Sabbath-keeping.

Mrs. White's position is essentially that of Captain Bates and other early Adventists, and even of contemporary Adventists. Thus if we refute her basic claim that the Sabbath and the fourth commandment are God's seal, confirmation by the "spirit of prophecy" of Bates' original thesis is neither grammatically, nor contextually tenable. In fact, we believe the Holy Spirit contradicts it. We submit, therefore, that the "seal" theory is a conjecture, not supported by sound exegesis. And as Mrs. White herself declared: "The Spirit was not given—nor can it ever be bestowed—to supersede the Bible; for the Scriptures explicitly state that the Word of God is the standard by which all teaching and experience must be tested."[8]

With Mrs. White's view *here* we are in full agreement, and she has well stated, "I recommend . . . the Word of God as the rule of your faith and practice. By that Word we are to be judged."[9]

If Seventh-day Adventists are to continue to place as much emphasis upon "the seal of the living God" (the fourth commandment) and the mark of the beast (future Sunday-observance) they need

[8] *The Great Controversy*, Introduction, p. vii; quoted in *Questions on Doctrine*, p. 90.
[9] *Early Writings*, p. 78; quoted in *Questions on Doctrine*, p. 90.

to re-examine the foundation of the "seal" concept, which is seriously deficient in the all-important areas of language and syntactical usage.

Space does not allow enlargement upon Mrs. White's statements about the Sabbath. However, in order to answer the Adventist charge that the papacy "changed" the day of worship from Saturday to Sunday, we must examine a statement by Mrs. White:

"I saw that God had not changed the Sabbath for He never changes. But the pope had changed it from the seventh to the first day of the week for he was to change times and law. . . . The pope has changed the day of rest from the seventh to the first day. He has thought to change the very command that was given to cause man to remember his creator. He has thought to change the greatest commandment in the Decalogue and thus to make himself equal with God or even to exalt himself above God. . . . The pope has made a breach in the holy law of God but I saw that the time had fully come for this breach to be made up by the people of God and the waste places built up."[10]

Now in this particular "vision," it is all very well for Mrs. White to declare her allegiance to the unchanging character of God; but when she says, "the pope has changed," "the pope has changed," "the pope has made a breach in the holy law of God," we believe that we are not amiss in asking, to which pope does she refer? Seventh-day Adventists agree with other evangelicals that there was no such office as the papacy until the elevation of Gregory the Great (Gregory I) in 590, despite the claims of Rome that the papacy began with Peter. Thus, by blaming the papacy, Adventists contradict their own statement that the change from the seventh day to the first began at least 250 years before Gregory I![11]

Adventists quote "stock" Roman Catholic sources as "proof" that the Catholic church did indeed change the Sabbath to Sunday. But why do they cite the testimony of Roman Catholic authorities to support this, and reject the same authorities when they contradict Adventist teaching on the Sabbath elsewhere? Many authoritative Catholic theological works state that the Apostles, following our Lord, considered the Jewish Sabbath fulfilled, and kept instead the first day of the week as the Lord's Day to commemorate His resur-

[10] *Early Writings,* pp. 33, 66.
[11] See *Questions on Doctrine,* pp. 166-69.

rection and the "new creation." Catholic authorities also state that the Roman Catholic church merely set its seal upon this early practice. This, coupled with the fact that neither Mrs. White nor any of her followers can name the particular pope who made the change, throws out their thesis for lack of historical data. Adventists cite a handful of references to "prove" that *some* people kept the Sabbath from Apostolic times, but they cannot prove that the great majority of early Christians did. In fact the evidence is overwhelmingly in favor of First Day observance or "The Lord's Day." Neither do the facts warrant the Adventists' assertion that the Lord's Day is the Seventh-day Sabbath.

Nor can it be proved that Daniel 7:25 refers to the papacy; that the Sabbath was kept in Eden or by the patriarchs; that it is "the seal of the living God"; and they cannot prove from history that the papacy changed the Sabbath, which many responsible Catholic theologians flatly deny.[12]

D. *The Catholic Church and the Sabbath*

Adventists' eager efforts to "prove" that the papacy changed the Sabbath sometimes act like a boomerang. One Catholic source which Adventists frequently quote is *The Convert's Catechism of Catholic Doctrine* by the Rev. Peter Geiermann (1910). On page 50 of the *Catechism* appear the following questions and answers: —

"Q. *Which is the Sabbath day?*"

"A. Saturday is the Sabbath day."

"Q. *Why do we observe Sunday instead of Saturday?*"

"A. We observe Sunday instead of Saturday because the Catholic Church, in the Council of Laodicea (A. D. 364) transferred the solemnity from Saturday to Sunday."[13]

Taken by itself, this quotation appears to give credence to the Adventist position; but Professor Geiermann went into more detail

[12] We have reviewed the subject in a number of leading Catholic sources and writings on papal edicts. The great majority deny the Adventist charge, and maintain that the Roman Catholic church only *confirmed* what the Apostles and early Christians recognized; i.e., the abolition of the Jewish Sabbath in favor of the New Testament Lord's Day which symbolizes the new creation inaugurated by the resurrection of Christ. Seventh-day Adventists have either not consulted leading Roman Catholic writers, or else are content to rely upon outdated Catholic writings in order to force the Roman church into Daniel 7:25 as the changer of times and laws, and justify their system of prophetic interpretation.

[13] Quoted in *Questions on Doctrine*, p. 170*n*.

in his book *A Manual of Theology for the Laity.* In this volume Professor Geiermann explains his statements in the *Convert's Catechism of Catholic Doctrine.* He says, "The first Christians, besides, kept Sunday holy also, because on that day the Saviour rose from the dead, and the Holy Ghost came down on the Apostles. Later on, however, a dispute arose between the Jewish and the Gentile converts respecting a day which must be kept holy. Many of the Jewish converts maintained that all converts were bound by the entire law of Moses. To remove this erroneous impression, and to free her children from the ceremonial law of Moses, the church decreed in the Council of Laodicea A. D. 364 that all Catholics should keep holy Sunday as 'the Lord's Day' (Apocalypse 1:10) as had been done since Apostolic times (Acts 20:7; I Cor. 16:2). This change the church was authorized to make by the power conferred upon her by Jesus Christ."[14]

Thus Professor Geiermann's statement shifts the basis of authority from the pope to the (1) Scriptures, (2) the testimony of the fathers, and (3) the practice of the overwhelming majority of Christians from Apostolic times. But, despite such evidence, the Adventists continue to maintain their Sabbatarian position. Some of them have even objected to utilizing Professor Geiermann's expanded statement. It should be remembered, however, that *they* introduced Geiermann's initial statements and are therefore under obligation to hear his clarification.

E. *Adventism Unmoved*

We conclude this section by quoting from Arthur E. Lickey's book, *God Speaks to Modern Man.*[15] The author therein doubtless gives the conclusion of many Seventh-day Adventists about the Sabbath:

"Not only is the Sabbath the memorial of the original creation but it is God's own appointed sign of redemption and sanctification. It is the symbol of the new birth, the spiritual creation. We read his words, 'Verily my sabbath ye shall keep, for it is a sign between me and you . . . that you may know that I am the Lord that doth sanctify you' (Exodus 31:13).

"The cross of Jesus Christ cast a glorious rainbow of heaven's

[14] *A Manual of Theology for the Laity,* p. 326.
[15] Review and Herald Publishing Ass'n., Washington, D. C. (1952).

redeeming love around the Sabbath of God on that holy day of rest nearly 2,000 years ago.

"The Sabbath emblem of creative power and the creator's gift of peace, unfurls its folds of sacred time over a rugged cross and a rock-bound tomb wherein lay the world's redeemer who died that men might live. The Lord of creation who made the Sabbath a memorial of his creative power says to us, 'My day, the Lord's Day, the Seventh Day, the Sabbath Day is the sign of my creative, redeeming, sanctifying power. It is at Calvary that you will find that saving power. The Sabbath and Calvary stand together for my creative redeeming power. What I have joined together, let no man put asunder."

Mr. Lickey's statement embodies what appears to be a mixture of law and grace. He goes beyond Ellen G. White and most other Adventists in making the Sabbath not only a memorial of creation but a "sign of redemption and sanctification . . . the symbol of the new birth, the spiritual creation." He does not quote Exodus 31:13 in full, for the verse begins, "Speak thou also *unto the children of Israel,* saying, Verily my sabbaths ye shall keep," etc. Then, in effect, he makes the Sabbath envelop the cross and the open tomb as the "emblem of creative power." This is peculiar language from the pen of one who claims to be "not under the law but under grace."

To me, the most shocking of Mr. Lickey's efforts to support seventh-day observance is the statement with which we closed the above quotations (which the author puts into the mouth of God) and climaxes by lifting the latter sentence of Matthew 19:6 from context: "What I have joined together, let no man put asunder." Matthew 19:6 however is part of a discussion of marriage, and has no bearing on the Sabbath. Mr. Lickey also incorporates the words of the Lord Jesus Christ into his apologetic for the Seventh-day Sabbath, which he seems to consider overshadows Calvary and the resurrection.

In a sense, however, Mr. Lickey does follow Ellen G. White who wrote that the Sabbath was "the greatest commandment in the Decalogue"[16] — greater, it appears, than the commandments against blasphemy, idolatry, murder, theft, false witness, adultery or covetous-

[16] ***Early Writings*, p. 65.**

ness! This position Mrs. White would find difficult to defend in the light of Old and New Testament teachings.

Mr. Lickey's position contradicts *Questions on Doctrine* and numerous other Adventist writings; his casual treatment of Scriptural context at this point is, we think, hazardous to the cause of Christian fellowship. It also provides fodder for certain critics of Adventism who, ignoring the majority position, seize upon such quotes.[17]

It is one thing for Adventists to argue about interpretation of the "spirit of prophecy," but quite another for one of their representative ministers to ascribe to God the Father and God the Son the forced interpretations of Scripture.

II. The Sabbath or the Lord's Day?

Seventh-day Adventists from the beginning have always attempted to equate the Sabbath with the Lord's Day. Their principal method for accomplishing this is arguments against their position, i.e., the Lord's Day as opposed to Sabbath observance.

They reason that since "the Son of Man is Lord also of the Sabbath" (Mark 2:27, 28), when John says he "was in the Spirit on the Lord's day" (Rev. 1:10), the Sabbath and the Lord's Day must be the same! The weakness of their position is that they base their argument on an English translation instead of on the Greek original. When one reads the second chapter of Mark and the first chapter of Revelation in Greek, he sees that there is no such interpretation inherent in the grammatical structure. The Greek of Mark 2:28 clearly indicates that Christ did not mean that the Sabbath was His *possession* (which the Adventists would like to establish); rather, He was saying that as Lord of all He could do as He pleased on the Sabbath. The Greek is most explicit here.

Nothing could be clearer from both the context and the grammar. In Revelation 1:10 the Greek is not the genitive of possession, which it would have to be in order to make *te-kuriake* (the Lord's) agree with *hemera* (day). John did not mean that the Lord's Day was the Lord's possession, but rather that it was the day dedicated to Him by the early church, not in accordance with Mosaic law, but in obedience to our Lord's commandment of love.

We may certainly assume that if the Sabbath had meant so much

[17] **See Author's note at end of this chapter.**

to the writers of the New Testament; and if, as Adventists insist, it was so widely observed during the early centuries of the Christian church, John and the other writers of Scripture would have equated it with the Lord's Day, the first day of the week. Scripture and history testify that they did not, and Adventists have, therefore, little Scriptural justification for their Sabbatarianism.

A. *Testimony of the Fathers*

The Church Fathers provide a mass of evidence that the first day of the week, not the seventh, is the Lord's Day. Some of this evidence is here submitted for the reader's consideration. In company with the overwhelming majority of historians and scholars, we believe that not only the New Testament but the following citations refute Sabbatarianism. We have yet to see any systematic answer to what the Christian church always believed.

1. *Ignatius, Bishop of Antioch,* in the year 110, wrote: "If, then, those who walk in the ancient practices attain to newness of hope, no longer observing the Sabbath, but fashioning their lives after the Lord's Day on which our life also arose through Him, that we may be found disciples of Jesus Christ, our only teacher."

2. *Justin Martyr*[18] (100-165): "And on the day called Sunday, all who live in cities or in the country gather together in one place and memoirs of the apostles or the writings of the prophets are read, as long as time permits. . . . Sunday is the day on which we all hold our common assembly because it is the first day on which God, having wrought a change in the darkness in matter, made the world; and Jesus Christ our Saviour on the same day rose from the dead."

3. *The Epistle of Barnabas* (between 120 and 150): "'Your new moons and your sabbaths I cannot endure' (Isaiah 1:13). You perceive how He speaks: Your present sabbaths are not acceptable to me but that which I had made in giving rest to all things, I shall make a beginning of the eighth day, that is a beginning of another world. Wherefore also, we keep the eighth day with joyfulness, a day also in which Jesus rose from the dead."

[18] Justin also wrote the famous "Dialogue with Trypho," a Jew, throughout which he refutes Sabbath-keeping as foreign to the gospel of grace and the spirit of Christianity. It is 142 chapters long.

4. *Irenaeus, Bishop of Lyons* (about 178): "The mystery of the Lord's resurrection may not be celebrated on any other day than the Lord's Day."

5. *Bardaisān* (born 154): "Wherever we be, all of us are called by the one name of the Messiah, namely Christians and upon one day which is the first day of the week we assemble ourselves together and on the appointed days we abstain from food."

6. *Cyprian, Bishop of Carthage* (200-258): "The Lord's Day is both the first and the eighth day."

7. *Eusebius* (about 315): "The churches throughout the rest of the world observe the practice that has prevailed from the Apostolic tradition until the present time so that it would not be proper to terminate our fast on any other day but the resurrection day of our Saviour. Hence, there were synods and convocations of our bishops on this question and they unanimously drew up an ecclesiastical decree which they communicated to churches in all places—that the mystery of the Lord's resurrection should be celebrated on no other than the Lord's day."

8. *Peter, Bishop of Alexandria* (about 300): "We keep the Lord's Day as a day of joy because of Him who rose thereon."

9. *Didache of the Apostles* (about 70-75): "On the Lord's own day, gather yourselves together and break bread and give thanks."

10. *The Epistle of Pliny* (about 112, addressed to the Emperor Trajan): "They [the Christians] affirmed . . . that the whole of their crime or error was that they had been wont to meet together on a fixed day before daylight and to repeat among themselves in turn a hymn to Christ as to a god and to bind themselves by an oath (*sacramentum*) . . .; these things duly done, it had been their custom to disperse and to meet again to take food—of an ordinary and harmless kind. Even this they had ceased to do after my edict, by which, in accordance with your instructions, I had forbidden the existence of societies."[19]

Thus it appears that from apostolic and patristic times, the Christian church observed the Lord's Day or the first day of the week;

[19] Book 10, epistle 96. Although Pliny does not state to which day of the week he refers, the foregoing quotations corroborate the N.T. record that Christians met on the Lord's Day or the first day of the week to partake of the Lord's Supper, and conduct church business (Acts 20:7; I Cor. 16:2). Such was *not* the practice of the early church concerning the Sabbath. See Dr. E. De Pressene, *The Ancient World and Christianity*.

further, the Jewish Sabbath, in the words of Clement of Alexandria (about 194) was "nothing more than a working day."

In their zeal to establish the authority of the Sabbath, Adventists either reject contrary evidence as unauthentic (and so conflict with the preponderance of scholastic opinion), or they ignore the testimony of the early church. Although they seem unaffected by the evidence, the fact remains that the Christian church has both apostolic and historical support for observing the Lord's Day in place of the Sabbath.

B. *"Authoritative Quotations"*

Recently the Adventist radio program *Voice of Prophecy* circulated a 31-page pamphlet entitled, "Authoritative Quotations on the Sabbath and Sunday." In it they quoted "leading" Protestant sources to "prove" that Sunday usurped the Sabbath and is a pagan institution imposed by Constantine in 321.

However, many of the sources quoted actually establish what the Adventists flatly deny; i.e., that the Seventh-day Sabbath is *not* the Lord's Day or the first day of the week, but is, in fact, the seventh day as its name indicates.

Since the Adventists are willing to quote these authorities to buttress their position in one area, surely they will give consideration to contradictory statements by these same authorities in another:

1. "The Lord's day did not succeed in the place of the Sabbath. . . . The Lord's Day was merely an ecclesiastical institution. . . . The primitive Christians did all manner of work upon the Lord's Day" (Bishop Jeremy Taylor, *Ductor Dubitantium,* Part 1, Book 2, Chap. 2, Rule 6, Secs. 51, 59).

2. "The observance of the Lord's Day [Sunday] is founded not on any command of God, but on the authority of the church" (*Augsburg Confession of Faith,* quoted in *Catholic Sabbath Manual,* Part 2, Chap. 1, Sec. 10).

3. "But they err in teaching that Sunday has taken the place of the Old Testament Sabbath and therefore must be kept as the Seventh day had to be kept by the children of Israel" (J. T. Mueller, *Sabbath or Sunday,* pp. 15, 16).

4. "They [the Catholics] allege the Sabbath changed into Sunday, the Lord's Day, contrary to the Decalogue as it appears, neither is there any example more boasted than the changing of the Sabbath

Day" (Martin Luther, *Augsburg Confession of Faith,* Art. 28, Para. 9).

5. "Although it [Sunday] was in primitive times and differently called the Lord's day or Sunday, yet it was never denominated the Sabbath; a name constantly appropriate to Saturday, or the Seventh day both by sacred and ecclesiastical writers" (Charles Buck, *A Theological Dictionary* (1830), p. 537).

6. "The notion of a formal substitution by apostolic authority of the Lord's Day [meaning Sunday] for the Jewish Sabbath (or the first for the seventh day) . . . the transference to it perhaps in a spiritualized form of the Sabbath obligation established by promulgation of the fourth commandment has no basis whatever, either in Holy Scripture or in Christian antiquity" (Sir William Smith and Samuel Cheetham, *A Dictionary of Christian Antiquities,* Vol. II, p. 182, article on the Sabbath).

7. "The view that the Christian's Lord's Day or Sunday is but the Christian Sabbath deliberately transferred from the seventh to the first day of the week does not indeed find categoric expression till a much later period. . . . The Council of Laodicea (364 A.D.) . . . forbids Christians from Judaizing and resting on the Sabbath Day, preferring the Lord's Day and so far as possible resting as Christians" (*Encyclopedia Britannica,* 1899 ed., vol. 23, p. 654).

Thus the Adventists have in effect destroyed their argument by appealing to authorities which state unequivocally that the first day of the week is the Lord's Day and that it was observed by the early Christian church from the time of the Apostles.[20]

It should also be carefully noted that in their "Authoritative Quotations" the Adventists overlook the fact that nearly all the authorities argue forcefully for the Lord's Day as the first day of the week, and state that legal observance of the Sabbath terminated at the cross (Col. 2:16, 17). The Adventists also, in their compilation of quotations appeal even to the Church of Jesus Christ of Latter-Day Saints (Mormon), and to Fulton Oursler, a Roman Catholic lay writer. The Mormons are a non-Christian cult, a fact which the Adventists admit; and Oursler, a layman, hardly represents the position of Rome.

On page 13 of this same pamphlet, the Adventists make mislead-

[20] See John 20:19, 26; Acts 20:7; I Cor. 16:1, 2; Rev. 1:10.

ing use of the ellipsis. The following is a direct quotation as it appears:

"Sunday (*dies-solis,* of the Roman calendar, day of the sun, because dedicated to the sun), was adopted by the early Christians as a day of worship. The sun of Latin adoration they interpreted as the 'sun of righteousness.' . . . No regulations for its observance are laid down in the New Testament, nor, indeed, is its observance even enjoined. Schaff-Herzog *Encyclopedia of Religious Knowledge,* 1891 ed., Volume 4, Article on Sunday."

Now here is the paragraph as it appears in the *Encyclopedia*:

"Sunday (*dies-solis,* of the Roman Calendar, day of the sun because dedicated to the sun), was adopted by the early Christians as a day of worship. The sun of Latin adoration they interpreted as the 'sun of righteousness.' SUNDAY WAS EMPHATICALLY THE WEEKLY FEAST OF THE RESURRECTION OF CHRIST, AS THE JEWISH SABBATH WAS THE FEAST OF THE CREATION. IT WAS CALLED THE 'LORD'S DAY,' AND UPON IT THE PRIMITIVE CHURCH ASSEMBLED TO BREAK BREAD (ACTS 20:7, I COR. 16:2). No regulations for its observance are laid down in the New Testament, nor, indeed, is its observance even enjoined; YET CHRISTIAN FEELING LED TO THE UNIVERSAL ADOPTION OF THE DAY, IN IMITATION OF APOSTOLIC PRECEDENCE. IN THE SECOND CENTURY ITS OBSERVANCE WAS UNIVERSAL."[21]

Such use of the ellipsis is not uncommon in certain Seventh-day Adventists' writings in connection with the Sabbath, the Lord's Day, etc. etc., and we regret that they resort to it in order to substantiate their position.

In this pamphlet they quote Martin Luther, despite the well known fact that Luther violently opposed Sabbatarianism. His refutation of his Sabbatarian colleague Dr. Carlstadt is a monument to his apologetic genius. Thus, to quote Luther in order to support the doctrine of the seventh day suggests that Adventists are not familiar with Luther's theology.

We admire the boldness of our Adventist brethren in their claims for the Sabbath but their boldness is misplaced and leads to a distorted concept of the value of the law of God; for, when a person

[21] Sentences in capital letters were omitted by the writer of the Adventist pamphlet on page 22. This mutilation of authoritative sources first occurs in *The Present Truth,* Vol. I, No. 9, published in the 1880's. So our Adventist brethren apparently failed to check the quotation's validity.

believes and teaches that "the fourth commandment is the greatest commandment in the Decalogue," it is apparent that he has no understanding of the spirit of the law. Volume IV of the *International Standard Bible Encyclopedia* represents the reasons why the Christian church observes the Lord's Day in preference to the Sabbath, and also clearly states (p. 2629-34) the Seventh-day Adventist position.[22] On page 2633 the Adventists contend: "According to church history the seventh day Sabbath was observed by the early church, and no other day was observed as a Sabbath during the first two or three centuries."

This sentence epitomizes the Adventist propensity for overstating their case; i.e., attempting to read "Sabbath" into "Lord's Day," which all leading authorities confute as we have seen.

III. Creation and the Sabbath

In many of their publications, Adventists reiterate their belief that 4004 B.C. is the date of the creation of the world.[23] This is commonly known as Ussherism, after Bishop James Ussher (1581-1656) who thought that by tracing the genealogy of individuals mentioned in Scripture, one arrives at 4004 B.C. as the date of creation.

The Adventists tenaciously hold the six-day creation concept; that is, six 24-hour days during which God created the earth. No doubt, one of the basic reasons for their tenacity is that their Sabbath theory would suffer a real setback if it could be shown Biblically and scientifically that the days of creation were actually eras or long periods of time during which the earth's great geological structures were formed. Of course we know that God could have created the earth in six literal days, but without contradicting Genesis, scientific evidence indicates that this was not the case.

In this connection, Ferguson and Bruun make the following statement: "Throughout the past century, each decade has seen fresh evidence uncovered by the geologists to substantiate their estimates of the all but incredible antiquity of this planet that we inhabit. It is not possible to enumerate here the eras, periods and epochs into which the scientists have divided the eons of geologic time, but only to analyze the methods by which they have calculated the ages required for the sedimentary deposits to form and harden into the

[22] Bible Question Column in *Signs of the Times*, Jan. 8, 1952.
[23] Bible Question Column in *Signs of the Times*, Jan. 8, 1952.

rocks they study. Their reckonings have recently been checked by delicate measurements based upon the rate at which radioactive elements like uranium disintegrate to form lead, and the figures thus obtained indicate that the earth has been circling in its particular orbit for a period in excess of four thousand million years."[24]

The particular method involving radiation to which these authors allude is known as the Carbon 14 method. Scientists believe that Carbon 14 is a radioactive form of carbon in a continuous state of creation in our atmosphere, and that quantities of it are absorbed by all living things. Granting this, and comparing the various amounts of Carbon 14 found in both plants and animals living today with the amounts of Carbon 14 retained in fossil structures of past ages, the relative ages of these fossils can be rather accurately approximated. Such calculation must allow for the fact that these authorities declare that it takes almost 6000 years for half of a certain amount of Carbon 14 to change into nitrogen. The amount of Carbon 14 in living things is at best minute, but a recent discovery by Dr. J. Laurence Kulp, Professor of Geochemistry at Columbia University and Director of Research for the Lamont Laboratories, now makes it possible for science to measure the amounts of Carbon 14 absorbed by animals or plants living 30,000 years ago.

On the basis of this discovery, the probable age of the earth has been more accurately estimated by physical science. Since almost all Old Testament authorities agree that it is virtually impossible to arrive at given dates by tracing chronologies, the Adventist position is all the more untenable.

To emphasize this fact, the following statement from the *International Standard Bible Encyclopedia* is enlightening: "If they [the Biblical writers] had intended the genealogies as the basis of chronology, surely they would have so used them. Then, an examination of some of the genealogies, as of Moses (Ex. 6:16-20) and that of our Lord (Matt. 1; cf. Kings and Chronicles) makes it perfectly clear that genealogies give the line of descent, but do not always include each step in the descent. In accord with the method of reckoning by events, the man that did nothing or lived an unworthy life is apt to be dropped out, as are the descendants of the detested queen

[24] W. K. Ferguson and Geoffrey Bruun, *A Survey of European Civilization* (1947), p. 5.

Athalia in the genealogy of our Lord. Then the words 'son' and 'daughter' and 'beget' and 'bare' do not, as usually with us, denote immediate descent, but any point in the descent however remote (Ex. 6:20; Num. 26:59; Gen. 46:16-18; Deut. 4:25; Isa. 51:2). Even the lists of the patriarchs, both antediluvian and postdiluvian, may not be added together to construct chronology, but denote the record of great world-rulers such as in later histories are called dynastic heads. Each birth record merely notes the time at which a line went off in which sometime, it may have been the tenth generation, the next dynastic head arose."[25]

Dr. J. Oliver Buswell of Covenant Theological Seminary, St. Louis, Missouri has, in this writer's opinion, presented the best concise case against the 24-hour-day creation in his pamphlet, "The Length of the Creative Days." Relative to this problem of the age of the earth and the language of Scripture, Dr. Buswell states: "The question before us is not what God can do or could have done in the creation of this world. God could have created the universe in an instant of time as in any length of time.

"The question is not how Scripture can be harmonized with geology or with any theory of cosmogony. Of course, we are thankful for any light from natural or historical facts upon the interpretation of the Scriptures. This, however, is a secondary question. The question before us does not lie within the field of those who specialize in the physical sciences.

"The question is, what do the Scriptures teach in regard to the length of the creative days described in Genesis 1:1 - 2:4? This is primarily a question of hermeneutics and exegesis.

"We hold that the word day is used here as elsewhere figuratively and represents a period of time of undesignated length. This does not mean that the several days correspond to periods into which the geologists have divided the physical history of the earth.

"Conservative scholars tell us that the headings of the Psalms are quite accurate, and that we have no reason to doubt that as stated in the heading, Moses is the author of the 90th Psalm. That being the case, we have in his own language a very clear reference to the attitude of God toward our earthly measures of time. Here we see

[25] ***International Standard Bible Encyclopedia,*** **Vol. I, p. 644A (1955).**

that a thousand years in God's sight are as only a day, 'yesterday' as only three or four hours, 'a watch in the night.'

"When one analyzes the metaphorical use of 'day' in both the Old and New Testaments, and understands that Scripture does not contradict findings of geologists, who demonstrated the fallacy of a literal 24-hour day, which is the essence of the Adventist position for Sabbath-keeping, the issue becomes clear."[26]

Dr. Buswell also makes an excellent comment on Genesis 1:14-19:[27] "It is obvious here that the visible function of the sun for 'days' and 'years' did not begin until the fourth day of the creative period. This fact was noted by St. Augustine long ago (See *City of God*, Book 11, Chapters 6, 7). The clear inference of Moses' teaching here is that the whole visible periodic function of the sun and the other heavenly bodies began to operate within the fourth day. It is hard to see how this fourth day could have been a literal 24-hour day."

We see, then, that far from the Scriptures teaching an ironclad, 24-hour creation day, the language of Moses, under the influence of the Holy Spirit, may indeed teach something which is in complete harmony with the findings of science.

"Seventh-day Adventists, as creationists, believe in the Genesis record of a fiat creation (Gen. 1:1-2:2), with the seventh day as God's recorded and attested rest day, and the Sabbath given as the perpetual memorial of that creation, blessed and sanctified (or set apart) for man. The sabbath had its inception *before sin entered the world* (Gen. 2, 3), and it was given to commemorate a completed creation. If sin had not entered, all would have kept the original Sabbath day."[28]

The founders of Seventh-day Adventism, and the one in whom Adventists believe the "spirit of prophecy" was manifested, Ellen

[26] J. O. Buswell, "The Length of the Creative Days," pp. 1, 2.

[27] "And God said, Let there be lights in the firmament of the heaven to divide the day from the night; and let them be for signs, and for seasons, and for days, and years: And let them be for lights in the firmament of the heaven to give light upon the earth: and it was so. And God made two great lights; the greater light to rule the day, and the lesser light to rule the night: he made the stars also. And God set them in the firmament of the heaven to give light upon the earth, and to rule over the day and over the night, and to divide the light from the darkness: and God saw that it was good. And the evening and the morning were the fourth day."

[28] *Questions on Doctrine*, p. 158.

G. White, all held this concept of creation. Thus their case rests very heavily upon a literal 24-hour-day creation theory which is contradicted by the findings of the majority of responsible scientists. Scores of volumes have been written on this subject, and we feel that the Adventist position sorely lacks conclusive scientific support. In view of the evidence from natural science, and certain accepted usages of the Hebrew of the Genesis account, the Adventist contention for a literal 24-hour Sabbath as the perpetual or eternal "seal" of God's creative power rests upon a shaky foundation which does not justify their dictum that those who reject the Adventist view of the sabbath are sinning against God. However, they own that God does not impute this transgression to our record, because of our ignorance. The Catholic doctrine of "invincible ignorance," it might be added, is no more dogmatic than is the Adventists' attitude on this point.[29]

IV. Primary Anti-Sabbatarian Texts

In more than one place, the New Testament comments unfavorably upon the practice of any type of legalistic day keeping. In fact, from the ascension of Christ on, the New Testament and early church observed the first day of the week or the Lord's Day, (Rev. 1:10), as we have endeavored to show. Besides the passages which contrast the Lord's Day with the Sabbath, the apostle Paul, Hebrew of the Hebrews and Pharisee of the Pharisees, the outstanding New Testament authority, apart from our Lord, on the Law of Moses, declared that the Sabbath as "the law" was fulfilled at the cross and was not binding upon the Christian (Col. 2:16, 17). Since the subject is so vast in scope, the reader is referred to the Bibliography, especially to Dr. Louis Sperry Chafer's *Grace,* and Norman C. Deck's *The Lord's Day or the Sabbath, Which?* These contain excellent refutations of Sabbatarianism. D. M. Canright in *Seventh-day Adventism Renounced* also deals exhaustively and ably with the Sabbath subject.

To narrow the issue down to simple analysis, we shall review the major New Testament texts, which in context and in the light of syntactical analysis refute the Sabbatarian concept, and sub-

[29] For proof that the Adventists believe that all who observe the Lord's Day in preference to the Sabbath are sinning against God, see *Questions on Doctrine,* p. 183: "Then those who still *continue* in transgression will receive the mark of the beast."

stantiate the historic position of the Christian church since the days of the Apostles and the Fathers.[30]

A. *Colossians* 2:13-17

Of all of the statements in the New Testament, these verses most strongly refute the Sabbatarian claim for observance of the Jewish Sabbath. Let us listen to the inspired counsel of Paul, not only the greatest of the apostles, but a Pharisee whose passion for fulfilling the law outdoes that of the most zealous Seventh-day Adventist: "And you, who were dead in trespasses and the uncircumcision of your flesh, God made alive together with him, having forgiven us all our trespasses; having canceled the bond which stood against us with its legal demands; this he set aside, nailing it to the cross. He disarmed the principalities and powers and made a public example of them, triumphing over them in him. Therefore let no one pass judgment on you in questions of food and drink or with regard to a festival or a new moon or a sabbath. These are only a shadow of what is to come; but the substance belongs to Christ" (Col. 2:13-17 RSV).

This translation, perhaps the best from the Greek text today, contains tremendously important teaching.

First, we who were dead have been made alive in Christ, and have been forgiven all trespasses and sins. We are free from the condemnation of the law in all its aspects, because Christ took our condemnation on the cross. As already observed, there are not two laws, moral and ceremonial, but one law containing many commandments, all perfectly fulfilled by the life and death of the Lord Jesus Christ.

"Therefore," the Apostle Paul boldly declares, "let no one pass judgment on you in question of food and drink or with regard to a festival or a new moon or a sabbath. These are only a shadow of what is to come; but the substance belongs to Christ."

In the face of this clear teaching, Sabbatarians revert to their dual-law theory and argue that Paul is referring only to observance of the Jewish ceremonial law, not to the Sabbath which, they insist, is a moral precept because it is one of the Ten Commandments.

[30] With few exceptions the church fathers and early historians maintain that Christians gathered together and worshiped on the Lord's Day (Rev. 1:10) or the first day of the week as we have set forth.

We have seen, however, that the Ten Commandments are but a fragment of the moral law encompassed by the commandment, "Thou shalt love thy neighbor as thyself" (Lev. 19:18, Rom. 13:9).

Sabbatarians, however, overlook the mass of contradictory evidence and appeal to certain commentators who do not analyze the uses of the word "sabbath," or exegete the New Testament passages where the word occurs. Such commentators are Albert Barnes, *Notes on the New Testament*; Jamieson, Fausset and Brown, *Critical and Explanatory Commentary*; and Adam Clark in his *Commentary*. If a commentator's opinion is not in accord with sound exegesis, it is *only an opinion,* and the commentators named above make no grammatical or textual analysis of the second chapter of Colossians!

Many New Testament commentators try to retain the moral force of the Sabbath (although all of these transfer it to the first day of the week) because it is the subject of the fourth commandment. For this serious theological error there is no warrant in the New Testament. Sabbatarians fail to mention that all the commentators whom they cite repudiate the Sabbath, and most of them teach that the true Sabbath was the Lord's Day (Rev. 1:10), carried over by the early church from apostolic tradition as a memorial to redemption, or the recreation of mankind through the regeneration power of the Holy Spirit. Adventists are therefore without historical or exegetical support when they make the Lord's Day the same as the Sabbath.

With regard to this passage, Adventists maintain that since the word in Colossians 2:16 (*sabbaton*) is in the plural, it means the ceremonial Sabbaths, not the weekly Sabbath, which they contend is still in effect. However, their argument seems to be that Colossians 2:16, 17 refers to sabbaths and feast days which were shadows of things to come, and thus are part of ceremonial law, but that the seventh-day Sabbath is not a shadow of redemption but a memorial of creation and part of the moral law. The leading modern translations, following the best New Testament scholars, render Colossians 2:16 as "a sabbath" or "a sabbath day" not "sabbath days" as in the King James Version. Their reason for doing this is well stated by W. E. Vine who wrote:

"*Sabbaton* or *sabbata,* the latter the plural form, was transliterated from the Aramaic word which was mistaken for a plural: hence the singular *sabbaton* was formed from it. . . . In the epistles the only direct mentions are in Colossians 2:16 'a sabbath day' (RV), which rightly has the singular . . . where it is listed among things that were 'a shadow of things to come'; i.e., of the age introduced at Pentecost and in Hebrews 4:4-11 where the perpetual *sabbatismos* is appointed for believers: . . . . For the first three centuries of the Christian era the first day of the week was never confounded with the Sabbath; the confusion of the Jewish and Christian institutions was due to declension from apostolic teaching."[31]

Supplementing Dr. Vine's statement is the comment of M. R. Vincent who declared: "Sabbath days (*sabbaton*), the weekly festivals revised correctly as *day*, the plural being used for the singular. See Luke 4:31 and Acts 20:7. The plural is only once used in the New Testament of more than a single day (Acts 17:2). In the Old Testament, the same enumeration of sacred seasons occurs in I Chronicles 33:31; II Chronicles 2:14; II Chronicles 31:3; Exodus 45:17; Hosea 2:11."[32]

As Dr. Vincent points out, the revisers' rendering of *sabbaton* in the singular accords with the use of the word throughout the New Testament. It is significant that in 59 of 60 occurrences in the New Testament, Adventists affirm that they refer to the *weekly* Sabbath; but in the 60th occurrence they maintain it does *not*, although *all* grammatical authorities contradict them.

With regard to Albert Barnes, whom the Adventists delight to quote because he agrees with their interpretation of Colossians two, (see p. 163) his comments are demolished by Dean Henry Alford, a truly great Biblical exegete whom the Adventists also frequently quote. Wrote Dean Alford concerning Colossians two: "Let no one therefore judge you (pronounce judgment of right or wrong over you, sit in judgment on you) . . . in respect of feasts or new moon, or sabbaths (i.e. yearly, monthly, or weekly celebrations). (The relative may refer either to the aggregate of the observances mentioned, or to the *last* mentioned, i.e. the Sabbath. Or it may refer to *all*.)"[33]

[31] *Expository Dictionary of New Testament Words*, pp. 311-13.
[32] *Word Studies in the New Testament*, Commentary on Colossians 2, p. 494.
[33] D. H. Alford, *The New Testament for English Readers*, pp. 1299, 1300; see his *Commentary on Colossians*, pp. 224-25.

After making significant comments on the grammar, Dean Alford went even further in his insistence that in verse 17, grammatically speaking, the Apostle Paul contrasts *all* the Jewish laws with their fulfillment in Christ, the former being a shadow, pointing forward to the real substance (*soma*), which was Christ.

Alford summed up his comments thus: "The blessings of the Christian covenant: these are the substance, and the Jewish ordinances the mere type or resemblance, as the shadow is of the living man. . . . We may observe, that if the ordinance of the Sabbath had been, *in any form* of lasting obligation on the Christian church, it would have been quite impossible for the Apostle to have spoken thus. The fact of an obligatory rest of one day, whether the seventh or the first, *would have been directly in the teeth of his assertion here: the holding of such would have been still to retain the shadow, while we possess the substance*. And no answer can be given to this by the transparent special-pleading, that he is speaking only of that which was *Jewish* in such observances: the whole argument being *general*, and the axiom of verse 17 universally applicable."[34]

We see, then, that from a grammatical standpoint if the Adventists insist that Colossians 2:16 refers only to ceremonial sabbaths, they run against the use of the word for weekly sabbaths in the New Testament; and, as Alford points out, if "sabbaths" be allowed, it must include all Sabbaths, weekly, monthly or yearly. On the other hand, if Adventists admit the correction of the revisers and render Colossians 2:16 "a sabbath day," its use in the New Testament still refers almost exclusively (see Acts 17:2) to the weekly sabbath, which Adventists maintain is permanent, although Paul deliberately classes it with the ordinances which Christ by His death nailed to the cross! (Col. 2:14).

Dr. J. B. Lightfoot, an acknowledged authority on New Testament Greek, makes this interesting observation:

"The word *sabbata* is derived from the Aramaic *shabbatha* (as distinguished from the Hebrew), and accordingly preserves the Aramaic termination of *a.* Hence it was naturally declined as a plural noun, *sabbata, sabbaton.* The New Testament *sabbata* is only once used distinctively as more than a single day, and there the plurality of

[34] *New Testament for English Readers*, p. 1300.

meaning is brought out by the attached numeral (Acts 17:2)."[35]

It is apparent therefore that the use of "sabbath" in the New Testament refutes the Adventist contention that in Colossians two it means sabbaths other than the weekly sabbath of the Decalogue. Since it is impossible to retain the "shadow" while possessing the "substance" (Col. 2:17), the Jewish Sabbath and the handwriting of ordinances "which was contrary to us" found their complete fulfillment in the person and work of the Lord Jesus Christ.

Seventh-day Adventists are also deprived of the support of Albert Barnes, because he admits that if Paul had *"used the word in the singular number, 'the sabbath,' it would then of course have been clear that he meant to teach that that commandment had ceased to be binding and that a sabbath was no longer to be observed."*[36]

Since Barnes makes this admission, and since modern conservative scholarship establishes the singular rendering of "sabbath" in the New Testament (see RSV, *et al.*), Adventists find even less support for their position.

We conclude our comments on this passage of Scripture by observing that in Numbers 28 and 29 which list the very "ordinances" referred to in Colossians 2:16, 17, the Sabbath is grouped with burnt offerings and new moons (Num. 28:1-15). Since these offerings and feasts have passed away as the shadow (*skia*), fulfilled in the substance (*soma*) of the cross of Christ, how can the seventh-day Sabbath be retained? In the light of this Scripture alone, this writer contends that the argument for Sabbath observance collapses, and the Christian stands under "the perfect law of liberty" which enables him to fulfill "the righteousness of the law" by the imperative of love.

B. *Galatians 4:9-11*

"But now that you have come to know God, or rather to be known by God, how can you turn back again to the weak and beggarly elemental spirits, whose slaves you want to be once more? You observe days, and months, and seasons, and years! I am afraid I have labored over you in vain" (RSV).

Paul's epistle to the Galatians was primarily a massive theological effort to bolster the young church against the Judaizers who added to

[35] *Commentary on Colossians*, p. 225.
[36] *Notes on the New Testament*, Colossians 2.

the gospel of grace "another gospel" (1:6), and sought to "pervert the gospel of Christ" (1:7).

Though steeped in Jewish lore and the law of Moses, Paul steadfastly opposed the Judaizers. The entire epistle to the Galatians is an apologetic against those who would seek to bring the Christian "under the law." After mentioning the errors into which the Galatian church had fallen, Paul, evidently with great disgust, remarks, "You observe days, and months, and seasons, and years! I am afraid I have labored over you in vain" (4:10, 11 RSV). In the Greek the expression "days, and months, and seasons, and years," matches both the Septuagint translation of the ordinances in Numbers 28 and 29, of which all Sabbaths are a principal part, and the ordinances mentioned in Colossians two. Paul was familiar with the Septuagint and quoted it, and the law, including the weekly Sabbaths, was so cherished by the Judaizers of his day that its legalistic observance called forth his strong words. Adventists insist that Paul meant ceremonial feasts and yearly sabbaths, not the weekly sabbath; but Paul's language, and the Septuagint translation of Numbers 28 and 29, refutes their objections. It is one thing to interpret your way out of a verse when your interpretation is feasible; it is another to ignore grammar, context, and comparative textual analysis (hermeneutics) as our Adventist friends and others appear to do. To substantiate their interpretation of Paul's statements they do not practice exegesis (taking out of), but eisegesis (reading into) the texts.

After studying Seventh-day Adventist literature, it is the opinion of this writer that the overwhelming majority of Seventh-day Adventists do not actually consider themselves "under the law." I believe they fail to realize that by trying to enjoin Sabbath observance upon other members of the Body of Christ, they are in serious danger of transgressing the gospel of grace. To them Paul says, "Tell me, you who desire to be under law, do you not hear the law? . . . Now before faith came, we were confined under the law, kept under restraint until faith should be revealed. So that the law was our custodian until Christ came, that we might be justified by faith. But now that faith has come, we are no longer under a custodian; for in Christ Jesus you are all sons of God, through faith" (Gal. 4:21; 3:23-26 RSV).

Bearing in mind that "the law" in its larger connotation includes the entire Pentateuch, it is apparent from Paul's language that one is "under the law" when he attempts to observe any part of it, because the Christian has been freed from the law. Seventh-day Adventists are doubtless Christians, saved by grace, but we do not find Scriptural warrant for their attempt to enjoin the Sabbath upon their fellow believers.

C. *Romans 13:8-10*

"Owe no one anything, except to love one another; for he who loves his neighbor has fulfilled the law. The commandments, 'You shall not commit adultery, You shall not kill, You shall not steal, You shall not covet,' and *any other commandment,* are summed up in this sentence, 'You shall love your neighbor as yourself.' Love does no wrong to a neighbor; therefore love is the fulfilling of the law."

It is really unnecessary to comment extensively upon the foregoing verses since they speak so plainly for themselves.

The Greek word *pleroma,* translated respectively "fulfilled" and "fulfilling" in Romans 13:8, 10 (RSV) appears 90 times in the New Testament and has the same basic meaning. The Apostle Paul surely understood this term; since the Adventists confess the divine inspiration of the Scriptures, they must concede that the Holy Spirit guided his pen. Quoting from the Decalogue upon which the Adventists rely for perpetual Sabbath-keeping, Paul declares, "The commandments . . . are summed up in this sentence, 'You shall love your neighbor as yourself.' Love does no wrong to a neighbor; therefore love is the *fulfilling* of the law." In verse eight the apostle declares, "He who loves his neighbor has *fulfilled* the law"; and since he quotes from the Decalogue as part of the law, the fourth commandment is also fulfilled, not by rigid observance of a given day, but by loving one's neighbor as oneself! Since it is impossible in the Christian context to love one's neighbor at all, apart from loving God as the prerequisite, the issue is clear. The false teaching that love of one's neighbor does not fulfill all the law of God comes from a failure to realize that our love for God and neighbor stems from God's initiating act of love in Christ. This law of love is first enunciated in Leviticus 19:18, which our Lord coupled with the commandment to "love the Lord thy God" (Deut. 6:4), and stated that observance of those two commandments fulfilled "all the law and the prophets."

While our Adventist brethren may seek to escape the implications of Colossians 2:14-17, and to explain away Galatians 4:9-11, in the present passage the Holy Spirit twice declares that love *fulfills* the law. They cannot exempt the Sabbath from this context without destroying the unity of the "Eternal Ten," hence their dilemma.

In Galatians Paul also declares, "The whole law is fulfilled in one word. You shall love your neighbor as yourself'" (5:14 RSV). So we see that Paul's theology rested upon the imperative of love. Therefore, it is my conviction that the Holy Spirit, not the Christian church, is the authority for the nullification of all sabbath-keeping. How any student of New Testament Greek could read the unmistakable language of the apostle and then exclude the Sabbath commandment from his argument, passes my understanding.

D. *Romans 14:4-6, 10, 12, 13*

"Who are you to pass judgment on the servant of another? It is before his own master that he stands or falls. And he will be upheld, for the Master is able to make him stand. One man esteems one day as better than another, while another man esteems all days alike. Let every one be fully convinced in his own mind. He who observes the day, observes it in honor of the Lord. He also who eats, eats in honor of the Lord, since he gives thanks to God; while he who abstains, abstains in honor of the Lord and gives thanks to God . . . Why do you pass judgment on your brother? Or you, why do you despise your brother? For we shall all stand before the judgment seat of God; . . . so each of us shall give account of himself to God. Then let us no more pass judgment on one another, but rather decide never to put a stumbling-block or hindrance in the way of a brother."

In this writer's opinion, and according to Romans 14, the Seventh-day Adventist is entitled to observe the seventh-day Sabbath if he feels that this is what God desires. Further than this, the Holy Spirit adjures us not to "pass judgment" on our fellow Christians regarding such matters as observance of days, and diet. I believe that Seventh-day Adventists, Seventh-day Baptists, and Sabbatarians of other religious groups have the right to worship on the seventh day in the liberty wherein Christ has made us free. It is wrong and unchristian to discriminate against Sabbatarians merely because they "esteem" the Sabbath above the first day of the week, or the Lord's Day. I suggest it is no more legalistic for them to observe the seventh day out of conviction than it is for the Christian church to observe the first day. It is a matter of liberty and conscience.

If Seventh-day Adventists, however, would follow the Biblical teaching of Romans 14 with regard to those who wish to observe Sunday, we would not have the conflict which has been generated by their dogmatic insistence that all should worship on the Sabbath. The sad fact is, however, that all Sabbatarians transgress the very counsels given by the Apostle Paul when he asks, "Who are you to pass judgment on the servant of another? It is before his own master that he stands or falls. And he will be upheld, for the Master is able to make him stand. . . . Why do you pass judgment on your brother? Or . . . why do you despise your brother? For we shall all stand before the judgment seat of God; . . . so each of us shall give account of himself to God. Then let us no more pass judgment on one another, but rather decide never to put a stumbling-block or hindrance in the way of a brother."

Of course Seventh-day Adventists feel that they are called upon to perpetuate or promulgate certain truths which they believe are to be found in the Word of God, and which they believe are to be emphasized in "these last days." Furthermore, the counsels of Ellen G. White, they believe, emphasize the importance of these truths. Granting their basic premise that God has indeed spoken to them concerning Sabbath observance, it is easy to see the source of their zeal. But this writer feels there is good evidence that the "spirit of prophecy" is not what they claim; and their "special truths" have, to say the least, questionable theological origins. Non-adventists reject the claims they make for Mrs. White, and merely because Adventists accept her counsel is no reason for other Christians to feel bound to do so. We repeat—the faith the Adventists place in "the spirit of prophecy" which has endorsed their "special truths," sincere though they may be, does not entitle them to contradict the counsel of the Holy Spirit as revealed in the Word of God. This I believe they have done. I could cite scores of references from contemporary Adventist writers who do indeed pass judgment* upon their Christian brothers and upon the Christian church at large, because the latter do not observe the seventh-day Sabbath. It is my opinion in these cases that they neglect the counsel of the Holy Spirit: "One man esteems one day as better than another, while another man esteems all days alike. Let everyone be fully convinced in his own mind. He who observes the day, observes it in honor of the Lord. . . . Happy is he who has no reason to judge himself for what he approves . . . for whatever does not proceed from faith is sin" (Rom. 14:5, 6, 22, 23 RSV).

By contending that other members of the Body of Christ should recognize "the spirit of prophecy," Seventh-day Adventists appear to juxtapose the "spirit of prophecy" with the Holy Spirit who says: "Then let us not pass judgment on one another but rather decide never to put a stumbling-block or hindrance in the way of a brother" (verse 13).

There can be little doubt that the great majority of Christians who worship on Sunday would never have discriminated against the Seventh-day Adventists, had the latter not insisted upon "passing judgment" on first-day observance as opposed to Sabbath-keeping. Although motivated by the best intentions and sincere in faith, Adventists have nevertheless put a stumbling-block or hindrance in the way of fellow Christians by their rigid Sabbatarianism. It is indeed unfortunate that such a source of strife exists among Christians.

The fourteenth chapter of Romans is a masterpiece on the subject of Christian liberty, not only in diet but in worship, and in the context of all Paul's writings on the subject it appears that Adventists ignore the plain teaching of Scripture about the observance of days. We ask, should they not be more charitable in the light of I Corinthians 13? They will thus avoid opposition from their fellow Christians.

These four passages from the writings of Paul reflect the position of the historic Christian church from the times of the fathers and the reformers to the leading exegetical commentators of our day. The reader should remember that Adventist arguments, although buttressed by selected Bible passages (sometimes cited out of context),

***Not of a final or eternal nature, however.**

must be studied in the clear light of these four passages which contain the comprehensive New Testament teaching on Sabbatarianism. The early Christian church met upon the *first* day of the week (I Cor. 16:2). The disciples received the Holy Spirit on the *first* day of the week; collections were taken for the saints on the *first* day of the week, and historic evidence establishes that the *first* day of the week was the Lord's Day, the memorial of the new creation in Christ Jesus which completely fulfilled the law in Christ.

No amount of argument by Adventists can alter these facts, and if we believe the Apostle Paul was inspired by the Holy Spirit it is apparent that we must reject Sabbatarianism. We do not judge Seventh-day Adventists for their Sabbath observance, and they in turn should extend the same charity to their fellow Christians. Only in the recognition of the principles of Romans 14 can true unity in the Body of Christ be realized. There can be no legislation of moral choice on the basis of "special revelation." This we believe is the case in Seventh-day Adventism, for it was Ellen G. White's "Vision" confirming Joseph Bates' "Seal of the Living God" concept as set forth in his pamphlet on the Sabbath that established Sabbatarianism in Seventh-day Adventism. The Bible must be the supreme court of appeal and authority; and the verdict of this court, it appears to me, invalidates the contentions of our Adventist friends.

Author's Note on "The Mark of the Beast"

The subjects of the Seventh-day Sabbath and the Mark of the Beast already have been covered in sufficient detail. However, it is often charged that Adventists teach that salvation depends upon observance of the seventh day as Sabbath, and that the mark of the beast (Rev. 13:16, 17) rests upon all Sunday-keepers. For this reason, the record should be examined.

One ex-Adventist layman writes that there are "characteristic false doctrines of the sect . . . the obligation of seventh-day Sabbath observance on the part of all professing Christians, the 'mark of the beast' for Sunday-keepers." Now if this charge were correct, we too would doubt the possibility of fellowship with Adventists. But such is not the case. Ellen G. White on a number of occasions pointedly denied what is claimed to be the position of the Adventist denomination on this point. Wrote Mrs. White: "No one has yet received the mark of the beast. The testing time is not yet come. There are true Christians in every church, not excepting the Roman Catholic communion. None are condemned until they have had the light and have seen the obligation of the fourth commandment. . . . Sunday-keeping is not yet the mark of the beast, and will not be until the decree goes forth causing men to worship this idol sabbath."[37]

In addition to this quotation, the Adventists have stated: "When Sunday observance shall be enforced by law and the world shall be enlightened concerning the obligation of the true Sabbath, then whoever shall transgress the command of God, to obey a precept that has no higher authority than that of Rome, will thereby honor popery above God."[38]

To sum up, the Adventists declare, "God surely does not hold men accountable for truth that has not yet come to their knowledge and understanding. . . . We hold the firm conviction that millions of devout Christians of all faiths throughout all past centuries, as well as those today who are sincerely trusting in Christ their Savior for salvation and are following Him according to their best light, are unquestionably saved. Thousands of such went to the stake as martyrs for Christ and for their faith. Moreover untold numbers of godly Roman Catholics will surely be included. God reads the heart and deals with the intent and understanding. . . . Seventh-day Adventists interpret the prophecies relating to the beast and the reception of his work as something that will come into sharp focus just before the return of our Lord in glory. It is our understanding that this issue will then become a worldwide test."[39]

The statement, then, that Seventh-day Adventists believe that anyone who is a Sunday-keeper *has* the mark of the beast or the mark of apostasy, is made without regard to the facts. Why do these critics attempt to make it appear that Adventists believe that their fellow Christians are lost? The authoritative statements of this denomination are available for all to read. Doubtless some Seventh-day Adventist writers have gone contrary to the teaching of the denomination, but to indict the entire denomination for the excesses of a few is neither ethical nor Christian.

[37] *Questions on Doctrine,* pp. 183-84.
[38] *Ibid.,* p. 178.
[39] *Ibid.,* p. 185.

CHAPTER SEVEN

THE SANCTUARY, THE INVESTIGATIVE JUDGMENT, AND THE SCAPEGOAT

The foundation of Seventh-day Adventism is its view of prophecy which is of the historicist school of interpretation, a school which maintains that prophecy is to be understood in the light of consecutive fulfillment in history. The exaggeration of this idea led William Miller and his followers to teach that the 2300 days of Daniel 8:14 were actually 2300 years. Figuring from 457 B.C., the now verified time of the decree to rebuild Jerusalem (Dan. 9:24),[1] the Millerites thought that 1843 would be the date for the second advent of Jesus Christ. Miller and his followers, among whom were James and Ellen G. White and other prominent Seventh-day Adventists, understood "the sanctuary" of Daniel 8:14 to be the earth which would be cleansed by Christ at the "great and terrible Day of the Lord," which they interpreted as the Second Advent of Christ. We have seen, however, that the Millerites were bitterly disappointed; and when Christ did not appear, Miller himself renounced the system and all resultant movements, including Seventh-day Adventism. But the early Seventh-day Adventists, relying upon the "vision" of Elder Hiram Edson, transferred the location of the sanctuary from the earth to Heaven, and taught that in 1844 Christ went instead into the second apartment of the sanctuary in Heaven (which contemporary Seventh-day Adventists term *the second phase* of His ministry), there to review the cases of those deemed to be worthy of eternal life. This phase of our Lord's ministry the Seventh-day Adventists call the "investigative judgment." It is a unique Arminian type theory intended, I believe, to discipline Christians by the threat of impending judgment and condemnation upon those whose cases are decided upon unfavorably by our Lord. When concluded, the Investigative Judgment will usher in the Second Advent of Jesus

[1] See Dr. Siegfried Horn and Lynn Wood, *The Chronology of Ezra 7,* Review & Herald Pub. Assoc., Washington, D. C.

Christ, according to the Seventh-day Adventist theology, and the devil, prefigured by the second or scapegoat of Leviticus 16 (Azazel), will bear away unto eternal destruction or annihilation his responsibility for causing sin to enter the universe. James White, a stalwart Seventh-day Adventist leader, when first confronted with the doctrine of the Investigative Judgment, opposed it *in toto,* giving in substance the very arguments put forth by all subsequent ex-Seventh-day Adventists. And it was only after considerable time that James White finally acceded to the doctrine of the Investigative Judgment. There are many critics of Seventh-day Adventism who, when approaching the Sanctuary, Investigative Judgment and Scapegoat concepts, deride and mock the early Adventists and their descendants for accepting such unsupported, extra-Biblical theories, but derision is not the answer, and it should be remembered that Adventists hold these doctrines in sincerity. Therefore, if they are ever to be persuaded of the mistaken nature of their faith, in these areas at least, only the facts of Scripture and the guidance of the Holy Spirit of God will bring it about.

The view of Hiram Edson, described in chapter one, is, so far as this writer is concerned, an attempt to escape the terrible calamity which befell the Millerite movement, and the disappointment and embarrassment that must have followed the failure of the Millerite prophecies and their interpretations of the Book of Daniel. We shall confine ourselves in this chapter, to the salient points of the theological issues raised by these special teachings or doctrines of the Advent message. In the matter of prophetic interpretation, this writer is convinced that the Holy Spirit has wisely veiled from the prying eyes and intellect of man many great truths which will doubtless be revealed toward the end of the age. It is not for us to judge whether the pretorist, historicist, or futurist schools of interpretation are correct, and we ought not overly to concern ourselves with when Christ is coming, whether before, during or after the Great Tribulation. Rather, we ought to be concerned *that* He is coming, because His coming is indeed "the blessed hope" of the Christian Church (Titus 2:13), which hope Adventists and non-Adventists alike who share the Christian message and faith, anticipate with joy.

I. The Sanctuary

Since the Seventh-day Adventists believe that the sanctuary to be cleansed is in heaven (Daniel 8:14), which the Millerites identified as the earth (a regrettable early mistake), we might ask, What is the purpose of the heavenly sanctuary and its cleansing? What are the Adventists really teaching?

The Book of Hebrews definitely sets forth a "heavenly sanctuary" of which Christ is the minister (Heb. 8:1, 2), and the writer of the epistle repeatedly contrasts the Lord Jesus Christ, our risen high priest, with the Aaronic priesthood. He shows that, as a priest after the order of Melchizedek, Christ derives His authority after the power of "an endless life" (Heb. 7:16), and that He was both *high priest and offering* on Calvary.[2] And this Adventists also emphasize.[3]

It is futile, therefore, to argue that the word "sanctuary" does not apply to Heaven or something of a heavenly nature, since the Scriptures teach that it does. But the Adventists' error is that they draw from the Scriptures interpretations which cannot be substantiated by exegesis but rest largely upon inference and deduction, drawn from theological applications of their own design.

In their Sanctuary teaching, the Adventists do indeed declare, in the words of Ellen G. White: "As anciently the sins of the people were by faith, placed upon the sin offering and through its blood transferred in figure to the earthly sanctuary, so in the new covenant the sins of the repentant are by faith placed upon Christ and transferred in fact to the heavenly sanctuary. And as the typical cleansing of the earthly was accomplished by the removal of the sins by which it had been polluted, so the actual cleansing of the heavenly is to be accomplished by the removal or blotting out of the sins that are there recorded."[4]

Here we have the very heart of Seventh-day Adventist teaching relative to the expiation of sin, which is that the sins of believers have been transferred, deposited or recorded in the heavenly sanctuary, and are now being dealt with in the Investigative Judgment.

Let us again listen to Mrs. White: "In the sin offerings presented

[2] Heb. 7:2, 4-7, 14, 16, 22, 25, 26; 8:1, 2, 6-8, 10; 9:2-12, 14, 23, 24, 26-28; 10:1-10, 12, 19-21.
[3] *Questions on Doctrine*, pp. 377-78, 667.
[4] *Great Controversy*, pp. 421-22.

during the year, a substitute had been accepted in the sinner's stead; but the blood of the victim had not made full atonement for the sin. It had only provided a means by which the sin was transferred to the sanctuary. By the offering of the blood the sinner acknowledged the authority of the law, confessed the guilt of his transgression, and expressed his faith in Him who was to take away the sin of the world; but he was not entirely released from the condemnation of the law. On the day of atonement the high priest having taken an offering for the congregation went into the most holy place with the blood and sprinkled it upon the mercy seat above the table to the law. Thus the claims of the law which demanded the life of the sinner were satisfied. Then in his character of mediator the priest took the sins upon himself and leaving the sanctuary he bore with him the burden of Israel's guilt. At the door of the tabernacle he laid his hands upon the head of the scapegoat, confessed over him all the iniquities of the children of Israel and all their transgressions and all their sins, putting them upon the head of the goat. And as the goat bearing these sins was sent away, they were with him regarded as forever separated from the people."

Mrs. White further stated, "Not until the goat had been thus sent away did the people regard themselves as freed from the burden of their sins."[5]

The Adventist teaching, then, is that Christ as our high priest transferred the sins of believers (i.e., the *record* of sins in Adventist thinking) to the heavenly sanctuary which will be finally cleansed at the conclusion of the great day of atonement, the Investigative Judgment having been concluded. Then the cases of all the righteous having been decided, their sins will be blotted out, followed by the return of the Lord Jesus Christ in glory. Mrs. White made it clear that the sin transferred to the sanctuary in Heaven would remain there until the conclusion of the Investigative Judgment and the subsequent cleansing of the sanctuary: "The blood of Christ, while it was to release the repentant sinner from the condemnation of the law, was not to cancel the sin; it would stand on record in the sanctuary until the final atonement; so then the type, the blood of

[5] *Patriarchs and Prophets*, pp. 355-56.

the sin offering removed the sin from the penitent but it rested in the sanctuary until the day of atonement."[6]

To substantiate this particular position, Adventists quote Acts 3:19 in the King James Version: "Repent ye therefore and be converted, that your sins may be blotted out *when* the times of refreshing shall come from the presence of the Lord."

The chief difficulty with the Adventist contention is that the Greek of Acts 3:19 does *not* substantiate their teaching that the blotting out of sins will take place as a *separate* event from the forgiveness of sins. According to modern translations (the Revised, the American Standard and the Revised Standard Versions), the text should read, "Repent therefore and turn again *that* your sins may be blotted out, *that* times of refreshing may come from the presence of the Lord." Peter was urging his listeners to repent, turn from their sins, in order to receive the forgiveness that comes only from the presence of the Lord. This text gives our Adventist brethren no support for their "heavenly sanctuary, investigative judgment" teaching.

II. Investigative Judgment

The Bible explicitly declares that when one accepts Christ as Lord, God freely forgives all his sins and ushers him from spiritual death to spiritual life solely on the merits of the perfect life and death of the Lord Jesus Christ. To this Adventists fully agree, and this makes their teaching on Investigative Judgment inconsistent. In John 5:24 the Greek deals a devastating blow to the Seventh-day Adventist concept of Investigative Judgment: "He that hears my word and believes him that sent me has everlasting life and shall not come under *judgment* but is passed from death to life" (literal translation).

Christians, therefore, need not anticipate any Investigative Judgment for their sins. True, we shall "all appear before the judgment seat of Christ to receive the deeds done in the body" (II Cor. 5:10), but this has nothing to do with any investigative judgment. It is a judgment for rewards. Several judgments are mentioned in the Bible, but in this writer's opinion not one passage substantiates the "investigative judgment" theory—for theory it truly is, relying upon out-of-context quotations and supported by the "spirit of prophecy." They

[6] *Ibid.*, p. 357.

are welcome to this dogma, but faithfulness to New Testament teaching forbids the idea that "the blood of Christ, while it was to release the repentant sinner from the condemnation of the law, was not to cancel the sin; it would be on record in the sanctuary until the final atonement," or "blotting out." The Scriptures clearly teach, "If we confess our sins he is faithful and just to forgive us our sins and to cleanse us from *all* unrighteousness" (I John 1:7). Further evidence of the completeness of the forgiveness of God and the cleansing power of the blood of Christ is found in the first chapter of the Book of Hebrews, where the Holy Spirit informs us that Christ as "the image of God," "upholds all things by the word of his power" and that on Calvary "he by himself purged our sins" (Heb. 1:3).

For the word translated "purged" or "purification" the Holy Spirit chose the Greek word *katharismon,* from which we derive *cathartic.* Hence it is said of the Lord Jesus and His sacrifice that He alone, "by himself," gave to our sinful spiritual natures the complete cathartic of forgiveness and purification on the cross. Christians may now rejoice that the Lord Jesus Christ is not engaged in weighing our frailties and failures, for "He knoweth our frame, he remembereth that we are dust" (Ps. 103:14). We cannot, therefore, accept the Adventist teaching on the investigative judgment since we are convinced that it has no warrant in Scripture. We must reject what we believe to be their un-Biblical concept that the sins of believers remain in the sanctuary until the day of blotting out of sins.

Our Adventist brethren, in teaching this doctrine, are overlooking the fact that "the Lord knoweth them that are his" (II Tim. 2:19) and it was no less an authority than the Lord Jesus Christ who declared, "I know my sheep" (John 10:14). The Apostle Paul declares that "Christ died for the ungodly . . . while we were yet sinners Christ died for us . . . when we were enemies we were reconciled to God by the death of his Son" (Rom. 5:6, 8, 10). This does not balance with the Seventh-day Adventist teaching of the heavenly sanctuary, the transfer of sins and the investigative judgment. In his epistle to the Colossians the Apostle Paul further declared, "Having made peace through the blood of his cross . . . you that were sometime alienated and enemies in your mind by wicked works yet now has he reconciled in the body of his flesh through death to present you holy and unblameable and unreprovable in his sight" (1:20-22). Once again the Holy Spirit declares that we are *now* reconciled through the death of Christ, *having been forgiven all* our trespasses through the blood of the cross (Col. 2:13).

Seventh-day Adventists, relying upon Daniel 8:14, Daniel 7:9, 10, Rev. 14:7 and 11:18, which refer to "judgment," and "books," attempt to "prove" that the investigative judgment is meant, but examination of each of these texts in context reveals the paucity of the claim. None of these texts has anything to do with any judgment *now* going on. Neither the grammar nor context supports such a contention. One can only base this interpretation on the Adventist premise that the historicist school of prophetic interpretation is the only accurate one, and by accepting the Adventist definition of the sanctuary and judgment. It is significant that non-Adventist Biblical scholars have never allowed these so-called "investigative judgment" interpretations, because there is no Scriptural warrant for them apart from implication and inference.

As mentioned previously, James White at first categorically denied the teaching of the investigative judgment and gave good reasons for his rejection. Although he later embraced this doctrine his objections are still valid:

"It is not necessary that the final sentence should be given before the first resurrection as some have taught; for the names of the saints are written in Heaven and Jesus and the angels will certainly know who to raise and gather to the New Jerusalem." . . . "The event that will introduce the judgment day will be the coming of the Son of Man to raise the sleeping saints and to change those that are alive at that time."[7]

Relative to the time for the beginning of the great judgment, James White quoted, "I charge thee therefore before God and the Lord Jesus Christ who shall judge the quick and the dead at [not before] his appearing in His kingdom" (II Tim. 4:1).[8]

Asked when he expected the judgment of Daniel seven to take place, James White stated, "Daniel in the night vision saw that judgment was given to the saints of the most high, but not to mortal saints. Not until the ancient of days comes will the little horn cease

[7] *A Word to the Little Flock* (1847), p. 24.
[8] James White in the *Advent Review*, August 1850; the brackets are his.

prevailing which will not be until he is destroyed by the brightness of Christ's coming."[9]

We see, then, that James White at the beginning rejected the investigative judgment with good reasons. But two more of his statements are quite revealing: He wrote, "The advent angel, Revelation 14:6, 7, saying with a loud voice, 'Fear God and give glory to him for the hour of his judgment is come' *does not prove* that the day of judgment came in 1840 or in 1844, nor that it will come prior to the second advent. . . . Some have contended that the day of judgment was prior to the second advent. This view is certainly without foundation in the Word of God."[10]

At that time, James White was on good Biblical ground, but he later forsook this position for the theories and prophetic speculation promulgated by his wife and other influential Adventist leaders. The Lord Jesus Christ Himself placed the judgment after His second advent when He said, "When the Son of man shall come in his glory, and all the holy angels with him, then shall he sit upon the throne of his glory: and before him shall be gathered all nations" (Matt. 25:31, 32). One need only read the following passages to see that the judgments of God upon believers and unbelievers are future events. Notice the language employed:

1. "The quick and the dead" "at His appearing in His kingdom" (Acts 10:42, I Pet. 4:5).
2. "The sheep and the goats when the Son of Man shall come in His glory" (Matt. 25:31-46).
3. "The wheat and the tares in the end of the world" (Matt. 13:24-30, 36-43).
4. "For we must all appear before the judgment seat of Christ that everyone may receive the things done in the body . . . whether it be good or bad" (II Cor. 5:10).
5. "So that everyone of us shall give account of himself to God" (Rom. 14:10-12).
6. "Every man's work shall be made manifest: for the day shall declare it" (I Cor. 3:13).

In addition to these verses which unmistakably indicate future judgment, the writer to the Hebrews declares, "As it is appointed

[9] *Ibid.*
[10] *Ibid.*

unto men once to die but after this the judgment" (Heb. 9:27). This, to any non-Adventist, is conclusive evidence that there is no investigative judgment now going on for believers to fear.

Hebrews 4:13 also exposes the faulty concept of investigative judgment: "Neither is there any creature that is not manifest in his sight: but all things are naked and opened unto the eyes of him with whom we have to do." Since our Lord knows the disposition of "cases" allegedly being reviewed in Heaven, what need is there for "investigative judgment"? We believe the Scriptures decidedly do not warrant such a doctrine.

Concluding our comments on the investigative judgment, note that rewards for believers will be meted out *after* the second coming of our Lord, or at "the resurrection of the just," for the resurrection of life (John 5:29, Luke 14:14). Even the Adventists concur in believing that the judgment of the wicked will *not* take place until the end of the millennial age (Rev. 20:11, 12; Matt. 25:31-46). Once again the investigative judgment theory conflicts with the Biblical teaching on judgment regarding both believer and unbeliever. To this writer's mind, the great error of the sanctuary and investigative judgment teachings is the premise that sins confessed by Christians are not fully dealt with until the conclusion of the investigative judgment, a position Scripture will *not* allow.

Adventists, in the opinion of conservative Biblical scholars, not to mention the liberal wing of Protestantism, are only speculating with their sanctuary and investigative judgment theories. Actually, most are agreed that they have created doctrines to compensate for errors in prophetic interpretation. But the very doctrines intended to solve their theological problems have in turn only increased their dilemma —a dilemma which they have yet to solve! Romans 8:1 declares, "There is therefore now no condemnation [i.e. *judgment,* (Greek)] to them who are in Christ Jesus"; and here every Christian's case must rest. We can never be indicted again for our sins nor convicted for them, because Christ has fully paid the penalty. For those who believe in "eternal security" there is *no* judgment for the *penalty* of sin, i.e., eternal separation from God. However, as II Corinthians 5:10 teaches, we shall be judged for how we lived as Christians. Seventh-day Adventists, we believe, needlessly subscribe to a doctrine which neither solves their difficulties nor engenders peace of mind. Holding as they do to the doctrine of the Investigative Judgment, it is extremely difficult for us to understand how they can experience the joy of salvation and the knowledge of sins forgiven. This is, however, true of so-called Arminian theology on the whole, which teaches that eternal life, given by God to the believer, is not really eternal in duration. According to this school, it is a conditional life, to be revoked by God when in His sight sufficient transgressions have occurred. Romans 11:29 declares, however, "The gifts and call of God are irrevocable" (RSV). God is fully aware of our past, present and future when He calls and reclaims us; His omniscience is our guarantee of eternal safety.

There is, however, clarification and summary of the doctrine of investigative judgment in *Questions on Doctrine:* "It is our understanding that Christ, as high priest, concludes His intercessory ministry in heaven in a work of judgment. He begins His great work of judgment in the *investigative* phase. At the conclusion of the investigation, the *sentence* of judgment is pronounced. Then as judge, Christ descends to *execute,* or carry into effect, that sentence. For sublime grandeur, nothing in the prophetic word can compare with the description of our Lord as He descends the skies not as a priest, but as King of kings and Lord of lords. And with Him are all the angels of Heaven. He commands the dead, and that great unnumbered host of those that are asleep in Christ spring forth into immortality. At the same time those among the living who are truly God's children are caught up together with the redeemed of all ages to meet their Saviour in the air, and to be forever with the Lord. . . . As we have suggested, Seventh-day Adventists believe that at the second coming of Christ the eternal destiny of all men will have been irrevocably fixed by the decisions of a court of judgment. Such a judgment obviously would take place while men are still living on the earth. Men might be quite unaware of what is going on in heaven. It is hardly to be supposed that God would fail to warn men of such an impending judgment and its results. Seventh-day Adventists believe prophecy does foretell such a judgment, and indeed point out the very time at which it was to begin. . . . When the high priest in the typical service had concluded his work in the earthly sanctuary on the Day of the Atonement, he came to the door of the sanctuary. Then the final act with the second goat, Azazel, took place.

"In like manner, when our Lord completes his ministry in the heavenly sanctuary, He, too, will come forth. When He does this, the day of salvation will have closed forever. Every soul will thus have made his decision for or against the divine Son of God. Then upon Satan, the instigator of sin, is rolled back his responsibility for having initiated and introduced iniquity into the universe. *But he* [Satan] *in no sense vicariously atones for the sins of God's people.* All this Christ fully bore, and vicariously atoned for, on Calvary's cross."[11]

It is apparent, then, that for Adventists the investigative judgment is something very real, and they believe that the final blotting out of their sins depends upon the results of that judgment, culminating in the final destruction (annihilation) of the wicked and Satan, typified by the scapegoat of Leviticus 16.

III. The Scapegoat

Perhaps no doctrine of Seventh-day Adventism has been more misunderstood than the teaching concerning the scapegoat (Lev. 16). Because of certain unfortunate choices of words by a few Adventist writers, the impression has been given that Adventists regard Satan as a partial sin-bearer for the people of God. This may be accounted for by the fact that in the early days of Adventism they built much of their theology on the typology of the Mosaic sanctuary, using almost exclusively the phraseology of the King James Version. Hence they got into difficulty when dealing with such involved Old Testament concepts as the scapegoat (Lev. 16). Not a few scholars, however, support the Seventh-day Adventist concept that Azazel represents Satan. Be that as it may, the important thing is the place of the scapegoat with regard to the atonement of Christ. Do Seventh-day Adventists believe that Satan eventually becomes their vicarious sin-bearer? Not at all! This writer is convinced that the Adventist concept of the scapegoat in connection with the day of atonement, the sanctuary and the investigative judgment is a bizarre combination of prophetic interpretation and typology; but it is by no means the

[11] *Questions on Doctrine*, pp. 422-23, 444.

soul-destroying doctrine that many people think it is. Let the Adventists speak for themselves:

"We take our stand without qualification on the gospel platform that the death of Jesus Christ provides the *sole* propitiation for our sins (John 2:2; 4:10); that there is salvation through no other means or medium and no other name by which we may be saved (Acts 4:12); and that the shed blood of Jesus Christ *alone* brings remission for our sins (Matthew 26:28). That is foundational.

"When Satan tempted our first parents to take and eat of the forbidden fruit, he as well as they had inescapable responsibility in that act—he the instigator, and they the perpetrators. And similarly, through the ages—in all sin, Satan is involved in responsibility, as originator and instigator, or tempter (John 8:44; Romans 6:16; I John 3:8).

"Now concerning my sin, Christ died for *my* sins (Romans 5:8). He was wounded for *my* transgressions and for *my* iniquities (Isaiah 53). He assumed *my* responsibilities, and His blood alone cleanses *me* from all sin (I John 1:7). Atonement for *my* sin is made solely by the shed blood of Christ.

"Concerning Satan's sin, and his responsibility as instigator and tempter, no salvation is provided for him. He must be punished for his responsibility. . . . He must himself 'atone' for his sin in causing men to transgress, in the same way that a master criminal suffers on the gallows or in the electric chair for his responsibility in the crimes that he has caused others to commit. It is in the same sense only that we can understand the words of Leviticus 16:10 concerning the scapegoat to make atonement with him.

"Satan is the responsible master mind in the great crime of sin, and his responsibility will return upon his own head. The crushing weight of his responsibility in the sins of the whole world of the wicked as well as the righteous—must be rolled back upon him. Simple justice demands that while Christ suffers for my guilt, Satan must also be punished as the instigator of sin.

"Satan makes no atonement for our sins. But Satan will ultimately have to bear the retributive punishment for his responsibility in the sins of all men, both righteous and wicked.

"Seventh-day Adventists therefore repudiate *in toto* any idea, suggestion, or implication that Satan is in any sense or degree our sin bearer. The thought is abhorrent to us, and appallingly sacrilegious.

"Only Christ, the Creator, the one and only God-man, could make a substitutionary atonement for men's transgressions. And this Christ did completely, perfectly and once for all, on Golgotha."[12]

To be sure, the Seventh-day Adventists have a unique concept of the scapegoat, but in the light of their clearly worded explanation, no critic could any longer with honesty indict them for heresy where the atonement of our Lord is concerned.[13] The Adventists have stated unequivocally that Jesus Christ is their sole propitiation for sin and that Satan has no part whatsoever in the expiation of sin. This writer agrees that Satan is the master criminal of the universe and that it is axiomatic, therefore, that he should suffer as the instigator of angelic and human rebellion. There are, of course, many interpretations of Leviticus 16 set forth by learned scholars, the great majority of whom are most certainly not Adventists; so at best the question is quite open. The *Abingdon Bible Commentary* (Methodist) relative to Leviticus 16 and the scapegoats states, "On the goats lots are to be cast, one for Jehovah and the other for Azazel. The translation 'Dismissal' in the Revised Version margin here (cf. removal in ASV margin) is inadmissible being based on a false etymology. What the word meant is unknown but it should be retained as a proper name of a wilderness demon."[14]

To this statement could be added the opinions of Samuel Zwemer, E. W. Hengstenberg, J. B. Rotherham and J. Russell Howden, the last of whom wrote in the *Sunday School Times* of January 15, 1927, "The goat for Azazel as it is sometimes misleadingly translated, typifies God's challenge to Satan. Of the two goats, one was for Jehovah signifying God's acceptance of the sin offering; the other was for Azazel. This is probably to be understood as a person being parallel with Jehovah in the preceding clause. So Azazel is probably a *synonym* for Satan."

Although Seventh-day Adventists have no exegetical support for their sanctuary and investigative judgment theories, one thing is certain: they have more than substantial scholastic support for assigning

[12] *Questions on Doctrine,* pp. 396, 398-400.
[13] See p. 51ff.
[14] See Author's Note at end of chapter.

the title "Satan" to Azazel in Leviticus 16 concerning the scapegoat, but where the Scripture does not speak specifically it is far wiser to withhold comment. Many critics, in their zeal to shred Seventh-day Adventism and classify it as "a dangerous non-Christian cult," lay much stress upon the scapegoat teaching. In the light of current Adventist statements concerning their concept of the scapegoat, the misunderstandings of the past have at last been brought out into the open, clarified, and presented in a plausible manner.

Much, much more could be written concerning the Seventh-day Adventist concepts of the sanctuary, investigative judgment and the scapegoat since they are inseparably linked together. But such writers as W. W. Fletcher (*The Reasons for My Faith*) and other ex-Seventh-day Adventists have exhaustively refuted the position of their former affiliation. The reader is urged to consider the Bibliography for additional information on this subject. The saving grace of the entire situation is that the Adventists fortunately deny the logical conclusions to which their doctrines must lead them; i.e., a negation of the full validity of the atonement of Christ which validity they absolutely affirm, and embrace with considerable fervor—a paradoxical situation at best!

AUTHOR'S NOTE

We could wish that some of the earlier unrepresentative Seventh-day Adventist statements on the scapegoat teaching had not been made, or better yet, that they were not still circulated in some quarters. However, to ignore their honest current declarations is, we believe, fundamentally unfair. It appears to us to be little more than blind prejudice. One recent review of the book, *Questions on Doctrine,* contains an error frequently found in critical writings. Imputing to their account a position the Adventists do not hold, the review then proceeds to destroy it as if, in the final analysis, it had both exposed and refuted a pernicious error. While it is true that the Seventh-day Adventists do believe that Azazel, in Leviticus 16, does represent Satan, their interpretation of it is far removed from this reviewer's straw man. After quoting the Seventh-day Adventist statement: "Seventh-day Adventists repudiate *in toto* any idea . . . that Satan is in any sense our sin bearer," this review states "but then two entire chapters are devoted to proving that Satan did bear our sin." It goes on to describe the Adventist position as "repulsive blasphemy" and "unholy twisting of the Scripture. If the Seventh-day Adventists were sound in everything but this and still held this one gross error, we would still have to consider them as an unscriptural cult."[15]

Now with some other portions of this review we are in agreement. But many of the statements show a marked predisposition toward removing various statements from context and placing them together to prove contradiction without respect to their setting. It ignores all the Seventh-day Adventist statements which contradict these out-of-context criticisms. The very chapter alluded to clearly shows that Adventists repudiate the meaning the reviewer has attached to the scapegoat concept. As we have noted, it is regrettable that this teaching has been so stated in some Adventist writings as to give the impression that the scapegoat represents Satan in the vicarious role of sin bearer, but the Adventists have clarified this beyond reasonable doubt in the large majority of their publications.

Questions on Doctrine clarifies the concept of the scapegoat in Seventh-day Adventist theology. For Adventists, when the Lord Jesus Christ returns He will place upon Satan the full responsibility for his role of instigator and tempter to sin. Since Satan caused angels and man to rebel against their creator, Adventists reason that Azazel, the scapegoat of Leviticus 16, is a type of Satan receiving the punishment due him. As we have seen however, Adventists repudiate the idea that Satan is their vicarious sin-bearer in any sense. They point out, and rightly so, that in Leviticus 16 only the first goat was slain as the vicarious offering. The second goat was not killed but was sent into the wilderness to die. Satan similarly bears the weight of guilt and final punishment culminating in the annihilation as the master criminal who has promulgated sin during the period of God's grace toward lost men. To quote the Adventists:

"Satan's death a thousand times over could never make him the savior in any sense whatsoever. He is the arch sinner of the universe, the author and instigator of sin. . . . Only Christ the Creator, the one and only God-man could make a substitutionary atonement for man's transgressions. And this Christ did completely, perfectly and once for all on Golgotha."[16]

[15] *The King's Business,* March 1958, pp. 22, 23.
[16] *Questions on Doctrine,* p. 400.

CHAPTER EIGHT

LAW, GRACE AND SALVATION

In order to understand the Adventist view of law and grace, especially in relation to eternal salvation, we must consider the Adventist antipathy towards antinomianism.

The very word "antinomian" (*anti*, against, and *nomos*, law) describes the conflict between those who believe that not only were the Ten Commandments abrogated at Calvary but even the principles underlying them were "abolished" so that the Christian is not bound by them; and those who believe that the Decalogue is as binding today as when it was given at Sinai.

From the beginning of church history, the great majority of evangelical Christians have been as strongly opposed to antinomianism as are the Adventists. Unfortunately however, the latter have tended to label antinomian anyone who disagrees with their definition of "the law of God." Consequently this has created a great problem in semantics which has disrupted the lines of communication, so to speak, between Adventists and other Christians. Although we believe in obeying the laws of God, and in good works as the evidence of saving faith, we strenuously object to "commandment keeping," to the extent of supposed spiritual superiority. A principal cause of their legalistic tendencies then is the Adventists' abhorrence of antinomianism.

By virtue of the fact that they obey the Fourth Commandment as well as the other nine, Adventists maintain that they alone are God's commandment-keeping church. To be sure, theologians have differed over the nature and extent of the moral law of God, and doubtless the controversy will continue until our Lord comes again. Any group, however, which feels they are the only ones that keep God's commands is likely to foment schism in the Body of Christ.

From their beginning, Adventists have concentrated upon "the law of God," and in *Questions on Doctrine* they devote 34 pages to the exposition of this subject. Although the Adventists repudiate legalism, that is, the doctrine that keeping the law merits salvation, a legalistic spirit does exist in some of their teaching. For example, although denying that the ceremonial law is binding upon Christians, they quote from it to defend their classifying certain foods as "unclean." Although Adventists reject antinomianism, in their desire to avoid the abuses of grace they actually abuse grace by magnifying the letter of the law. How Adventists arrived at this position has been well explained by D. M. Canright (*Seventh-day Adventism Renounced* [chapter xvii]). In one place, Canright sets forth a series of propositions which, in some areas, are exegetically irrefutable, and with which I am in full agreement.

Now let us examine the Adventist claim that the law is binding upon the Christian, as stated in their Fundamental Beliefs, *Questions on Doctrine,* and wherever their writings touch on this subject.

I. The Principle of Law

To begin with, we agree to the proposition that the principle underlying the moral laws of God is indeed eternal, and consistent with His character. However, we must distinguish between the principle of the law of God, and the expression of that principle in specific statutes such as those in the Pentateuch. Because Adventists do not seem to make this distinction, it appears to this writer that they relate law to grace, which is an unhealthy practice. They claim that "the Law" was in effect in Eden and during all the centuries thence to Sinai. Wherever the Bible speaks of "commandments" or "law," most Adventists apparently assume that it means the Decalogue. We must, however, clearly differentiate between the *principle* of the law of God and the *function* of the law of God as revealed in the Pentateuch. Not only the Adventists but many historic Protestant groups have failed to make this distinction, and so have been guilty of carrying over into the New Covenant some of the legalistic Jewish functions of the law.

A. *The Dual Law Theory*

In *Questions on Doctrine,* the Adventists distinguish between "the moral law of God — the Decalogue — and the ceremonial law," setting

[2] Pp. 130-31.

forth the distinctions in two columns.[2] In column one is the Decalogue which was spoken by God, written by Him on tables of stone, given to Moses and deposited in the Ark. It dealt with moral precepts, revealed sin, and is in effect today. They insist that Christians must "keep the whole law,"* (James 2:10) and that we shall be judged by this law (James 2:12). They believe that the Decalogue is established in the life of a Christian by faith in Christ (Romans 3:31), and that Christ magnified the law (Isaiah 42:21), which Paul described as "spiritual" (Romans 7:14).

In column two, Adventists analyze the law of ceremonial ordinances, which were abolished at the cross. They contrast this with "the moral law of God — the Decalogue," stating that the latter was not abolished because it was separate from the ceremonial law. Concerning the ceremonial law, Adventists teach that it was spoken and written by Moses, and given to the Levites who deposited it by the side of the Ark, and that it governed ceremony and ritual. This law prescribed offerings for sins but the apostles gave no commandment to keep it, and the Christian is not bound by it, nor can he be blessed by it. Indeed, they say "the Christian who keeps this law loses his liberty"; it "was abolished by Christ," and was "the law of a carnal commandment" containing nothing of a moral nature, the Decalogue being "the moral law of God."

Now although there are both moral and ceremonial aspects of the law in the Pentateuch, as well as civil and judicial, nowhere does the Bible state that there is any such juxtaposition of ceremonial with moral law. In fact, the whole Bible teaches that "the law was given through Moses" (John 1:17) and that it is essentially a *unit*, a fact which the Adventists have overlooked. We make this observation after comparing the application of the term "law" in the Old and New Testaments.

To illustrate: As noted above, the Adventists claim that the law of Moses and the Decalogue are separate, the one being ceremonial, the other "the moral law of God." Therefore, although the ceremonial law was abolished at the cross, the moral law remains in effect; and so they insist in "commandment-keeping," not to *earn* salvation, but as it works out in the practice of many, to *retain* salvation. If, how-

***As a sign of obedience to God.**

ever, the ceremonial law and the Decalogue are inextricably bound together, and if both are referred to as "the law," the distinction which the Adventists and others make between them is fictitious. To prove this is to nullify their interpretation concerning "the moral law." Let us examine the Scriptures to see whether such a distinction as they propose can be sustained.

The highest authority on this subject is the Lord Jesus Christ. When speaking of "the law," He alluded to both moral and ceremonial precepts; e.g., Mark 10:19 (moral); and Luke 5:12-14 (ceremonial). The Gospels abound with similar references to "the law," without distinguishing between the moral and the ceremonial, and certainly not teaching that they are separate codes.

We do not mean that the law has no moral and ceremonial aspects, for it has, but they are only aspects, not separate codes or units. They are parts of the one law which "was our schoolmaster to bring us unto Christ, that we might be justified by faith" (Gal. 3:24). The apostle Paul, certainly an authority on "the law," dogmatically affirms that the role of the schoolmaster has *ceased* and that the Christian is "dead to the law." Note, also, that the word "schoolmaster" is in the singular, which destroys the Adventist notion that there is more than one law. If the moral law were separate from the ceremonial law, instead of both being aspects of one law, Paul would have had to write that the *laws* were our *schoolmasters* to bring us to Christ, and that now "we are no longer under *schoolmasters*." But he knew and taught that the law was a unit and that it was perfectly fulfilled as such in the life of our Lord and on the cross of Calvary.

By His perfect life, the Lord Jesus met all the requirements of the moral aspect of the law; by His death, He fulfilled all the ceremonial ordinances which prefigured His incarnation and sacrifice. He Himself said, "Think not that I am come to destroy the law, or the prophets: I am come not to destroy, but to fulfill. For verily I say unto you, Till heaven and earth pass, one jot or one tittle shall in no wise pass from the law, till all be fulfilled" (Matt. 5:17, 18).

Which law did Christ fulfill? If he fulfilled only the ceremonial law as the dual law theory states, the moral law is yet to be satisfied. But "Christ is the *end* of the law for righteousness to every one that believeth" (Romans 10:4); and as we have shown, there are no distinct codes such as moral and ceremonial law. The distinction is arbitrary and contradicts the declaration of Scripture that the believer lives by a higher principle: "The law of the Spirit of life in Christ Jesus which hath made us free from the law of sin and death" (Rom. 8:2).

In order to maintain the dual law theory against the Biblical declaration that the one law has divisions or aspects, Adventists must explain why, in at least 20 passages in the New Testament, a dozen of them in the words of Jesus Christ, the Holy Spirit teaches that there are not two laws, but one; that this law is not only in the five books of Moses but in the Prophets and the Psalms as well. Christ looked upon moral, ceremonial and prophetic precepts as parts of the one law which pointed to His life, ministry, death, and resurrection, as He said to His disciples that first Easter day, "These are the words which I spake unto you, while I was yet with you, that all things must be fulfilled, which were written in the law of Moses, and in the prophets, and in the psalms concerning me" (Luke 24:44).

A study of the passages listed in footnote 3 will convince the reader that the law is one gigantic structure comprised of moral, ceremonial, civil, judicial and prophetic aspects,[3] all of which were grouped by Christ and the apostles under the heading of "the law," and which structure was completely fulfilled in the life and death of the Lord Jesus Christ who instituted the universal principle of divine love as the fulfillment of every aspect and function of the law. Our Lord said, "Therefore all things whatsoever ye would that men should do to you, do ye even so to them: for *this is the law* and the prophets. . . . Thou shalt love the Lord thy God with all thy heart, and with all thy soul, and with all thy mind. This is the first and great commandment. And the second is like unto it, Thou shalt love thy neighbor as thyself. On these two commandments hang *all the law* and the prophets" (Matt. 7:12, 22:37-40).

Instead of the Adventist belief that the law must be "kept" as a sign of obedience to God, Christ here teaches that the Christian obeys God when he obeys the supreme commandment of love. This

[3] See John 8:17, referring to Deut. 19:15; John 10:34, to Psa. 82:6; John 12:34, to Psa. 72:17 and 102:23-27; John 15:25, to Psa. 35:19 and 69:4; and John 19:7, to Lev. 24:14. In these passages, moral, ceremonial, and prophetic aspects are all spoken of as "the law." For further Scriptural teaching, the reader is invited to look up Matt. 5:17, 18; 7:12, 11:13, 12:5, 22:36, 23:23; Luke 2:22, 24, 27; 5:17, 10:26, 16:14-17; 24:44, and John 1:45.

teaching is reiterated by the greatest of the apostles, who wrote to the Galatians, "All the law is fulfilled in one word, even in this: Thou shalt love thy neighbor as thyself" (Gal. 5:14). Obviously, if we love our neighbors as ourselves, we do so because we love God with all our hearts, souls, and minds. If we do not so love God, we cannot love our neighbors as ourselves. Thus on this "great commandment" rests the law in all its aspects.

Note the language of these passages, for they indicate the strong emphasis given by our Lord. In Matthew 22:40 Christ uses the Greek word *"holos,"* translated 65 times in the New Testament as "all," 43 times as "whole," twice as "every whit," once "altogether," and once "throughout." With these renditions all lexicons agree, so there can be no linguistic doubt that the all-inclusive principle which binds and seals all aspects of the law into a unit, to be fulfilled in the life of a believer because it has been fulfilled by the Saviour, is once again declared to be "love."

The apostle Paul uses an entirely different word to sum up the unifying principle of the law and the only principle which Scriptures say fulfills it. This is the Greek word *pas*.

In the New Testament *pas* is translated 748 times as "all," 170 times as "all things," 117 times as "every," 41 times as "all men," 31 times as "whosoever," 28 times as "everyone," 12 times as "whole," and 11 times as "every man." We see then how the Holy Spirit rendered linguistically impossible any escape from the clear declaration that the principle of love indeed *fulfills* all the precepts of the law in their *entirety* since the two terms used most frequently in the New Testament to describe inclusiveness were utilized by both Christ and Paul to enunciate this vital issue.

Finally, notice Paul's powerful admonition to the believers at Rome: "Owe no man anything but to love one another: for he that loveth another *hath* fulfilled the law. For this, Thou shalt not commit adultery, Thou shalt not kill, Thou shalt not steal, Thou shalt not bear false witness, Thou shalt not covet; *and if there be any other commandment*, it is briefly comprehended in this saying, namely, Thou shalt love thy neighbor as thyself. Love worketh no ill to his neighbor: therefore love is the fulfilling of the law" (Rom. 13:8-10).

In this context the greatest authority on the law in the New Testament, next to Jesus Christ, used the very emphatic Greek word *etera* which is translated 42 times in the New Testament as "other." Unquestionably the Apostle Paul not only considered the law a unit of which the Decalogue is only a part (quoting five of the Ten Commandments), but he indicated the rest of the law — ceremonial, civil, and judicial — by the word "other." Thus if one is to be a true "commandment-keeper," he has only to obey the divine principle of love, and God looks upon this as fulfillment of "the law." The Holy Spirit does not specify the moral, ceremonial, or civil law. He emphatically states that love is the fulfillment of "the law"; a tremendously important statement, to say the least!

It is significant that in the thirteenth chapter of Romans, after quoting five of the ten commandments which the Adventists steadfastly affirm constitute "the moral law," the apostle conspicuously omits what the Adventists maintain is God's great "seal" — the Sabbath. In fact, the words "any other commandment" must include even the Sabbath in the law of love. Nowhere is this more decidedly emphasized than in the usage of a peculiar term which appears but twice in the New Testament; here in Romans 13:9, and again in Ephesians 1:10. The term in question is the Greek *"Anakephalaioutai"* which in both instances means "to sum up, to repeat summarily, and so to condense into a summary . . . to bring together."[4]

We see then that the Apostle Paul, under the inspiration of the Holy Spirit, taught in both Romans 13:9 and Ephesians 1:10 that as God in the fullness of time intended to "gather together" (KJV) or "sum up" (RSV), those whom He had chosen in Christ, in like manner He has forever condensed or summed up, comprehended or gathered together, the law in all its aspects and divisions under the all-embracing principle of love. By not adhering strictly to the established laws of sound Biblical interpretations,[5] Seventh-day Adventists seem to have overlooked this fact in the New Testament. In the course of our study of Seventh-day Adventist literature we have been impressed by the fact that some Adventists will cite texts largely out of their context and grammatical structure in what appears to be an attempt to enforce an arbitrary theory of two laws (moral and ceremonial) upon the believer in the age of grace. In so doing, they

[4] Thayer, *Greek-English Lexicon,* pp. 38, 39.

[5] Hermeneutics and exegesis, i.e., comparative study and grammatical analysis of texts.

violate that principle which the Apostle Paul states "sums up or condenses" all of the commandments of the entire law, perfectly fulfilling them under the one heading, "the great commandment," upon which, our Lord declared, "hang all the law and the prophets," the imperative of love.

On page 131 of *Questions on Doctrine* it is stated that the ceremonial law is now "abolished" (Eph. 2:15); and, "the Christian who keeps this law is not blessed," but "loses his liberty" (Gal. 5:1, 3). Nevertheless, Adventists religiously observe some ceremonial laws, especially with regard to "unclean food." Now, although they deny that their rejection of "unclean" food is based on Mosaic prohibitions, all their literature on the subject appeals to the very law which they insist has been "abolished." Under the covenant of law, nowhere but in the Mosaic ceremonial aspects of the law are people forbidden to eat oysters, clams, lobsters, crabs, reptiles, rabbits, and swine's flesh, but the Adventists still claim the validity of such prohibition. We wish that they would be consistent in following their dual law theory and abandon their "unclean foods" restriction which binds them to what even they admit is an abolished ceremonial teaching; a teaching which they also declare can cause the Christian to "lose his liberty" and miss the blessing of God.[6] Writing on this subject of unclean foods with apostolic authority and in the power of the Holy Spirit, the Apostle Paul unequivocally declared, "Therefore let no one pass judgment on you in questions of food and drink." And he warns Timothy that in the latter days some persons will "enjoin abstinence from foods which God created to be received with thanksgiving by those who believe and know the truth. For everything created by God is good, and nothing is to be rejected if it is received with thanksgiving, for then it is consecrated by the Word of God and prayer." Finally he sums it up thus: "I know and am persuaded in the Lord Jesus that nothing is unclean in itself; but it is unclean for anyone who thinks it unclean. . . . For the kingdom of God does not mean food and drink but righteousness and peace and joy in

[6] They vainly endeavor to meet this argument by declaring that these food laws were not ceremonial or typical but laws of hygiene and were in vogue even before the Mosaic dispensation. *Questions on Doctrine*, pp. 622-24. But why appeal always to Moses?

the Holy Spirit; he who thus serves Christ is acceptable to God and approved by men."[7]

From these texts it is apparent that Adventists limit their own liberty in Christ by voluntary bondage to ceremonial precepts, and it is the dual law theory which has largely caused their confusion and the consequent error of law-keeping.

For this teaching, which lapses so easily into legalism, we find no Biblical authority since it is demonstrably true that the law of Moses and the Decalogue are a unit described throughout Scripture as "*the* law," and the fact that the Decalogue was written on stones (Exodus 31:18), and the law of Moses written in a book (Exod. 24:4, 7, Deut. 31:24), in no way proves that one is moral and the other ceremonial. As we have seen, the law of Moses, written in a book, and deposited by the Levites by the side of the Ark, deals not only with ceremonial ritual matters, but with those moral precepts contained in the Decalogue itself. One could not be fulfilled, as Christ prophesied and accomplished, and the other left unfulfilled, for then God's sacrificial plan would not have been consummated at Calvary.

B. *"Law" in the New Testament*

When New Testament writers spoke of "the law," they usually meant all five books of Moses,[8] which contain moral, ceremonial and civil ordinances. It was national and applied only to Israel and to anyone who became an Israelite. Nowhere in Scripture is it applied to anyone else. Although the Gentiles, as Paul says, "have not the law," its great moral principle applied to them, so that the Gentiles "do by nature that which is contained in the law"; but they did not come under Law as given to Israel.

Acts 15:23-32 describes how the leaders of the Christian church at Jerusalem, all Jews, were very careful not to impose the demands of the law upon the Gentiles. For them, the complete "law"—moral, ceremonial and civil—had been fulfilled, and the one law to observe now was to love God and your neighbor. St. Augustine remarked, "Love God, and do as you please," for if we truly love God with heart, soul, mind and strength, we do only those things which please Him. This is "the law" of the New Testament, the only guide

[7] Col. 2:16; I Tim. 4:3-5; Rom. 14:14, 17-18 (RSV).

[8] Compare: I Cor. 14:34, Gen. 3:16; Rom. 7:7, Exod. 20:17; Matt. 22:36-39, Deut. 6:5 and Lev. 19:18; Matt. 12:5, Num. 28:9, 10.

for the Christian. We are "no longer under the law, but under grace," and the function of the "schoolmaster" (Gal. 3:24) has forever and irrevocably ceased.

Let us see how these first Christian leaders solved the problem of "the law":

"And they wrote letters by them after this manner; The apostles and elders and brethren send greetings unto the brethren which are of the Gentiles in Antioch, Syria and in Cilicia. Forasmuch as we have heard, that certain which went out from us have troubled you with words, subverting your souls, saying, Ye must be circumcised, and keep the law: to whom we gave no such commandment: It seemed good unto us, being assembled with one accord to send chosen men unto you. . . . We have sent therefore, Judas and Silas. . . . For it seemed good to the Holy Ghost, and to us, to lay upon you no greater burden than these necessary things; that ye abstain from meats offered to idols, and from blood, and from things strangled, and from fornication: from which if ye keep yourselves, ye shall do well. Fare ye well" (Acts 15:23-25, 27-29).

Since "the law" includes the precepts of the Pentateuch, and certain sections of the Psalms and Prophets, this message to the Gentiles contradicts all dual law teachers who insist that we must for any purpose "keep the law." We know from a comparison of the New Testament with the Old that the Decalogue of itself is not the entire moral law of God, as our Adventist brethren often insist, for there are many other commandments, which are neither *inferred, implied* nor *contained* in the Decalogue but which are just as moral as anything appearing in Exodus 20.[9] Although nine of the Ten Commandments are enunciated in the New Testament, we have seen that they are "comprehended, summed up or condensed" in the words of Paul, in the great commandment of love (Rom. 13, Gal. 5). So the Adventists have no argument against the total fulfillment of all the law by the life and death of our Saviour.

In Acts 15:24, the leaders of the church in Jerusalem reiterate this principle in their letter to the Gentiles in Antioch, Syria and Cilicia: "Certain which went out from us have troubled you with words, subverting your souls, saying, Ye must be circumcised, and keep the law: to whom we gave no such commandment."

[9] See Lev. 19:18.

Now although Seventh-day Adventists affirm (see Chapter Three, section VII) that law-keeping cannot merit salvation, nevertheless they teach that by breaking the law one forfeits salvation. They invoke a principle which was fulfilled in the life and death of Christ; and in so doing they place themselves in direct opposition to the great law of love enunciated by Christ and the apostles, and are in effect putting "a yoke upon the neck of the disciples which neither our fathers nor we were able to bear" (Acts 15:10). To those who invoke the law as the criterion of obedience in the Christian life, the Word of God replies, "We gave no such commandment" (Acts 15:24).

Paul's phrase "any other commandment" in Romans 13:9 of course includes abstinence from meats offered to idols, blood, things strangled and fornication, for love of God would enjoin discernment and obedience in all these things.

To support their argument that a Christian must obey the commandments, Adventists and other Christian bodies cite such passages as the following: "If ye love me keep my commandments"; "He that hath my commandments, and keepeth them, he it is that loveth me" (John 14:15, 21). "And hereby we do know that we know him, if we keep his commandments. He that saith, I know him, and keepeth not his commandments, is a liar, and the truth is not in him. . . . And whatsoever we ask, we receive of him, because we keep his commandments, and do those things that are pleasing in his sight. . . . He that keepeth his commandments dwelleth in him and he in him. And hereby we know that he abideth in us by the Spirit which he hath given us. . . . By this we know that we love the children of God, when we love God, and keep his commandments. For this is the love of God, that we keep his commandments: and his commandments are not grievous" (I John 2:3, 4; 3:22, 24; 5:2, 3).

We too yield to the authority of those verses; but the fallacy of the position lies in the concept that the word "commandments" always refers to the Ten Commandments, which they maintain are "the moral law of God." This claim cannot be substantiated from Scripture, in fact, it is contradicted by the Bible. Let us see how the Lord Jesus and the Apostle John applied the words "commandments" and "law." First, consider the conversation of our Lord with the lawyer in Luke 10:25-28:

"And, behold, a certain lawyer stood up, and tempted him, saying, Master, what shall I do to inherit eternal life?

"He said unto him, What is written in the law? how readest thou?

"And he answering said, Thou shalt love the Lord thy God with all thy heart, and with all thy soul, and with all thy strength, and with all thy mind; and thy neighbor as thyself.

"And he said unto him, Thou hast answered right: this do, and thou shalt live."

Clearly, the Lord Jesus did not subscribe to the Seventh-day Adventist view that "commandment-keeping means keeping all of the Ten Commandments," none of which He mentions in this passage. Christ did not say, "Keep the Ten Commandments, especially the fourth one, and thou shalt live." He said, in effect, "Obey the law of love upon which all the law and the prophets rest, and thou shalt live." This refutes the Adventist claim that when Jesus spoke of commandments he meant *only* the Decalogue.

Among those who listened to our Lord's discourse in the Upper Room was the Apostle John, who records the "new commandment . . . That you love one another as I have loved you" (John 13:34). To this commandment John refers in the passages quoted from his First Epistle. Nowhere does he mention the Decalogue or any part of the moral law of God. Instead, he writes: "This is his commandment, That we should believe on the name of his Son Jesus Christ, and love one another, as he gave us commandment. . . . And this commandment have we from him, That he who loveth God love his brother also" (I John 3:23, 4:21). And in his Second Epistle he says, "I beseech thee, not as though I wrote a new commandment unto thee, but that which we had from the beginning, that we love one another. And this is love, that we walk after his commandments. This is the commandment, That, as ye have heard from the beginning, ye should walk in it" (II John 5, 6).

What then does John mean when he speaks of "commandment" or "commandments"? In his own words he means ". . . that which we had from the beginning, that we love one another. And this is love, that we walk after his commandments. This is the commandment, That, as ye have heard from the beginning, ye should walk in it" (II John 5, 6).

How different from ironclad obedience to what many, including

Adventists, sometimes call "The Eternal Ten"! By "the righteousness of the law," and fulfillment of the law, Christ and all the New Testament writers mean *not* the Ten Commandments but the eternal law of *love.* The motivating power of the universe, love, is to motivate obedience to God. By loving Him and one another, we fulfill all moral law. The chief function of the law was to reveal sin and to "slay" the soul, that righteousness might come by faith, and it was given for the unregenerate, *not* the redeemed: "Knowing this, that the law is not made for a righteous man but for the lawless and disobedient, for the ungodly and for sinners, for unholy and profane, for murderers of fathers and murderers of mothers, for manslayers" (I Tim. 1:9).

C. *The Charge of Pharisaism*

By believing they are God's commandment-keeping church, Adventists have exposed themselves to the charge of Pharisaism. Because they monopolize such passages as the following, they give the impression of claiming to be the only people on earth: (1) "Which keep the commandments of God"; (2) "They that keep the commandments of God, and the faith of Jesus"; and, (3) "Blessed are *they that do his commandments,*[10] that they may have the right to the tree of life, and may enter in through the gates into the city" (Rev. 12:17, 14:12, 22:14).

We admire the desire of our Adventist brethren to obey the commandments of God; but, we ask, what commandments? If they answer, "The Decalogue," we reject their effort to bring us under bondage, for we "are not under the law, but under grace" (Rom. 6:14). If some fail to recognize that "the law" of the New Testament is love for God and for one another, and that it fulfills and supersedes all previous embodiments of divine principle, then the issue is clear. Such people speak like "a noisy gong or a clanging cymbal," because they do not give supremacy to the "new" and "great commandment."

Concluding this section on the principle of law, we may sum up our position briefly:

[10] All the oldest and best Greek manuscripts of Rev. 22:14 read "They that wash their robes," so the verse gives no support whatever for "commandment keeping." This fact well-informed Adventists recognize, but a large segment still attempt to utilize certain faulty and incorrect English translations to "prove" their position.

The Adventist insistence that there are two separate codes of laws, the moral and the ceremonial, and that the former is in effect today and the latter was abolished at the cross, finds, we believe, no exegetical or theological basis in Scripture. We have also shown that they select numerous texts out of context and juxtapose them in order to validate their contention. We have seen that the greatest of all commandments is not included in the Decalogue or "the moral law." And yet upon this great commandment, love for the Lord and for one's neighbor, "hang all the law and the prophets." The nineteenth chapter of Leviticus is alone sufficient to refute the dual law theory, for it contains *moral, ceremonial* and *civil* laws sometimes all appearing in the same verse, and yet Leviticus is called by Christ, "the law," as are the other four books of Moses.

The Adventist contention that since the Ten Commandments were spoken by God, inscribed on stone and placed within the Ark, they are superior to the law written by Moses in a book and placed by the side of the Ark, is fallacious. This is true because the book placed by the side of the Ark actually contains *more* moral law than does the Decalogue itself. It is therefore, superior to the Decalogue, at least in scope.

The Bible refutes the Adventist contention that the law was in force in Eden and that it was known to Adam, Noah, Abraham and the patriarchs. Not one verse of Scripture can be cited free from inference, deduction and implication, that teaches such a doctrine. The Word of God frequently states, "*The law* was given by Moses. . . . Did not Moses give you *the law*. . . . If therefore perfection were by the Levitical priesthood, for under it the people received *the law*. . . . The covenant, that was confirmed before of God in Christ, *the law*, which was 430 years after, cannot disannul . . . The Lord our God made a covenant with us in Horeb. The Lord made not this covenant with our fathers, but with us" (John 1:17, 19, Hebrews 7:11, Gal. 3:17, Deut. 5:2, 3, 4 through verse 22). The Adventists' contentions, therefore, concerning the eternal nature of the Decalogue and the time of its application to man, are mere conjecture. Although we admit that the principle of the law was, in effect, written upon the hearts of men by the Holy Spirit, so that they were judged by it (Rom. 2), there is a vast difference between the principle of the law and the embodiment of that principle in a given code (Sinaitic-Mosaic), which the Adventists fail to recognize.

Finally, the Old Testament Scriptures all teach the unity of the law. Christ endorsed it, and the Apostles pointed out that its chief purpose was to condemn man and show him his need of redemption that he might come to Christ, the author and fulfiller of *all* the law. We who are "led of the Spirit are not under the law" (Gal. 5:18); for "love is the fulfilling of the law" (Rom. 13:10). This love energizes us to "walk not after the flesh, but after the Spirit" that in us "the righteousness of the law might be fulfilled"[11] (Rom. 8:4). In Jeremiah 31:31-34 the prophet states that under the new covenant God would write His law "in their inward parts, and write it in their hearts." In II Corinthians 3:3 the Apostle Paul declares that Christians are "the epistle of Christ . . . written not with ink, but with the Spirit of the living God; not in tables of stone, but in fleshy tables of the heart." The motive for obedience to this law is the imperative of Love—"We love Him because He first loved us" (I John 4:19).

The great foundational moral law of the universe is therefore declared to be unchanging love. This is vastly different from the national or Mosaic law given only to Israel. That law was designed to be fulfilled, even though it was based upon the eternal principles of the moral character of God (Col. 2:14-17). And when its fulfillment did take place and the character of God was imputed to the believer and imparted to his life by the power of the indwelling Spirit, the entire Mosaic system passed away; but the eternal principle, its foundation, remained, and is operative today as the law of love, the supreme "commandment" and the only "law" under which the Christian is to live.

The concept of Law in Seventh-day Adventism, then, leads them to the un-Biblical and at times legalistic position that although they are "under grace," by failing to "keep the commandments" they are in danger of coming "under law" again.

The Word of God, however, describes the Christian under grace as "dead to the law" and "alive unto God" (Gal. 2:19), and nowhere

[11] Not the embodiment of carnal prohibitions or commandments.

is it taught that one can "come alive" again so that the function of the law is resumed.

II. The Relationship of Grace to Salvation

Although Adventists lay great stress on "commandment-keeping" and "obedience to the moral law of God as contained in the Ten Commandments," they devote a large portion of their writings to the New Testament doctrine of grace. As we saw in Chapter Three, Seventh-day Adventists believe in salvation by grace alone, and vehemently deny that "law" plays any part as a basis for redemption.[12] In their own words, "Salvation is not now, and never has been, by law or by works; salvation is only by the grace of Christ. Moreover, there never was a time in the plan of God when salvation was by human works or effort. Nothing men can do or have done, can in any way *merit* salvation.

"While works are not a *means* of salvation, good works are the inevitable *result* of salvation. However, these good works are possible only for the child of God whose life is inwrought by the Spirit of God. . . . One thing is certain, man cannot be saved by any effort of his own. We profoundly believe that no works of the law, no deeds of the law, no effort however commendable, and no good works —whether they be many or few, sacrificial or not—can in any way justify the sinner (Titus 3:5; Romans 3:20). Salvation is wholly of grace; it is the gift of God (Rom. 4:4, 5; Eph. 2:8)."[13]

These and many similar clear-cut statements in current authoritative Seventh-day Adventist literature reveal that, despite the "dual law theory" and the peculiar concept that the law is still operative in the life of the believer, Adventists confess the basis of their salvation to be grace, and grace alone, the only basis upon which God deigns to save the fallen children of Adam.

In Chapter 14 of *Questions on Doctrine,* Adventists spell out their allegiance to divine grace as the only channel of salvation: "According to Seventh-day Adventist belief, there is, and can be, no salvation through the law, or by human works of the law, but only through the saving grace of God."[14]

[12] See Author's Note at end of chapter.
[13] *Questions on Doctrine,* pp. 141-42.
[14] P. 135.

Christians who are familiar with historical theology know that the Adventist position on law, though tinged with legalism, has its roots in the basic Arminian position that one receives salvation as a free gift of God; but, once he has received this gift, the believer is responsible for its maintenance and duration, and the chief means of accomplishing this is "commandment-keeping" or "obedience to *all* the laws of God."

Since Adventists are basically Arminian, we may logically deduce that, in a sense, their salvation rests upon legal grounds. But the saving factor in the dilemma is that by life and by world-wide witness, Adventists, like other so-called Arminians, give true evidence that they have experienced the "new birth," which is by grace alone, through faith in our Lord and His sacrifice upon the cross. One would be callous and uncharitable indeed not to accept their profession of dependence upon Christ alone for redemption, even though there is inconsistency in their theological system.

Some Christians make a great issue of the teaching of "eternal security," and perhaps rightly so because it is an important truth. However, no matter how strongly we may feel about it, our conviction does not entitle us to judge the motives and spiritual condition of other believers in this respect. This is our principal reason for taking the position that Seventh-day Adventists are Christians who believe the historic gospel message. They cannot rightly be called non-Christian cultists or "Judaizers," since they are sound on the great New Testament doctrines including grace and redemption through the vicarious offering of Jesus Christ "once for all" (Heb. 10:10) and give evidence of "life in Christ."

For many centuries, there has been much controversy over the juxtaposition of the principles of law and grace in the Scripture. If evangelicals today were asked, "Do you believe that grace and law are in direct opposition?" the answer in most cases would be a strong affirmative. Through the years, confusion has been caused by the abuse of both principles by two groups of equally sincere Christians. One group believes that all law has ceased; the other that the Ten Commandments are still God's standard of righteousness and must be obeyed or salvation is forfeit. What both groups have failed to grasp is that the great conflict is not between law and grace as such; rather, it centers around a proper understanding of their relationship and respective functions.

We have established that love is the ground and source of the doctrine of grace, but the law was necessary to expose the sinfulness of sin and the depth of man's moral depravity. When law becomes the ground of salvation or of restraining the Christian from practicing sin, it intrudes upon the province of grace. When a Christian is not controlled by love, grace is abused and its purpose is nullified. All law is fulfilled by love, as our Saviour and the apostles taught, but the Christian can never please God if he obeys for fear of the law. Life under law binds the soul, for the tendency is for man to obey not because he wants to please God but because he fears God's judgment. Under grace, love works upon the regenerate heart, and what was legalistic duty under law becomes gracious obedience under grace. Actually, grace and love demand more than the law, which to the Pharisees required only outward obedience. Grace commands us to "do the will of God from the heart" (Eph. 6:6). Seventh-day Adventists declare that they obey the law not out of fear but out of love for God, but it is to be regretted that in a large proportion of their literature on the subject, they declare that the keeping of the law is necessary to *maintain* salvation, and thus they introduce the motive of fear instead of the Biblical imperative of love.

The Apostle John defined the issue when he wrote, "The law was given by Moses, but grace and truth came by Jesus Christ" (John 1:17). As a governing principle, a measure of righteousness, a schoolmaster and an instrument of death, the law was supplanted by grace — the unmerited favor of God. All believers in the Lord Jesus Christ, having passed from death to life through the sacrifice of the Son of God, possess the divine nature and righteousness. Because He first loved us, we are compelled and impelled to love and serve Him. In obedience to the great law of love, the Christian fulfills the *righteousness* of the law (not the law itself; this Christ alone did); and by the transforming power of the indwelling Holy Spirit he will "walk not after the flesh, but after the Spirit" (Rom. 8:4).

Seventh-day Adventists believe, we repeat, that they are saved by grace. As "Arminians," however, they are often prone to believe that their remaining saved depends on "commandment-keeping." They are not alone in this error, for it is characteristic of most of those who embrace Arminianism.

III. The Author of Salvation

Because He took our sins upon Himself, in obedience to His Father's will, the Lord Jesus "became the author of eternal salvation unto all them that obey him" (Heb. 5:8-10). This truth Seventh-day Adventists believe. They strongly assert their belief in the deity of the Lord Jesus Christ, His equality with the Father, and His perfect, sinless human nature, and expound these truths in detail.[15] However, they teach that before his incarnation the Lord Jesus Christ bore the title of Michael the archangel.[16] This interpretation differs greatly from that of Jehovah's Witnesses who believe that Christ was a created being and that "He was a god, but not the almighty God who is Jehovah."[17] The Adventists make this very clear: "We emphatically reject the idea . . . and the position held by the Jehovah's Witnesses. We do not believe that Christ is a created being. We as a people have not considered the identification of Michael of sufficient prominence to dwell upon it at length either in our literature or in our preaching. . . . We believe that the term Michael is but one of the many titles applied to the Son of God, the second person of the Godhead. But such a view does not in any way conflict with our belief in His full deity and eternal pre-existence, nor does it in the least disparage His person and work."[18]

Although a number of authoritative commentators support the Adventist view, the New Testament, we believe, does not warrant this conclusion.[19] Most of the evidence that the Adventists submit is from the Book of Daniel, the rest from the Apocalypse. By comparing such designations as "angel of Jehovah," "angel of the Lord," "Prince," and "Michael," the Adventists conclude that Michael is another title for the Lord Jesus Christ. But Seventh-day Adventists maintain that although he is called "the arch angel" (*archangelos* or "first messenger"), he is *not* a created being since, in the Old Testament, "angel of Jehovah" is a term of Deity. In the light of this, we do not judge them because of their view of Michael, but call the

[15] *Questions on Doctrine,* pp. 35-41, 50-65.
[16] *Ibid.,* pp. 71-86.
[17] *Let God Be True,* pp. 34-35, Watchtower Bible and Tract Society, Brooklyn, N. Y. (1946).
[18] *Questions on Doctrine,* p. 71.
[19] Matthew Henry, *Commentary*; J. B. Rotherham, *The Emphasized Old Testament*; George Rowlinson, *Pulpit Commentary*; T. Robinson, *Preacher's Homiletic Commentary.*

reader's attention to the ninth verse of the Book of Jude, which says, "Yet Michael the archangel, when contending with the devil he disputed about the body of Moses, *durst not* bring against him a railing accusation, but said, The Lord rebuke thee."

The word translated *durst* in the King James Bible is the archaic past tense of "dare"; so Michael "did not dare" bring against Satan a railing or blasphemous (*blasphemos*) judgment. The Greek word for "dare" is *tolmao* and appears 16 times in the New Testament, and in the negative always means "not daring through fear of retaliation." Thus if Michael was Christ, according to the Seventh-day Adventists, "He did not dare" to rebuke Satan for fear of retaliation.

Adventists agree that 15 times in the New Testament *"tolmao"* carries the meaning indicated. But, since its use in Jude nine refutes their notion that Michael is a title of Christ, they *reverse* its meaning here! As the Adventists know, none of the commentators to whom they appeal has grammatically analyzed or diagrammed the passage in the Greek or for that matter commented upon exclusive usage of *tolmao* in the Scripture of the New Testament. The agreement of such commentation therefore gives no validity whatever to the Adventists' misuse of *tolmao*. The preincarnate Christ, the *Logos*, having the nature of God (John 1:1), certainly would not refer the creature Satan to God the Father for rebuke. While He was on earth, Christ the Creator rebuked Satan many times.[20] Would He then fear him during His preincarnate life? Scripture belies this.

The Adventist explanation is: "The devil, the prince of evil, could rightly be said to deserve a railing accusation, but to such a thing Michael would not stoop. To say that Michael *could not,* in the sense that he did not have the power or the authority to do so, would not be true. It is not that Michael *could not,* in the sense of being restricted, but rather that he would not take such an attitude."[21]

This statement appears to be an attempt to escape the fact that the word "dare" (*tolmao*) in the New Testament always connotes fear, including its use in Jude nine. The text teaches that because Michael did not have the authority to rebuke Satan, "he did not dare" to do so through fear of superior retaliation. There is no implication that Michael's position was so high that he "would not stoop." The con-

[20] See Matt. 4:10; 16:23; Luke 4:8; Mark 8:33.
[21] *Questions on Doctrine,* p. 80.

text, grammar and root meaning of *tolmao* belie the Adventists' attempt to make this text support their view of Michael. All authorities on Greek grammar agree that the Adventist interpretation violates the classic and New Testament usage of *tolmao*.

Thus the Adventist statement about Michael is neither linguistically nor Scripturally accurate. Although they repudiate the Jehovah's Witnesses' position, they wrest this passage from its true meaning, and read into it their own theory concerning Michael as Christ.

In conclusion, we are convinced of the sincerity of the Adventists' claim to regeneration, and allegiance to the New Testament principle of saving grace. We appreciate their high regard for the law of God, and their desire to obey it. We cannot agree, however, with their insistence upon linking "commandment-keeping" to observance of the ceremonial law, especially with regard to "unclean" foods. We feel, moreover, that they err in saying that Michael is a title of Christ, and we believe that we have shown that they violate the linguistic and Scriptural meaning of Jude nine.

Author's Note

One of the chief critics of Seventh-day Adventism is a vocal ex-Adventist printer of Minneapolis, a man who has written much against his former church. Writing in *The Sword of the Lord,* August 2, 1957, he bitterly assailed Seventh-day Adventists as willful deceivers. Since his writings are repeatedly quoted by most of the other critics we shall discuss his charge, but in the interest of brevity we shall confine ourselves to one of his chief areas of criticism, law and salvation in Seventh-day Adventist theology.

This critic quotes the book, *Steps to Christ,* by Mrs. Ellen G. White in the following manner: "The condition of eternal life is now just what it has always been . . . perfect obedience to the law of God."

He then maintains that Seventh-day Adventism teaches this and on the surface it appears that he has proved his point; namely, that to Adventists salvation is a combination of grace, faith in Christ, plus the keeping of the law. A closer look at the statement in the context from which the critic removed it, however, serves to refute this position. Wrote Mrs. White in the very same context: "We do not earn salvation by our obedience for salvation is the free gift of God to receive by faith. But obedience is the fruit of faith . . . here is the true test. If we abide in Christ and the love of God dwells in us, our feelings, our thoughts, our actions will be in harmony with the will of God as expressed in the precepts of His Holy law. . . . Righteousness is defined by the standard of God's holy law as expressed in the ten precepts given on Sinai. That so-called faith in Christ which professes to release men from the obligation of obedience to God is not faith but presumption. 'By grace are ye saved through faith.' But 'faith if it has not works is dead.' Jesus said of Himself before He came to earth, 'I delight to do thy will O my God. Yea, thy law is within my heart.' And just before He ascended again to Heaven, He declared, 'I have kept my Father's commandments and abide in his love.' The Scripture says, 'Hereby we do know that we know him, if we keep his commandments. He that saith he abides in him ought also himself to walk even as he walked,' because 'Christ also suffered for us, leaving us an example, that ye should follow his steps.'

"The condition of eternal life is now just what it always has been—just what it was in Paradise before the fall of our first parents—perfect obedience to the law of God, perfect righteousness. Since we are sinful, unholy, we cannot perfectly obey a holy law. We have no righteousness of our own with which to meet the claims of the law of God. But Christ has made a way of escape for us. He lived on earth amid trials and temptations such as we have to meet. He lived a sinless life. He died for us and now He offers to take our sins and give us His righteousness. If you give yourself to Him and accept Him as your Saviour, then sinful as your life may have been for His sake you are counted righteous. Christ's character stands in place of your character and you are accepted before God just as if you had not sinned.

"So we have nothing in ourselves of which to boast. We have no ground for self exaltation. Our only ground of hope is in the righteousness of Christ imputed to us by His Spirit working in and through us."[22]

In the light of Mrs. White's complete statement on this subject

[22] *Steps to Christ,* pp. 36-49 (paperback ed. 1945).

we see that our critic omitted her principal thesis, that we are saved by grace. There are not a few instances of similar carelessness on the part of the writer of this article. The result is that his work is largely discredited and discounted by those who know the proper methods of research.

Seventh-day Adventists are well aware of the law and grace problem and in *Questions on Doctrine* they state:

"There has been regrettable misunderstanding as to our teaching on grace, law, and works, and their interrelationships. According to Seventh-day Adventist belief, there is and can be, no salvation through the law, or by human works of the law, but only through the saving grace of God. This principle, to us, is basic."[23]

Further the Adventists state: "Salvation is not now, and never has been, by law or works; salvation is only by the grace of Christ. Moreover, there never was a time in the plan of God when salvation was by human works or effort. Nothing men can do or have done can in any way *merit* salvation.

"While works are not a *means* of salvation, good works are the inevitable *result* of salvation. . . . One thing is certain, man cannot be saved by any effort of his own. We profoundly believe that no works of the law, no deeds of the law, no effort however commendable, and no good works—whether they be many or few, sacrificial or not—can in any way justify the sinner (Titus 3:5; Rom. 3:20). Salvation is wholly of grace; it is the gift of God (Rom. 4:4, 5; Eph. 2:8)."[24]

Ellen G. White, certainly an authoritative voice in Adventism, summarized it thus: "Christ is pleading for the church in the heavenly courts above, pleading for those for whom he paid the redemption price of his own lifeblood. Centuries, ages, can never diminish the efficacy of this atoning sacrifice. The message of the gospel of His grace was to be given to the church in clear and distinct lines, that the world should no longer say that Seventh-day Adventists talk the law, but do not teach or believe Christ."[25]

[23] P. 135.
[24] *Questions on Doctrine,* pp. 141-42.
[25] *Testimonies to Ministers,* p. 92.

CHAPTER NINE

THE "REMNANT CHURCH"

One of the teachings of Seventh-day Adventist theology which has hindered fellowship with other denominations is that of the "Remnant Church." A survey of their literature from the early days of the movement indicates that Adventists consider themselves a "special people" called by God to perform a special mission which will culminate in the second coming of Christ (see *Questions on Doctrine,* chapters III, IX and X). The Adventists state, "We believe that the prophecy of Revelation 12:17 points to the experience and work of the Seventh-day Adventist Church." It is evident that the Adventists consider themselves especially favored by God, for Revelation 12:17 says: "And the dragon was wroth with the woman, and went to make war with the remnant of her seed, which keep the commandments of God, and have the testimony of Jesus Christ."

Although it is possible to have fellowship with Seventh-day Adventists, we cannot accept the "remnant church" concept which is exclusivism, in the light of the Biblical teaching concerning the unity of the Body of Christ. The Adventists officially state: "We do not believe that we alone constitute the true children of God—that we are the only true Christians—on earth today."[1] Doubtless they are sincere in this profession, but their special teachings cause them to cling to the spiritual exclusivism which through the years has caused much friction between themselves and other members of the Body of Christ.

In general, Seventh-day Adventists believe that certain "forgotten and neglected truths" need re-emphasis in our day and age. In their own words, "There are special truths for today that we have been called of God to give. We definitely feel that we must emphasize certain neglected truths, must restore others that most Protestant bodies no longer stress, and must continue the work of the Reforma-

[1] *Questions on Doctrine,* p. 187.

tion."[2] This conviction is based on their particular interpretation of the Book of Revelation, not on systematic theology or textual values.

The historicist school, however, is but one of several methods of interpreting apocalyptic literature, and it is disheartening to note that our Adventist brethren build their teaching about the "remnant church," "which keep the commandments of God and have the testimony of Jesus Christ," upon this particular school of interpretation and do not recognize the claims of other schools of interpretation. It is well to have a method of interpretation, and admirable to be consistent in practicing it. Nevertheless, it is inconsistent with Scripture and the principles of comparative textual analysis, language and syntactical study, to make such an interpretation the criterion for judging the spirituality of other members of the Body of Christ. This, sad to say, the Seventh-day Adventists unfortunately do.

As we have seen in an earlier chapter, the concept of the Seventh-day Sabbath and the "mark of the Beast" arose during the early days of the Advent movement. Men formulated this doctrine from their own interpretations of highly symbolic and apocalyptic Scripture which they believed was "confirmed" by the spirit of prophecy supposedly manifested in the writings of Ellen G. White. Seventh-day Adventists are entitled to this method of interpretation and application, but when they presume to designate the distribution of the gifts of the Holy Spirit, and the manifestation of those gifts in the Christian church, we must vigorously dissent. In this connection, they positively teach that "He has raised up a movement—known as the Seventh-day Adventist church—for the express purpose of making it, in a special way, the depository and exponent of this message." In the words of Ellen G. White, "God's remnant people, standing before the world as reformers, are to show that the law of God is the foundation of all enduring reform, that the Sabbath of the fourth commandment is to stand as a memorial of creation, a constant reminder of the power of God. In clear, distinct lines they are to present the necessity of obedience to all the precepts of the Decalogue."[3]

The Apostle Paul wrote to the Corinthians: "For as the body is one, and hath many members, and all the members of that one

[2] *Ibid.*, pp. 188-89.
[3] *Ibid.*, pp. 194-95.

body, being many, are one body: so also is Christ. For by one Spirit are we all baptized into one body, whether we be Jews or Gentiles, whether we be bond or free; and have been all made to drink into one Spirit. For the body is not one member, but many. If the foot shall say, Because I am not the hand, I am not of the body; is it therefore not of the body? And if the ear shall say, Because I am not the eye, I am not of the body; is it therefore not of the body? If the whole body were an eye, where were the hearing? If the whole were hearing, where were the smelling? But now hath God set the members every one of them in the body, as it hath pleased him. And if they were all one member, where were the body? But now are they many members, yet but one body. And the eye cannot say unto the hand, I have no need of thee: nor again the head to the feet, I have no need of you. Nay, much more those members of the body, which seem to be more feeble, are necessary. . . . There should be no schism in the body; but (that) the members should have the same care one for another. And whether one member suffer, all the members suffer with it; or one member be honoured, all the members rejoice with it. Now ye are the body of Christ, and members in particular" (I Cor. 12:12-22, 25-27).

This passage is the divine indictment of the Seventh-day Adventist doctrine of the "remnant church." For the apostle clearly states that God has set every member in the Body of Christ as it has pleased Him. Do Adventists have a revelation which supersedes that of First Corinthians? Do the writings of the "spirit of prophecy" empower them to contradict God's Word? We think not! By characterizing themselves as "the remnant church," and recognizing other members of the Body of Christ as only "presently potential members of that final 'remnant' company as defined in Revelation 12:17,"[4] Adventists unintentionally sow schism in the Body. In this they do not exercise "the same care one for another," as the Holy Spirit has instructed us to do.

The "remnant church" concept is also linked inseparably to Adventists' belief that they *alone* constitute "God's commandment-keeping church." This expression occurs frequently in the writings of Ellen White and other Adventist authors. It has resulted in a spirit

[4] *Ibid.*, p. 196.

of pharisaism of which not a few Adventists appear to be guilty. This legalistic attitude says in effect, "We are keeping *all* the commandments of God because we keep the Fourth Commandment, the Seventh-day Sabbath, while Sunday keepers do not." As the result of interviews with a large number of Adventists, it is my conclusion that they firmly maintain this position. They hasten to add, however, that although Sunday-keepers are definitely transgressing the laws of God, He does not impute their sin to them because "they have not received light on the subject." In all kindness, I must say that such an attitude of condescension often discourages fellowship between Adventists and non-Adventists.

The Word of God, on the other hand, clearly teaches that no one really keeps the commandments of God, no one is really capable of obeying His laws, for all are sinners (I John 1:8). Instead, whether regenerate or unregenerate, man is still a sinner, and "sin is the transgression of the law" (I John 3:4). Since Scripture calls sin the transgression of the law, defines all unrighteousness as sin (I John 5:17), and declares that "all have sinned" (Rom. 3:23), it is obvious that even Seventh-day Adventists cannot really obey the law of God. Keeping the Fourth Commandment does not alter the fact that they by nature are consistent and constant "transgressors of the law," because they are still in the flesh and are subject to sin and the desires which render meritorious obedience impossible (Rom. 3:23, I John 3:4). James, the half-brother of our Lord, makes this unmistakably clear: "For whosoever shall keep the whole law, and yet offend in one point, he is guilty of all. For he that said, Do not commit adultery, said also, Do not kill. Now if thou commit no adultery, yet if thou kill, thou art become a transgressor of the law" (James 2:10, 11).

When Seventh-day Adventists claim to be "God's commandment-keeping church," they contradict the declaration of God throughout Scripture that it is impossible to "keep" God's law (Rom. 3:23, I John 3:4, I John 1:8). Only the perfect, imputed righteousness of the Lord Jesus Christ compensates for our constant infraction of the law of God. "The law was our schoolmaster to bring us unto Christ, that we might be justified by faith," so "we are not under the law but under grace" (Gal. 3:24, Rom. 6:14).

To see the result of what is exclusivism in Seventh-day Adventist theology, one need only study the following quotations from Course 2, Lesson 9, of the Twentieth Century Bible Course of the Review and Herald Publishing Association, Takoma Park, Washington, D.C.:

"The New Testament Church was called to come out and be separate (II Cor. 6:17). The apostate church united with the world, the state, and paganism. Protestant churches separated partially from apostasy. Today God is calling for complete separation from Babylon. Babylon means confusion. From the Papal confusion and mixture of truth and error, her mixture of the church and the world and the church and state, God says come out. From apostatizing Protestantism, clinging to unbiblical doctrines, uniting with the world, federating with false systems and beliefs, seeking to reform the world by civil law, God says come out" (p. 2).

Such an attitude toward fellow Protestants and members of the Body of Christ helps to explain why there are often unhappy relationships between Seventh-day Adventists and other Christians. Those who indict fellow believers as "apostates" should realize that they are causing offense and weakening the possibilities of unity and fellowship in the Body of Christ.

Question II in this Bible course is significant: "Upon what commandment will the great test come?" *Answer:* "Upon the fourth commandment the test will come. God said that the Papal power would think to change the time of his law—Daniel 7:25. The Papacy says, 'By my divine power I abolish the sabbath day and command you to keep holy the first day of the week.' And lo, the entire civilized world bows down in reverent obedience to the command of the Catholic Church. She claims the change is 'a mark of ecclesiastical power.' This Sunday mark will be enforced by law (Rev. 13:15-17). God sends a worldwide warning against it (Rev. 14:9, 10). Those who do not receive the mark 'keep the commandments of God and the faith of Jesus' (Rev. 14:12). Which do we choose? The Sunday sabbath of the Papacy, or the Bible sabbath of the fourth commandment?"

According to this concept, the great test of the end of the ages will not be primarily fidelity to Christian living, the preaching of the gospel of Jesus Christ or "the defense of the faith once delivered unto the saints," but the observance of the Decalogue, especially its fourth precept. It is a sobering thought to realize that over a million earnest people are committed to the highly speculative and questionable apocalyptic interpretations laid down by the founders of Seventh-day Adventism.

In connection with this doctrine of the "remnant church," it is apparent that many present-day Adventists have somewhat mellowed in attitude. In early Adventist literature it was not uncommon to read that all who were outside the denomination and rejected the seventh day were outside the "remnant church" and already possessed the "mark of the Beast." In its current literature, however, the Adventist Church is attempting to harmonize all writing with the official position on this subject. For example, the new book, *Questions on Doctrine,*[5] repeatedly states that God's children are in all denominations, and that the majority keep the first day instead of the seventh-day Sabbath.[6] If the Seventh-day Adventists truly believed that they *alone* constituted the completed remnant church of Revelation, to the exclusion of all members of the Body of Christ who are not Sabbatarians, fellowship with them would be impossible. However, since they do not so believe, what they do claim (though disconcerting) should not bar them from fellowship with Christians of other denominations. I have met thousands of Adventist ministers, missionaries, church leaders and laymen, and neither the "remnant church" doctrine nor any other divergent view has prevented our wholehearted fellowship. This has been not only my experience, but that of many other Christians who have dealt with responsible Adventists.

We conclude this chapter with what we believe is another sobering thought for all Seventh-day Adventists who are willing to face the facts of history.

Questions on Doctrine states that the Seventh-day Adventist denomination is "the depository and exponent of this message"; further, that its mission is "that of persuading men to make ready for the day of God, by calling them to accept Heaven's special message and thus to join with us in proclaiming God's great truth for these days."[7] If this be true, Adventists are woefully bereft of outstanding personalities by which to substantiate their claim.

[5] Pp. 154-96.
[6] Even Ellen G. White says, "The great body of Christ's true followers are still to be found in these communions." *The Great Controversy,* p. 390.
[7] *Ibid.,* p. 195.

It is highly significant that during more than a century since the founding of the Seventh-day Adventist denomination, God has raised up in evangelical Christianity giants of the faith, such as Charles G. Finney, Dwight L. Moody, Gypsy Smith, Billy Sunday, and Billy Graham, whose world-wide evangelistic campaigns dwarf the combined efforts of the Seventh-day Adventist denomination over the same period. Adventists themselves admit that Almighty God certainly blessed these great preachers. To go one step farther, if the Adventists' claim to special divine favor is to be allowed, they must explain to the other members of the Body of Christ why all the aforementioned servants of God failed to espouse the "special message" of Seventh-day Adventism! Not one of those men embraced the Adventists' "sanctuary truth," "investigative judgment," "spirit of prophecy," "health reform," "Seventh-day Sabbath," "conditional immortality," or the "remnant church" concept. Yet God blessed them and their ministries with results beyond the Seventh-day Adventists' fondest dreams. Indeed, we would ask, Why has there not appeared some great, outstanding Seventh-day Adventist Bible teacher, evangelist, or leader of national or international standing comparable to these? Yet Adventists claim that they are *the* depository of God's special truths for the end of the age.

We do not wish to belittle the accomplishments of the Adventists, for God has blessed and increased them in their comparatively short history. They have established many hospitals and publishing houses and have pioneered mission projects throughout the world. Nevertheless, it is obvious to the student of the Word of God that their success has resulted from their faithful preaching of the gospel of Jesus Christ, since God has promised to bless His Word despite whatever human interpretations and doctrines may be appended. It has *not* been due to the proclamation of their "special truths." To establish their doctrine of the "remnant church," the Seventh-day Adventists must prove from history that they are entitled to their claim; but I think the testimony of history overwhelmingly controverts them. The record of the Christian Church in the United States reveals beyond doubt that whenever Almighty God has energized men to seek the salvation of souls, in every great evangelistic movement He has passed over the Seventh-day Adventist denomination and chosen men who did not and do not hold their "special truths." The Adventists may attempt to explain this away one way or another, but the bare facts themselves cannot be explained away. Their claim to be the "remnant people," the "depository of special truths for this age," and "God's commandment-keeping church," does not square with either the teaching of the Word of God or the history of the denomination. If their claim were valid, could God remain consistent and still use Finney, Moody, Smith, Sunday, and Graham—all opponents of the "special message" of Seventh-day Adventism (revealed, the Adventists say, by God Himself)—while He virtually ignored His especially anointed "remnant people"? Yet this is precisely what God has done, if the record of history is to be believed.

It is thus all to the good that Seventh-day Adventists recognize non-Adventists as born-again believers, not possessing the mark of the Beast even though the great majority of non-Adventists observe Sunday and pay little heed to the "special truths" of the Advent message. Nevertheless, they must realize that their position fosters schism in the Body of Christ, and any exclusivistic doctrine that divides Christians is to be regretted and rejected as erroneous. Dogmatic adherence to speculative interpretation has constituted a massive barrier to understanding and fellowship between Adventists and other Christians. Fellowship must be encouraged wherever possible, for this is the Scriptural injunction, but so long as Adventists maintain inflexibility where the "remnant church" concept and other "special truths" of the Advent message are concerned, Seventh-day Adventists must expect that Christians of other denominations will be cautious in according fellowship on an unlimited, unrestricted basis.

May God grant us the wisdom to understand and obey the counsel of His Holy Spirit, who has decreed "that there should be no schism in the body: but that the members should have the same care one for another" (I Cor. 12:25).

Part III

In Retrospect

CHAPTER TEN

THE PROBLEM OF FELLOWSHIP— A GREAT CONTROVERSY

In Chapter Two we discussed psychological factors in the growth and development of the Seventh-day Adventist denomination, and saw that Seventh-day Adventists have historically isolated themselves from the main stream of Christianity. In justification we could cite the abuse, ostracism and misrepresentation to which they have been subjected; nevertheless the onus rests, we believe, largely upon the Adventists. Be that as it may, Seventh-day Adventists and their fellow Christians must one day review their conduct before the bar of eternal justice, so we shall not attempt here to judge that phase of the problem, since it is not for us to do so; also there are other considerations far more pressing and practical.

We have also seen that although Seventh-day Adventists regard Ellen G. White as the great counselor and messenger of the Lord to their denomination, they have pointedly ignored her numerous recommendations that they seek fellowship with Christians of other denominations. She herself describes the attitude of the Advent people in this connection as "positively unfaithful."

There can be no doubt that the exclusivism of Seventh-day Adventists and their readiness in early years to seize upon the common custom of public debates have set most Christians against them as a group. These traits, coupled with the many inflammatory assertions which they have published about Sunday as the "mark of the Beast," the "remnant church," "144,000," and their unfortunately divisive presentation of "special truths," have caused Seventh-day Adventists not only to alienate their fellow Christians but to create hostility and prejudice against Adventism in general.

The writer has assembled scores of volumes and hundreds of pamphlets, tracts and articles by Seventh-day Adventist writers which bear out these contentions, and many Adventists who have had wide association with other groups admit this. In a word, Seventh-day Adventists have discouraged fellowship with Christians of other communions because they have overemphasized their so-called "special truths." Also, they have assumed that their fellow Christians know what Seventh-day Adventists believe relative to the cardinal doctrines of the Christian faith. Sad to say, this is not the case. Many Christians still are under the impression that the "special truths" of the Advent message are the *principal* doctrines of Seventh-day Adventism, and what they have seen they have disliked, because of the Adventists' lack of love and tolerance in the presentation of their beliefs.

I. The Ministry — Attitudes and Relationships

The background of the whole problem of fellowship, then, is anything but simple. Indeed, it is complex and checkered, and one can see the objections raised on both sides of the fence.

The principal problem facing us is how to achieve fellowship between Adventists and non-Adventists who recognize their common Christian faith but apparently cannot attain spiritual communion interdenominationally. They are separated by the wall of prejudice erected by the Orthodoxy vs. Adventism conflict of the last hundred years. We need only turn to the new Seventh-day Adventist volume, *Questions on Doctrine,* which presents the current position of the denomination, to see that Seventh-day Adventists today eagerly desire and encourage fellowship with Christians of other communions who love the Lord Jesus Christ and are seeking a common basis of fellowship. Relative to the position of Seventh-day Adventists where other Christians are concerned, the official Adventist source just mentioned states:

"We believe the majority of God's children are still scattered . . . throughout the world, and of course the majority of those in Christian churches still conscientiously observe Sunday. We ourselves cannot do so, for we believe that God is calling for reformation in this matter. But we respect and love those of our fellow-Christians who do not interpret God's Word just as we do. . . . Finally, we would say with all the earnestness and directness we can command, that we repudiate any implication that we alone are beloved of God and have a claim upon heaven. . . . We fully recognize the heartening fact that a host of true followers of Christ are scattered all through the various churches of Christendom, including the Roman Catholic communion. These God clearly recognizes as His own. Such do not form a part of the Babylon portrayed in the Apocalypse."[1]

This and many similar declarations in the Adventist volume indicate that Seventh-day Adventists have repudiated the concept that all who disagree with them are a part of apostate "Babylon" and that they are the only ones who "have a corner on Heaven." They have also stated in numerous places their desire for fellowship with Christians of other denominations. Leading Adventist periodicals (*The Ministry, Signs of the Times, et al.*) have devoted much space to this subject, over the last few years particularly. Seventh-day Adventists, far from opposing Christian fellowship, are apparently in favor of it and are willing to co-operate in any way short of compromising their principles, to effect the proper relationship with their fellow Christians.

On the other side, however, there has been a tendency on the part of Christians in some circles to strenuously deny fellowship to Seventh-day Adventists, and they have industriously erected straw men supported by quotations from outdated and repudiated Adventist literature. They claim thus that they are guarding evangelical Christianity from the supposed deadly infiltration of the "Adventist wolf." Before discussing four of their favorite objections to fellowship with Seventh-day Adventists, I wish to point out that these critics have misunderstood the Bible definition of Christian fellowship. They have redefined the word "fellowship," as a condition which requires: a) corporate worship, b) financial interchange, and c) intermissionary sponsorship. This is not the Biblical position. The Bible teaches that Christians may pray together, worship God together, partake of communion together, assist each other toward the attainment of common goals, and edify one another through Christian love and ethics. And the only requirements for Biblical fellowship are adherence to fundamental doctrinal truths, abstinence from overtly divisive practices, and love for one another as Christ commanded us (John 13:34, 35).

Take the Apostle Paul as an example of Biblical fellowship. For years, Paul was an avowed enemy of the Christian faith. After his conversion on the Damascus Road, many Christians could not believe

[1] *Questions on Doctrine*, pp. 192, 196, 197.

that he who once destroyed the faith now preached it. But when they saw that by the power of God he preached the Gospel and contended for the faith of Jesus, they "glorified God in him," and at Jerusalem he was formally given "the right hand of fellowship" by the ruling elders, James and Peter.

If it were true, as some Christians contend, that Seventh-day Adventists do not hold the great fundamentals of the faith,[2] then we would have Biblical ground for refusing fellowship. But what about the Adventist who confesses every cardinal doctrine of the Christian faith, gives evidence of regeneration by the Holy Spirit, and desires to live the Christian life? If we disagree with him on certain secondary points of theology, none of which affect the destiny of the soul, and allow that disagreement to separate us from him, we usurp the authority of the Holy Spirit. Are we not attempting to impose standards of fellowship which are nowhere expressly taught in the Word of God?

The divine program for fellowship in the Body of Christ is based upon the very nature of God Himself—love. Love has been conspicuously absent from both the words and actions of those who have so violently opposed fellowship with Seventh-day Adventists.

We have systematically pointed out the areas of disagreement between Adventism and Orthodoxy. The fellowship we have advocated, the nature of which has already been described, is the only kind which the Bible teaches. Nowhere did we suggest going beyond what is prescribed by Scripture and enjoined by the Holy Spirit upon all those who name the name of Christ in sincerity. It is interesting to note that those who have opposed fellowship with Seventh-day Adventists give evidence by their criticism that they never carefully evaluated the Biblical basis.

II. Objections to Fellowship

The following leading example pretty well sums up the major objections to fellowship with Seventh-day Adventists:

"In recent months a sustained attempt has been made to push aside the peculiar doctrines of Seventh-day Adventism and to admit the group to the true family of evangelical churches. . . . Wide

[2] Which they do; see Chapter Three.

controversy has been stirred by this, for many do not feel that the situation regarding this cult has been changed at all.

"This reviewer feels that a number of comments must be made on this attempt to bring Seventh-day Adventists into the fellowship of evangelicals. (1) Despite the supposed change of heart on the part of the group leaders, not one of their peculiar doctrines which would stamp them as heterodox in past years has been abandoned. In this connection, it must be insisted that the changes of heart on the part of leaders take a long time to percolate down to the laity, if they ever do. (2) Literature which has been used to propagate these doctrines in the past . . . is still being distributed by the headquarters of the group. (3) Although the leaders are giving assurance of their adherence to evangelical truth and their belief in salvation by grace, these same assurances have been given down through the years even by Ellen G. White. Nevertheless, the law has been set forth as necessary to salvation, Satan carried away the guilt of our sins, an investigative judgment of Christians is being carried on by Christ in the heavenly sanctuary, and the Sabbath is being observed. (4) Perhaps the most serious effect of these articles is the hindrance to the evangelicalism of those still ensnared by the legalism of false doctrines of the cult, and the number of instances in which Christian relatives and friends of such persons have been lulled into a false sense of security because Seventh-day Adventism has been labeled as entitled to fellowship among true evangelicals. (5) If Seventh-day Adventists should be admitted to evangelical fellowship so should Roman Catholicism, which is staunch in its adherence to basic Christian doctrine. But one is no more justified in brushing aside the heterodoxy of Seventh-day Adventism than in treating the deviations of Roman Catholicism as unimportant."[3]

The preceding objections can easily be refuted by returning to the facts.

(1) No attempt was ever made to "push aside the peculiar doctrines of Seventh-day Adventism." As the reader has seen, we have only suggested that Adventists be recognized as Christians and admitted to fellowship on the basis of spiritual life in Christ, and their large area of doctrinal agreement with historic Christianity. The review further states, "Not one of their peculiar doctrines which

[3] ***Bibliotheca Sacra,*** **April 1956, pp. 189, 190.**

have stamped them as heterodox in past years has been abandoned." The Adventists have repudiated the concept of the sinful nature of Christ, the "mark of the Beast" for Sunday keepers, the infallibility of Ellen G. White, the vicarious nature of the scapegoat transaction (see Chapter Three), positions held by some members of the Adventist denomination and which had appeared prominently in their literature for some years.

Relative to the brief comment that decisions of the leaders take a long time to "percolate down to the laity, if they ever do," this writer thinks that the Seventh-day Adventist leadership is far more capable of determining the over-all theological position of their denomination than are the critics. An interesting and relevant sidelight is the fact that copies of *Questions on Doctrine* were actually sent around the world to every conference and division of the Adventist denomination, and to every major school and editorial house for their approval, an approval which was overwhelming and resounding.[4]

(2) The review states that the literature which teaches some of the divergent views of Seventh-day Adventism is still in circulation in Adventist stores. This is true, but it must be remembered that it will take time for divergent literature within the denomination to be brought under editorial control and harmonized with the declared denominational position. The Adventists are seriously studying this problem.

(3) To further substantiate this critique of Adventism, the review pointedly contradicts what the Adventists have now published as their true position. It states that "the law has been set forth as necessary to salvation, Satan carried away the guilt of our sins," etc. In these particular areas, chapter 3 of the new Adventist volume completely repudiates these contentions.

(4) The review intimates that granting fellowship to Adventists will hurt the cause of Christ. This is pure conjecture, and he has produced no evidence to support this contention. There are some instances where Christians of other denominations have come into conflict with Adventists in various areas of theology, but this is true

[4] Added to this, the General Conference, meeting in Quadrennial session in Cleveland in 1958, thought the book was sufficiently in harmony with Adventist views to preclude any necessity of even reviewing the issue. Its approach was apparent to all, as was its acceptance.

of many groups within Christendom, and to draw any such drastic conclusion as it does is totally unwarranted by the facts.

(5) This article's final objection to fellowship is that "if Seventh-day Adventists should be admitted to evangelical fellowship so should Roman Catholicism with its staunch adherence to basic Christian doctrine."

The whole point of this objection is, of course, absurd to any student of systematic theology and church history, for it is a well known fact that Roman Catholicism *adds* to fundamental truths many teachings which affect the basic foundations of the Christian faith; such teachings as the mass, papal supremacy, the authority of tradition above the Scriptures, auricular confession, worship of the Virgin and the saints. Now this is not true of the Adventist "special truths," unless one wishes to deduce from some of their teachings what the Adventists themselves most heatedly deny. Not one of the deviations in Seventh-day Adventism is a deviation from the cardinal doctrines of the Christian faith which are necessary to salvation. This is not true of Roman Catholicism, so the critic's attempt to equate Roman Catholicism and Seventh-day Adventism does not stand the test of history or theology.

These objections to fellowship with Seventh-day Adventists, then, reveal lack of familiarity with primary sources where the Adventist controversy is concerned.

III. The Biblical Basis of Fellowship

Underlying the whole fellowship controversy, of course, is the basic misunderstanding as to what constitutes true Biblical unity and fellowship within the Body of Christ. Many who oppose the acceptance of Adventists quote numerous passages to bolster their case, but generally speaking the passages refer to those who deny the fundamental doctrines of the faith, not those who have doctrinal aberrations of a comparatively minor nature.

In connection with this the following facts are essential to a proper understanding of the problems involved. The Bible clearly teaches that the mystical Body of Christ contains two groups of people, the obedient and the disobedient sheep. Beyond this the Scriptures also teach the existence of spiritual wolves who have all the appearance of sheep, and yet, in the words of our Lord, they are "false prophets" (Matt. 7:15-23). The Bible declares that where the sheep are concerned, they are capable of blasphemy (I Tim. 1:20); they confuse other Christians by teaching erroneous doctrine (II Tim. 2:18); they are sometimes guilty of severe moral lapses (I Cor. 5); they divide the church (Rom. 16:17); and, further, that they sometimes reject apostolic doctrine (II Thess. 3:6). It is said of these disobedient sheep that they sow schism within the Body of Christ. In the sixteenth chapter of Romans, verse 17, the Apostle Paul distinctly teaches that the obedient sheep are to mark the disobedient sheep who cause dissension (*dichostasias*) and commit scandalous offenses (*scandalon*). The Apostle Paul says not only to mark them, but to avoid them, a position he qualifies in II Thessalonians 3:14: "Do not count him as an enemy but admonish him as a brother." Paul notes in I Corinthians 3:3 that carnality, envy, and strife exist in the Christian church among the sheep and in Galatians 5:20 he enumerates the "works of the flesh." In his first epistle to Timothy, Paul speaks of Hymenaeus and Alexander both of whom were doubtless Christians, and whom he "delivered to Satan that they might learn not to blaspheme." He followed this same procedure in I Corinthians 5 with those guilty of severe moral lapses. It is obvious therefore that doctrinal and moral error are linked together as grounds for separation from fellowship within the category of sheep. However, this only obtains, if and only if doctrinal schism is being fostered in the Body of Christ. To illustrate this, a person may believe in the a-millennial concept of eschatology and teach Sunday School in a church that is pre-millennial. So long as the a-millennial Christian does not cause division, schism, etc. within the church by teaching his interpretation as a pet doctrine, he can remain in fellowship. But when he uses his position as a lever to cause dissension, then separation from fellowship is the inevitable result. (Rom. 16:17). In Paul's second epistle to Timothy he points out that Hymenaeus and Philetus have erred concerning the truth, teaching that the resurrection has passed. Paul states that they "over turn" the faith of the saints (*anatrepousin*), and it is obvious that he separates them from fellowship by apostolic authority until they repent of this false doctrinal position. It is interesting to note that the same Greek word for "over turn" is utilized in Titus 1:11, where Paul gives the same advice to Titus concerning Christians, declaring that they must be silent (muzzled) since they are "upsetting whole families!" The Apostle says, "rebuke them sharply that they may be sound in the faith" (1:13). The context here demands that Christians are being spoken of though they are manifestly disobedient sheep and false teachers. II Timothy 2:18 then dovetails perfectly with Titus 1. Further on in his epistle to Titus, Paul speaks of a Christian who is a heretic or a factious man (3: 9, 10). Paul says "after the first and second admonition (or warning) reject him" from fellowship. To be in line with his previous council (II Thess. 3:6, 14) the Titus reference can only mean such a rejection is pending repentance and subsequent restoration.

In the Thessalonian epistle (II Thess. 2:15) Christians are told "to be firm and to hold to the tradition [or teachings, (*paradoseis*)] which you were taught by us either by word of mouth or by letter." In the third chapter, the apostle declares, "If any one refuses to obey what we say in this letter, note that man and have nothing to do with him that he may be ashamed. Do not look on him as an enemy but warn him as a brother" (RSV). The tradition or doctrine of the Apostles, for that is what the word means in this context, must refer to the previously discussed teaching concerning the return of the Lord (ch. 2), as well as to the moral issue of a Christian "who is living in idleness and not in accord with the tradition which you received from us" (II Thess. 3:6).

Paul here mixes moral and doctrinal issues together and says in a nutshell, if a man will not work to earn his bread, following our tradition, have nothing to do with him that he may repent, and if he is not listening to the doctrine which we teach, on the same basis, have nothing to do with him. However, he clearly maintains that we should not count him as an enemy but as a brother and strive to lead him to repentance.

Disobedient sheep, then, can be false teachers and schismatics, who sew division, scandal, and heretical teachings in the Body of Christ, and they must be dealt with in the same way as moral offenders until they repent. This is an exceptionally clear exegetical teaching of the Scriptures. Our attitude toward the erring brother or disobedient sheep is to be one of admonishment and restoration (Matt. 18:15; II Thess. 3:14, 15), but one point is clear—that disobedient sheep exist and must be disciplined accordingly.

To make an application here in the light of the New Testament position we should be careful to remember as previously noted, that anyone who unduly magnifies any teaching, whether it be true or false, which causes the faith of fellow Christians to be "unsettled" or if it promulgates division and schism, those who do this must in the words of Paul be "marked" and "avoided," "admonished," and if need be, "rejected" until they cease such practices.

Thus the men who split Christian churches and sow dissension, whether it be on the mode of baptism or communion or the issues of so-called "special truths," fall under the apostolic injunction; this is one area of true Biblical separation justified on both doctrinal and moral grounds, the same language being used interchangeably for both offenses.

As we have seen, relative to the obedient and the disobedient sheep, there can be little doubt as to the existence of both and the methods of detecting serious aberrations as well as the methods and attitudes obedient Christians ought to apply toward erring brothers. They are still believers, albeit in error; they must be dealt with as believers in obedience to our Lord and the doctrine of the apostles. Where schismatic sheep are involved the statement from Dr. Hodge in his famous article, *Unity of the Church*, cogently sums up our conviction. Dr. Hodge maintains that "there can be conscientious differences of opinion on questions of doctrine and order, so as to render harmonious action in one and the same externally united body impossible. It is better to separate than to quarrel and oppress. Two cannot walk together unless they be agreed. External union is the product and expression of internal union. The former cannot be safe or desirable when pressed beyond the latter. One of the greatest evils in the history of the church has been the constantly recurring effort to keep men united externally, who are inwardly at variance. Such forced union must be insincere and pernicious. It led to persecution and hypocrisy and the suppression of the truth. Where two bodies of Christians differ so much, either as to doctrinal order or as to render their harmonious action in the same ecclesiastical body impossible, it is better that they should form distinct organizations. . . . We may lament over such differences in the separation, alienation, jealousies, and conflicts which they are apt to produce, but no wise man would act as if the differences did not exist. They are facts which must be recognized and taken into account. We may labor to remove them and to produce such unity of opinion as to render external union practical and desirable, but until such unity is obtained all attempts to external union are premature and injurious." (*Eternity*, June 1958, p. 27).

Let us keep in mind then the issue of discipline within the Christian church; the problem of the obedient and disobedient sheep; let us not forget the very real existence of the wolves. The issues are plain for anyone to honestly evaluate. We should understand our responsibility to fellowship with Christians of all denominations whether they be Baptist, Methodist, Presbyterian or Seventh-day Adventist. No one has suggested organizational union and, in the light of Dr. Hodge's statement, this would be impossible where Adventism and Orthodoxy is concerned. On the other side of the picture, however, the Adventists are not "wolves" who deny the foundations of the faith, rather, at the very worst they might at times be classed as "disobedient sheep" who have from time to time sown schism within the Body of Christ. But in this they are not alone as other groups in reputable denominations have been guilty of the same. Today, Seventh-day Adventists are happy to fellowship with Christians of other denominations. By and large they are not eager to emphasize areas of disagreement which cause schism, but rather to fellowship upon the large majority of truths which all Evangelicals hold in common. We must never forget that a Baptist who divides churches on the basis of immersion, a Presbyterian who sows schism on the basis of Calvinism, or a Methodist who "unsettles" the faith of fellow believers by using the Arminian concept of salvation, is just as guilty as any Seventh-day Adventist who might use his "special truths" to instigate similar unfortunate schismatic activities.

Whatever it might be that causes Christians to become divisive and unloving must be dealt with by the church as a whole. None must be allowed to "overturn" the faith of other sheep.

It is in this area, and this area alone, where valid objection to fellowship with Seventh-day Adventists could be raised, and it is our conviction that the Seventh-day Adventist on the whole does not qualify for such judgment in our day!

As previously stated, the problem of fellowship, though basically simple, has thus been made extremely complex. There is no panacea for this confusion except the profound doctrine of love as revealed in Scripture. But it is far better to recognize a brother in Christ, and to fellowship with him here than it is to regret not having done so before the judgment seat of God where we shall appear to review the deeds done in the body. Since we must spend eternity with Adventists who are Christians, it is more advantageous to know them and learn to love them as fellow-Christians here, while there is opportunity for fellowship and the pursuit of a common objective, i.e., the winning of the lost to Christ and the strengthening of the unity of the Church "which is His body."

During the course of the preparation of this book, the author delivered a series of lectures in the field of comparative religion in a well-attended Baptist church in upper New York State. The closing lecture of the series was on Seventh-day Adventism, and the pastor of the local Adventist church and his parishioners were invited to attend the service. Throughout the lecture we contrasted the teachings of Adventism with those of historic orthodoxy, pointing out our areas of agreement and disagreement; and concluded, as is our custom, with a question and answer period during which questions from the floor were presented and answered. At the close of the period, the Adventist minister rose and stated that for the first time in his ministry he had heard an objective presentation and critique of Seventh-day Adventism, and further stated that he was delighted to be in Christian fellowship with a church which would present so objective a study. The result was that both Adventists and Baptists realized for the first time their oneness in the Christian faith. At the close of the meeting, they joined in a profitable half hour of true fellowship. The church paper summed up the entire meeting as follows:

CULT SERIES HELPS UNDERSTANDING

"Closer understanding of the cults and their growth resulted from a series of Wednesday evening meetings on the subject conducted by Rev. Walter Martin, contributing editor of *Eternity* Magazine. While warning of the work of the *Watchtower* of the Jehovah's Witnesses and Christian Science, he pointed out in an inspiring meeting on the last night of the series that the Seventh-day Adventists are close to us in their beliefs, accepting the basic doctrines of the Trinity, salvation through the grace of God and the blood of Christ, His absolute deity, the inspiration of the Scriptures and many others. He

> urged a closer fellowship with these people that we might emphasize our points of agreement rather than disagreement, and together better serve our Lord. Many Adventists were present at the meeting and expressed a desire for such fellowship."

This is the Biblical basis of fellowship. And when it was practiced in this meeting and in many subsequent meetings in other localities, the unity of the Body of Christ was realized. In that town, today, fellowship continues with apparently little friction; indeed this anecdote more than any series of factual propositions illustrates the fruit of applying the true Scriptural principle of fellowship to all Christians.

CONCLUSION

In our study of Seventh-day Adventism, we have seen how a denomination was born and how it reached its present position after many years of theological controversy and debate born within and without the denomination. We have attempted to compare the basic theology of Seventh-day Adventism with that of historic orthodox Christianity, and have seen that many Adventist doctrines such as the Seventh-day Sabbath, "soul sleep," the annihilation of the wicked, and Arminianism (which causes apprehension among some evangelicals) were derived from pre-Adventist sources. The Seventh-day Sabbath was taken from the Seventh-day Baptists, as was immersion. Conditional immortality was taught by Martin Luther, William Tyndale, John Wycliffe and other great figures of church history. Arminianism, or the belief that one can fall from grace, was borrowed from the theology of the Remonstrant school of Arminianism and John Wesley, and many evangelicals still hold this view. At worst, then, Seventh-day Adventism is guilty of heterodoxy and eclecticism, or borrowing from many sources for its theological structure. This structure, however, is essentially orthodox as evidenced by their statements on cardinal doctrines of the Christian faith catalogued in Chapter Three.

This writer, a Baptist minister, in no sense endorses the "special truths" of the Adventist message. But in order to be objective and in the light of certain selected passages of Scripture which definitely deal with these problems (especially the Sabbath), we must not allow these aberrations to blind us to the facts, that clearly reveal Seventh-day Adventists to be sincere Christians.[1]

We hope that many who have looked upon Adventists as dangerous non-Christian cultists will revise this view. In the providence of God, and in His own good time, we trust that evangelical Christianity as a whole will extend the hand of fellowship to a group of sin-

[1] No denomination is, *per se*, "Christian"; but in the generally accepted sense we are employing the term as descriptive of the Seventh-day Adventist denomination.

cere, earnest fellow Christians, distinguished though they are by some peculiar views, but members of the Body of Christ and possessors of the faith that saves.

After reaching this decision on Seventh-day Adventism, based upon a prolonged and exhaustive factual first-hand analysis of the denomination as it is today, I realized that consternation and bitterness might result from the publication of these findings. Many may feel that I have "gone overboard" on Seventh-day Adventism and that I am attempting to "whitewash" the movement. Neither charge is true. I have simply presented an objective, first-hand analysis of Adventism—free, I believe, from the strong prejudices that have characterized the writings of the past one hundred years on the subject.

In summing up we should like to make the following observations regarding these critical writings on Seventh-day Adventism. All popular critics of Seventh-day Adventism seem to share the disconcerting habit of quoting one another. From their writings, past and present, it would be a simple matter to prove that many of them consistently draw from repudiated and unrepresentative Adventist literature for their polemics; notably, *Bible Reading for the Home Circle, Signs of the Times* and other "stock references." Ignoring the over-all picture of Adventist theology, they maintain that isolated quotations actually represent the entire denomination. Second, these critics repeatedly refer to the former Adventist, D. M. Canright, whose criticisms in the field of Adventism vs. Historic Christian theology are basically sound in many areas, but whose judgments and quotations concerning other areas of Adventist theology, and the character of Ellen White, reflect personal prejudice and are often outdated.

Third, often the critics tend to violate publishing ethics by printing private correspondence without permission, deleting paragraphs by illegal use of the ellipsis, and sometimes even citing references that do not exist. It is one thing to criticize a man's beliefs; it is another to misrepresent his beliefs and then submit your misrepresentations as a valid analysis. Yet this is precisely what many critics have done. And finally, they have not hesitated to denounce noted Christian leaders as "ill-informed, easily duped and heretofore trusted editors."[2]

[2] *Sword of the Lord*, p. 7.

All this because these editors had the courage, common honesty and Christian charity to seek to right great wrongs on both sides of the Adventism-Orthodoxy controversy.

Finally, we stand firm with the critics in opposition to already specified areas of Adventist teaching. But we cannot risk our perspective, good judgment and ethics merely to win an argument.

It should be carefully pointed out that not all critics are destructive. Quite a number of constructive articles and comments about Seventh-day Adventism have been written by persons attempting an objective analysis. Unfortunately some of these attempts have been inconsistent in the presentation of material and lacking in primary information.

These critics generally do not wish to commit themselves to anything too favorable to the Adventists. An illustration of this is a recently published two-part article, "What of Seventh-day Adventism?"[3]

On page 13 of the second article we read: "We must ask whether Seventh-day Adventist views . . . violate the doctrine of grace and consequently involve the error of Galatianism." The writer then states, "We must affirm that all of the Seventh-day Adventist people who truly accept Christ as the Son of God and Saviour are regenerate believers and brothers in Christ—despite theological accretions and legalistic attitudes."

Less than 10 lines further, with startling inconsistency, the article says: "It is the opinion of this writer that SDA *does* mix grace and works and thus falls into the error of Galatianism against which Paul writes." On page 14 it declares, "beyond dispute . . . in the SDA system, salvation is *not* by grace alone but by faith plus works."

We need only comment that if Seventh-day Adventists are willfully guilty of Galatianism as charged, then according to the Apostle Paul they are doubly anathematized by God Himself (Galatians 1:8, 9), and in no sense can they be considered Christian. Thus, after paving the way for condemnation of Adventism he accepts them as "regenerate believers and brothers in Christ despite theological accretions and legalistic attitudes"—something one cannot logically do *if* they are guilty of the error in Galatians.

[3] *Christianity Today,* March 31 and April 14, 1958.

We are in sympathy with some of the things these articles say, but they seem to indicate a desire to avoid an appearance of conciliation toward Seventh-day Adventism for fear of provoking some of the more vocal and less-informed elements of the Christian public.

It may seem to some that we have dealt with the critics as though we espouse the Adventist cause. Nothing could be further from the truth. Our main desire is to treat the Adventists as we ourselves would want to be treated. In adopting this attitude, it is inevitable that we should come into conflict with those critics of Adventism who have not thoroughly investigated its teaching and so are prone to misrepresent them.

We believe, however, that Christian people will weigh and accept verifiable evidence. In our research we have been interested in facts alone, not in the emotional reactions of adherents to either side of the controversy. We believe that these facts conclusively show the right of Adventists to be called Christians and we further believe that other Christians should recognize them as fellow-believers and extend fellowship to them, within the New Testament definition of fellowship. Many problems, however, remain to be solved in Adventist publications, public relations, missionary activities, and other fields of endeavor. Adventism today, we believe, presents a unified picture of a Christian denomination, but the fact that we recognize it as such does not mean as some infer, that we either accept or are in sympathy with certain tenets of its theology or activity.

We urge those who have further questions about Adventism to read *Questions on Doctrine,* the recent comprehensive volume of Adventist theology which has been prepared and published in full collaboration with the General Conference leadership of Seventh-day Adventists.

As we draw toward the end of the ages, and as Israel continues to bud and the desert blossoms as a rose before our wondering eyes, Christians of all denominations should re-examine their basis of fellowship with one another.

By so doing, we may, by God's grace, usher in a new era of understanding and spiritual growth in the Church at large, which according to the Scripture, is "Christ's Body." It is toward this goal, in the light of the "blessed hope" of our Lord's return, that we have endeavored to present *The Truth About Seventh-day Adventism.*

BIBLIOGRAPHY*

I. *Writings of Ellen G. White*

Early Writings, Review and Herald Publishing Association, Takoma Park, Maryland
The Story of Redemption, Review and Herald
Education, Review and Herald
Child Guidance, Review and Herald
Messages to Young People, Review and Herald
The Adventist Home, Review and Herald
Christ's Object Lessons, Review and Herald
The Ministry of Healing, Review and Herald
Counsels on Diets and Foods, Review and Herald
Evangelism, Review and Herald
The Great Controversy, Pacific Press Publishing Association, Mountain View, Calif.
The Acts of the Apostles, Pacific Press
The Desire of Ages, Pacific Press
Prophets and Kings, Pacific Press
Patriarchs and Prophets, Pacific Press
Testimonies to Ministers, Pacific Press
Testimonies for the Church, Vols. 1 - 9, Pacific Press
Christian Experience and Teachings, Pacific Press
Index to the Writings of Ellen G. White, Pacific Press
Thoughts From the Mount of Blessings, Pacific Press
Steps to Christ, Review and Herald

II. *Seventh-day Adventist Publications*

Anderson, R. A., *The Shepherd Evangelist,* Review and Herald Publishing Association, Takoma Park, Maryland
Anderson, R. A., *Unfolding the Revelation,* Pacific Press
Andreasen, M. L., *What Can a Man Believe?,* Pacific Press
Andreasen, M. L., *The Sanctuary Service,* Review and Herald
Andreasen, M. L., *The Book of Hebrews,* Review and Herald
Andreasen, M. L., *The Sabbath,* Review and Herald
Branson, W. H., *In Defense of the Faith,* Review and Herald

*** Due to the tremendous amount of material dealing with Seventh-day Adventism, this is but a partial bibliography of the vast wealth of data available. I have selected those works, both pro- and anti-Adventist, which I feel condense the salient points under study in this volume and which are still for the most part in print.**

Froom, Leroy E., *The Prophetic Faith of Our Fathers,* Vols. 1-4, Review and Herald
Froom, Leroy E., *The Coming of the Comforter,* Review and Herald
Haynes, Carlyle B., *Life, Death and Immortality,* Southern Publishing House, Nashville, Tenn.
Daniels, A. G., *The Abiding Gift of Prophecy,* Pacific Press
Reed, W. E., *The Bible, The Spirit of Prophecy, and The Church,* Review and Herald
Spicer, W. A., *Our Day in the Light of Prophecy,* Review and Herald
Odom, R. L., *Sunday in Roman Paganism,* Review and Herald
Jamison, T. Housel, *A Prophet Among You,* Pacific Press
Horn, Sigfried H. and Wood, Lynn H., *The Chronology of Ezra Seven,* Review and Herald
The Seventh-day Adventist Bible Commentary, Vols. 1 - 5
Genesis - John, Review and Herald
Problems in Bible Translation, General Conference, Seventh-day Adventists, Takoma Park, Washington, D.C.
Haynes, Carlyle B., *The Gift of Prophecy,* Southern Publishing Association, Nashville, Tenn.
Wilcox, Milton C., *Questions Answered,* Pacific Press
Nichol, Francis D., *The Midnight Cry,* Review and Herald
Nichol, Francis D., *Answers to Objections,* Review and Herald
Nichol, Francis D., *Ellen G. White and Her Critics,* Review and Herald
Smith, Uriah, *Daniel and the Revelation,* Vols. 1 and 2, Review and Herald
Robinson, D. E., *The Story of our Health Message,* Southern Publishing House
Bible Readings for the Home Circle, Review and Herald
Werner, A. J., *Fundamentals of Bible Doctrine,* Review and Herald
Wilcox, F. M., *The Coming Crisis,* Review and Herald
Spalding, Arthur W., *Sister White,* Review and Herald
White, James, *Life of William Miller,* Review and Herald
Wheeler, Ruth, *His Messenger,* Review and Herald
Daniels, Arthur G., *Christ our Righteousness,* The Ministerial Association of Seventh-day Adventists, Takoma Park, Washington, D.C.
Bunch, Taylor G., *The Ten Commandments,* Review and Herald
Walker, Allen, *The Law and The Sabbath,* Southern Publishing Association
Straw, W. E., *Origin of Sunday Observance,* Review and Herald
Haynes, Carlyle B., *Seventh-day Adventists, Their Work and Teachings,* Review and Herald
Johns, Varner J., *The Secret Rapture and the Antichrist,* Pacific Press
Everson, Charles T., *The Rich Man and Lazarus,* Southern Publishing Association
Bollman, Calvin P., *Sunday, Origin of its Observance in the Christian Church,* Review and Herald
Sabbath-School Quarterly (Magazine) — Assorted copies

How to Handle Objections, prepared by the publishing department of The Secretaries of the Southern Union Conference, Southern Publishing Association
Haynes, Carlyle B., *When a Man Dies,* Review and Herald
Everson, Charles T., *Who Are the Angels?,* Review and Herald
Odom, R. L., *How Did Sunday Get Its Name?,* Southern Publishing Association, Nashville, Tenn.
Richards, H. M. S., *Hard Nuts Cracked,* Southern Publishing Association
Voice of Prophecy Bible Course (Correspondence)
Haskell, S. N., *Bible Hand Book,* Review and Herald
Twentieth Century Bible Course (Correspondence Course)
Odom, Robert L., *The Final Crisis and Deliverance,* Southern Publishing Association
General Conference Young Peoples Department of Missionary Volunteers, pamphlet, *Studies in Bible Doctrine,* Senior Missionary Volunteer, Review and Herald
Review and Herald (Magazine) — Assorted copies
Signs of the Times (Magazine) — Assorted copies
These Times (Magazine) — Assorted copies
The Ministry (Magazine) — Assorted copies
Compilation, *Bible Readings for the Home,* Review and Herald, 1956
Bunch, Taylor G., *Behold the Man,* Southern Publishing Association
Maxwell, Arthur S., *The Coming King,* Pacific Press
Haynes, Carlyle B., *From Sabbath to Sunday,* Review and Herald
Nichol, Francis D., *The Certainty of my Faith,* Review and Herald
Haynes, Carlyle B., *The Christian Sabbath, Is It Saturday or Sunday?,* Southern Publishing Association
Cottrell, Roy F., *The True Sabbath,* Southern Publishing Association
Moseley, Calvin Edwin, *The Lord's Day,* Southern Publishing Association
The Bible Made Plain, a series of short Bible studies for the home circle upon the fundamentals of the Christian faith, Review and Herald
Wilcox, Milton C., *The Lord's Day, The Test of the Ages,* Pacific Press
Dixon, Louis J., *Law or Grace,* Southern Publishing Association
Marsh, F. L., *Evolution, Creation and Science,* Review and Herald
Andreasen, M. L., *God's Holy Day,* Review and Herald
Haynes, Carlyle B., *Marks of the True Church, Its Divine Identification,* Review and Herald
Lickey, Arthur E., *Fundamentals of the Everlasting Gospel,* Review and Herald
Maxwell, Arthur S., *Your Friends the Adventists,* Pacific Press
Froom, Leroy E., *Finding the Lost Prophetic Witness,* Review and Herald
Seventh-day Adventist Church Directory, United States and Canada, Review and Herald
Church Manual, General Conference of Seventh-day Adventists, Takoma Park, Washington, D.C.
Seventh-day Adventist Year Book, 1957, Review and Herald

III. *General*

Canright, Dudley M., *Seventh-day Adventism Renounced,* B. C. Goodpasture, Nashville, Tenn.

Chafer, Louis Sperry, *Grace,* Van Kampen Press, 1947

Canright, D. M., *Life of Mrs. E. G. White,* B. C. Goodpasture, Nashville, Tenn., 1948

Talbot, Louis T., *What's Wrong with Seventh-day Adventism?,* Dunham Publishing Company, Findlay, Ohio

Talbot, Louis T., Articles on Seventh-day Adventism, The King's Business, Selected Issues

Rowell, J. B., *Seventh-day Adventism Examined,* Challenge Publishing Company, Norwalk, California

Smith, Oswald J., *Who Are The Seventh-day Adventists and What Do They Teach?,* Hugh Warren, Wesley Press and Publishing House

Putnam, C. E., *Legalism and The Seventh-day Question, Can Sinai Law and Grace Coexist?,* The Bible Institute Colportage Association, Chicago

Pollock, A. J., *Seventh-day Adventism Briefly Tested by Scripture,* The Central Bible Truth Depot, London, England

Bliss, Sylvester, *Memoirs of William Miller,* Boston, 1853

Dungan, D. R., *Sabbath or Lord's Day, Which?,* Harbinger Book Club, Nashville, Tenn.

Biederwolf, Wm. Edward, *Seventh-day Adventism, the Result of a Predicament*

Smith, Oswald J., *Who Are The False Prophets?,* The Peoples Press, Toronto, Canada

Canright, D. M., *The Lord's Day or The Sabbath,* pamphlet abridged from *Seventh-day Adventism Renounced*

Jones, E. B., *Forty Bible-Supported Reasons Why you Should not be a Seventh-day Adventist,* Designed Products, Oak Park, Ill.

Jones, E. B., *The Answer and the Reasons,* eye-opening information regarding Seventh-day Adventism, Designed Products

Jones, E. B., *Free Indeed,* The Author's Testimony Concerning His Deliverance from Seventh-day Adventism, Designed Products

Dictionary of American Biography, Charles Scribner's Sons, New York

Booth, A. E., *Seventh-day Adventism, What is It?,* (Vol. 12, Article on William Miller)

Ironside, H. A., *What Think Ye of Christ?,* Loizeaux Brothers Publishers, N.Y.C.

Feinberg, Charles L., *The Sabbath and the Lord's Day,* Van Kampen Press

Miller, William, *Apology and Defense* (pamphlet), August, 1845

Miller, William, *A Few Evidences of the Time of the Second Coming of Christ* (Mss. 1831)

The Advent Shield and Review (Millerite), 1844—Assorted copies

The Advent Herald (Millerite)—Assorted copies

Pickering, Ernest, *Can We Fellowship with Seventh-day Adventists?,* THE

VOICE of the Independent Fundamental Churches of America, October, 1956

Davies, Horton, *Christian Deviations,* Chapter on Seventh-day Adventism, Philosophical Library, New York

Van Baalen, J. K., *The Chaos of Cults,* Wm. B. Eerdman Publishing Co., Revised edition, 1956, chapter on Seventh-day Adventism

Canright, D. M., *Hard Nuts for Seventh-day Adventists* (Tract)

Ferguson, Charles W., *The New Books of Revelation,* Doubleday Doran, 1929, chapter on Seventh-day Adventism

Irvine, Wm. C., *Heresies Exposed,* Chapter Seventh-day Adventism, Loizeaux Bros., N.Y.

Sanders, J. Oswald and Wright J., Stafford, *Some Modern Religions,* Chapter on Seventh-day Adventism, Inter-Varsity Press, England

Fletcher, W. W., *The Reasons for My Faith,* William Brooks & Co., Limited, Sydney, Australia

Deck, Norman C., *The Lord's Day or The Sabbath, Which?,* Bridge Printery, Ltd., Sydney, Australia

Jones, E. B., *The Historical Background of Seventh-day Adventism, Seventh-day Adventism and the Gospel of Grace,* etc., Articles in the Sunday-School Times, 1954

Meyer, F. B., *The Religious Bodies of America,* Concordia Publishing House, section on Seventh-day Adventism

Jones, E. B., *Seventh-day Adventists Counterfeit Gospel,* Christian Victory Magazine, February, 1952, Denver, Colorado

Auchincloss, Douglas, *Peace with the Adventists, Time* Magazine, Dec. 31, 1956, pp. 48-49

"Seventh-day Adventists and the Date of Creation," Editorial, *The Examiner* Magazine, March-April, 1952

Buswell, J. Oliver, *The Length of Creative Days,* Monograph, Shelton College, 1950, N.Y.C.

Dugger, A. F., *The Bible Sabbath Defended,* The Church of God Publishing House, Stanbury, Missouri

Hulbert, Terry C., *Seventh-day Adventism Weighed in the Balances,* The Discerner Magazine (This edition entirely given over to a refutation of Seventh-day Adventism), Oct. - Dec., 1956

Barnhouse, Donald Grey, *Are Seventh-day Adventists Christian?* Article *Eternity* Magazine, Sept. 1956

Martin, Walter R., *Seventh-day Adventism Today,* Article *Our Hope* Magazine, Nov. 1956

Martin, Walter R., *Are Seventh-day Adventists Evangelical?, Christian Life* Magazine, October 1956

Martin, Walter R., *The Truth About Seventh-day Adventism,* Series of Articles in *Eternity* Magazine, October, November, and January, 1956, 1957

Baer, James E., *The Seventh-day Adventists,* Series of Articles entitled "The Bible and Modern Religions," *Interpretation,* Journal of Theology, January, 1956

IV. *Magazine Articles*

Bibliotheca Sacra, April, 1956

Christianity Today

"What of Seventh-day Adventism?" by Harold Lindsell	Part I, March 31, 1958 Part II, April 14, 1958
"Another Look at Adventism" by Herbert S. Bird	April 28, 1958
"A Seventh-day Adventist Speaks Back" by Frank H. Yost	July 21, 1958

Eternity, September, 1956

Eternity, June, 1958

King's Business, The, April, 1957

King's Business, The, March, 1958

Signs of the Times, January 8, 1952

Sword of the Lord, The, August 2, 1957

NOTE:

In addition to the above-listed books, the author has consulted standard theological works, exegetical commentaries, word studies, concordances, and translations of the Bible, as well as many, many other publications, too numerous to list at this time. The writings of William Miller and the Millerite Movement have been largely omitted from the Bibliography for the sake of space and due to the fact that almost all of them are out of print now. For a complete list see F. D. Nichol's *The Midnight Cry,* pp. 531 - 561, Review and Herald Publishing Association, Washington, D.C.

Index

INDEX

INDEX

INDEX